CRIME AND CRIMINALITY

SOCIAL, PSYCHOLOGICAL, AND NEUROBIOLOGICAL EXPLANATIONS

EHOR BOYANOWSKY

CRIME AND CRIMINALITY

SOCIAL, PSYCHOLOGICAL, AND NEUROBIOLOGICAL EXPLANATIONS

UNIVERSITY OF TORONTO PRESS

ISBN 978-1-4875-0562-2 (cloth)   ISBN 978-1-4875-3243-7 (EPUB)
ISBN 978-1-4875-2389-3 (paper)   ISBN 978-1-4875-3242-0 (PDF)

Library and Archives Canada Cataloguing in Publication
Title: Crime and criminality : social, psychological, and neurobiological
    explanations / Ehor Boyanowsky.
Names: Boyanowsky, Ehor, 1943– author.
Description: Includes bibliographical references and index.
Identifiers: Canadiana 20190144009 | ISBN 9781487505622 (hardcover) |
    ISBN 9781487523893 (softcover)
Subjects: LCSH: Criminology. | LCSH: Crime. | LCSH: Criminal behavior.
Classification: LCC HV6025 .B69 2019 | DDC 364.2—dc23

We welcome comments and suggestions regarding any aspect of our
publications—please feel free to contact us at news@utorontopress.com or visit us
at utorontopress.com.

Every effort has been made to contact copyright holders; in the event of an error or
omission, please notify the publisher.

University of Toronto Press acknowledges the financial assistance to its publishing
program of the Canada Council for the Arts and the Ontario Arts Council, an
agency of the Government of Ontario.

Canada Council   Conseil des Arts
for the Arts   du Canada

ONTARIO ARTS COUNCIL
CONSEIL DES ARTS DE L'ONTARIO
an Ontario government agency
un organisme du gouvernement de l'Ontario

Funded by the   Financé par le
Government   gouvernement
of Canada   du Canada

Canada

For Cristina, who insisted I persevere

In memoriam
Lesia Vera Dayneka, 1933–2019

Nothing is easier than to condemn the evildoer; nothing is more difficult than to understand him.

—attributed to Fyodor Dostoyevsky

There are many evil systems, but few really evil people.

—Dmitri (Mike) Boyanowsky

CONTENTS

FIGURES AND TABLES

FIGURES

TABLES

ACKNOWLEDGMENTS

I thank the great teachers whom I have been so fortunate to have had, beginning with Donald Wilkes in grades 7 and 8, a former British army captain, who treated us, obstreperous but keen adolescents, with firmness and tolerance and taught me the rules and beauty of grammar. Jim Sturgis and Janet Sturgis imbued me with the love of history, language (including Latin), and English literature. Adele Roloff's vivaciousness and passion for French were irresistible.

Finally, I am grateful to my University of Wisconsin graduate school advisor and mentor, Vernon Allen, who held out the intellectual enterprise as the highest calling a person could embrace, and who, tragically, died so very young.

I am fortunate to have had many dedicated research assistants, most prominently Alison Barnes, Robyn McElveen, Jonathan Yasayko, Majid Najafabadi, Irina Malin, and Anna Von Bischoffshausen whose conscientiousness and special skills provided crucial information and diagrams for the completion of this book. I wish them well in their future endeavors.

Finally, I am first of all grateful to my initial editor, Anne Brackenbury, whose patience, tolerance, professionalism, and relentless insistence on phlegmatic excellence and clarity have made this book better than I could have hoped. And to the editorial and production staff at the University of Toronto Press, whose intrepid questioning and conscientious attention to detail removed any error or ambiguity in the text.

INTRODUCTION

This book is intended for readers who strive to understand the conditions under which crime occurs, especially violent crime but also serious crime committed by groups and corporations that harms thousands, even millions of people or the environment and wildlife. You may be an interested citizen or someone reading this text as a student of an introductory criminology, law, or criminal psychology course, but you will not be exposed merely to reams of theories stacked up in historic sequence.

For North American readers, the book compares some significant differences in the law and how it is administered in the United States and Canada. The first chapter also touches upon how the law differs internationally, and in order to allow the reader to make comparisons, tables for prominent countries allow a quick scan to give a perspective on similarities and differences.

For those who wish to read densely written volumes that describe the dozens of theories that have been promulgated over the past 150 years, I recommend picking up *Criminological Theory: Past to Present* by Cullen and Agnew (2011) or *Criminal Behavior: A Psychological Approach* by Bartol and Bartol (2017). Both are comprehensive reviews of formidable size (about 600–700+ pages) that list most of the perspectives but do not synthesize them into an organic whole so that having read through the chapters you would have a grasp of how the different levels of analysis relate to an overall explanation. That overall understanding, however, is what this book does provide.

Thus this book, rather than favoring social or psychological or neurobiological levels of explanation, can be best described as an eclectic synthesis, which is usually the best way to account for most phenomena studied scientifically. For example, creationism is a grand unidimensional theory to explain the world, no other level of analysis necessary, whereas natural selection accounts for life forms produced by genetics, climatic conditions, and favorable ecological niches existing at the appropriate time. Creationism requires no further elaboration to account for the existence of life forms (God did it, end of story), whereas Darwin's natural selection requires identification of the specific conditions that promote certain forms of life and not others.

The usual rule for accepting competing theories is parsimony: that is, the theory that can explain the phenomenon or more phenomena being studied with fewer constructs is to be preferred. In that sense creationism wins and appeals to many people, but it doesn't unravel the specific paths followed by all living organisms including humankind. At the other end of the spectrum, explaining everything in terms of instinct rather than the will of God is also a parsimonious explanation. So too, it explains very little if you challenge, for example, whether aggression is completely instinctive versus learned. If instinctive, when and how does it emerge? Why are some people more aggressive than others? If purely instinctive, can aggression and violence be modified or even eliminated in individuals, groups, or the human race? Those strongly supporting the instinct hypothesis usually do not want a lot of society's financial or other resources wasted on trying to reduce aggression or eliminate it, e.g., through therapy, whether behavioral or even in psychodynamic in-depth form to produce rehabilitation, or through ameliorating the conditions under which violence occurs, such as by providing supplemental income to needy single mums and their children. They think all such attempts would be futile. Those individuals, it follows, would also more likely be in favor of capital punishment as the only remedy for perpetrators in whom aggression is so uncontrolled that it has led to murder of another human being. Or if they oppose capital punishment—perhaps, ironically, on religious grounds because "Vengeance is mine; I will repay, saith the Lord"

(Romans 12:19, KJV)—those who think violence instinctive would insist on prison sentences truly lasting the whole life of the offender.

Persons who favor the learning explanation for aggression and violence are more likely to believe that negative early experience in infancy may have created the potential for aggression and violence and so are less likely to stamp offenders with the "mark of Cain," a biblical reference to one who has been condemned to misbehave from birth. Thus, to avoid such antisocial tendencies, society must devote more resources to mothers and children (perhaps, in our emerging egalitarian families, to "both" parents and children) so that they can cope with the stresses of child rearing without damaging their offspring. As a corollary, that faction would also believe that more learning and unlearning, hence successful rehabilitation, is possible. And so "life sentences" would comprise only 25 years and could be reduced with significant signs of rehabilitation. Consequently, the onus is placed on society rather than merely attributing criminal behavior to unfortunate genetic combinations.

Because these parsimonious explanations of aggression and violence are unsatisfactory, this book is an eclectic explanation, and the relative contribution of each factor listed above may vary from one instance to another. So some criminology theories explain crime wholly by bad societal conditions, others by bad genetic constitution, others by faulty physical health or mental health or cognitive functioning. This book, *Crime and Criminality*, recognizes all of their contributions but points out that, in some circumstances, one factor is more significant while, in other circumstances, other factors in different proportions create the critical mass producing criminal behavioral outcomes. In other words, an eclectic explanation accounts for what are the necessary and sufficient conditions for a certain outcome. Perhaps most important is that it challenges many of the positions espoused in criminology, a highly politicized discipline, with new theories and conclusions based on the latest empirical findings and advanced thinking. Even seasoned veterans in research, practice, and instruction will be startled by the concepts and theories presented and, I believe, will learn a great deal by reading this book.

The resulting formula or algorithm allows you to plug in the factors that produce a certain outcome. We all use algorithms, e.g., people +

music + drinks = party. And you can add factors to change the outcome, e.g., people + music + food = dinner party. Using such a method is how TV commercials try to come up with a winning combination to promote their products. I hope you enjoy the process of discovery as I intend it to be both informative and entertaining. Do keep in mind as you read the book that, as a result of its approach, truly comprehending each chapter is necessarily dependent on having read and assimilated the previous chapters. Reading chapters in isolation you will be sometimes puzzled by why certain premises or information is missing. Those can be found in the previous chapters. So too, case studies presented early will be eventually analyzed in later chapters as relevant theory and research emerges.

Chapter 1 sets out to tackle the thorny problem of what actually is a crime and what is not. Crime is examined from the perspectives of both history and culture, especially in the United States and Canada. To highlight the differences that exist in the world, the chapter presents several anecdotes that may startle the reader, and, at the end of the chapter, some of the most relevant countries are profiled and compared culturally and in how they administer justice. Readers may be surprised by the diversity.

Chapter 2 examines the shortcomings in dividing crime merely into mala in se (offenses that are wrong irrespective of law) and mala prohibita (offenses prohibited by law but not inherently wrong) and investigates how the courts evaluate the gravity or seriousness of crime. Postmodern theorists argue that all crime is a social construction, that is, made up or defined arbitrarily by society. Postmodern theory derived from symbolic interaction theory argues that there is no arbitrary reality, so truth is whatever the particular cultural group decides it is. This postmodern idea is derived from a branch of philosophy known as phenomenology in which reality is not really accessible. By contrast, this chapter argues that violence is a physical phenomenon naturally existing in the real world and is separate and independent from aggression, which infers motivation. Rather, a multidimensional model is proposed that demonstrates the relationship between them and how the seriousness of different types of crimes can be calculated. The intended result is to allow the reader and the courts to consider, compare, and assess the relative gravity of crimes as diverse as murder and pollution.

Chapter 3 delves into the nature of criminality. Why do some people become criminals, committing not just one crime but several, perhaps throughout life? It begins with a letter to the *New York Times* that could have been written today but was written over 105 years ago, arguing that explanations based on genetics or biology in general are merely letting the guilty relieve themselves of responsibility, that wrongdoers must take the rap for what they perpetrate rather than passing the buck (i.e., by claiming the devil or my genes or my family made me do it).

Four different case studies of crimes purportedly derived from different causes are described. There follows a discussion of the constitutionality of criminality: what the constitution of the individual comprises in criminality's various manifestations. That is, the chapter addresses whether criminality can be found entirely within the individual person or just when the situation is factored in as well.

Chapter 3 follows the historical development of biogenetic constitutional theories beginning with Lombroso, their decline over the years, and their unexpected resurgence with the discovery of the relationship between multiple physical and/or physiological anomalies and aggressive criminal behavior. The case studies of chapter 3 are discussed and analyzed for main probable causal factors. Recent research using modern brain imaging effects has established the connections among genes, the brain, and offending posited 150 years ago.

Chapter 4 covers the phenomenon of psychopathy and psychopaths. Moving from a historical chronicling of the disorder to the modern identification of it and its pernicious effects on society, the chapter describes various individuals who have been identified as psychopathic and then delves into their psychophysiological anomalies, perhaps causally implicated in their lack of empathy, lack of fear, and inability to anticipate the consequences of their actions. Several case studies are examined in the light of recent research.

Chapter 5 proceeds to identify crucial stages wherein trauma and disruptive events interfere with normal development and investigates how criminality emerges as part of the emotional developmental process of the individual using the overall theoretical scheme of Freud as a basic framework for stage progression. Case studies to illustrate the traumas and other theories such as learning theory are discussed.

Chapter 6 in *part one* traces the stages of cognitive development in the child, integrating the theories of Pavlov, Skinner, Piaget, Freud, and Kohlberg. Research that tests whether achieving a certain cognitive stage of moral development influences behavior is discussed.

In *part two*, case studies of extremely violent individuals are explained by neurological research that shows that stimulation of the amygdala, anterior hypothalamus, or caudate nucleus directly triggers aggression or produces calm and even affection.

Chapter 7 provides an in-depth exploration of the origins of delinquency, including 1) social learning and situational factors, integrating the theories of Bandura, Akers, and sociological approaches; 2) familial factors; 3) effects of the media; 4) peer group and gang influences; and 5) political structure and mass conflict and how in the chaos of open civil war almost everyone is affected. A model outlining the different types of evolved and devolved society is presented.

Chapter 8 presents a model revealing how the structure of society interacts with all the individual idiosyncrasies of its citizens to suppress or minimize crime among its populace, or by contrast, to promote it, especially the performance of atrocities against groups identified as outgroups or the enemy. It becomes increasingly difficult from Tier 1 to Tier 5 to avoid crime and violence.

Chapter 9 examines the phenomena of partner or spousal abuse and child abuse. There follows a discussion of the perspective identifying men in patriarchal society as the perpetrators. However, research over the last 30 years has revealed that once the data get past reports to police, victims of domestic violence and aggression are almost as often male as female and that homosexual and lesbian relationships have elevated levels of domestic violence. The causes—individual, cultural, and societal—are evaluated, and explanations based on social learning paradigms as well as individual predilections are considered.

Child abuse is covered historically as well as analyzed within the same framework of individual idiosyncrasy, cultural values, and the transmission of accepted punitive regimes dealing with children across generations. Recommendations for reducing the incidence of child abuse are discussed.

Chapter 10 may startle the reader by arguing, as Darwin emphasized, that we are creatures of our environments and that the physical environment determines a great deal of our reactions, emotionally, cognitively, and socially, through violence and aggression as a function of **ambient temperature**, especially heat stress. Some of the findings are among the oldest and most robust in the study of crime and criminality. Causal theories have ranged from geographic, sociological, and cultural to psychophysiological. Recent work on the neurophysiology of aggression and violence has found that brain function changes caused by both heat and cold are precursors to antisocial behavior. Cross-cultural findings in the United States, Canada, Europe, and the Far East reveal that violent crime increases as environmental temperature increases. Implications for dealing with crime and climate change are discussed.

Chapter 11 explores the relatively new and inchoate criminological phenomenon of crimes against the environment.

Part one describes how coping with toxic waste produced locally has led to the destruction of natural resources such as fish and forests, as well as to the contamination of the environment upon which people depend. Case studies focusing on pulp mill pollution, the ocean, and landfills of hazardous waste demonstrate that disease and death can be prevalent even in the allegedly sophisticated and democratic countries of the United States and Canada. And we examine the problem of how to evaluate the actions of corporations and governments as they cut economic corners or regard potentially deadly situations as mere misdemeanors versus outright criminal acts.

Part two traces the trafficking of hazardous waste in Canada, the United States, and internationally as corporations and even countries try to rid themselves of the poisonous detritus of industry. Although a north-south axis of movement of waste is hypothesized and poignantly horrendous case studies exist, there appears to be hope as countries such as the United States and Canada create facilities for dealing with the waste, ironically making it more profitable for traffickers to follow the law than to engage in nefarious, illegal activities.

Chapter 12 traces the development of technology in the history of conquest, business, and crime. The use of computers in the present day to engage in cybercrime is discussed at the end of this narrative, beginning with avoiding long distance charges in the late twentieth century to committing large-scale fraud or waging ideological warfare with corporations or other countries.

CHAPTER ONE

WHAT IS A CRIME, WHAT IS NOT?

In this chapter, we will explore how acts can vary in their criminality by jurisdiction, by the historic time in which they occur, and by how much consensus there is regarding their gravity, or "badness." The two mechanisms by which society operates are **norms** that are defined as, first, the appropriate behavior expected of the average citizen and, second, **community standards** (e.g., of tolerance) that refer to the amount of deviation from the norm (in behavior or even in existence) that the same community will tolerate in its citizenry.

CIRCUMSTANCES AND CULTURAL DIFFERENCES DEFINE CRIME: CASE STUDIES

Ian Thomson, an older man living alone in a relatively remote location in the country, is awakened in the middle of the night by the sound of breaking glass. He grabs his gun and looks out the window to where three men wearing balaclava masks are throwing **Molotov cocktails** against his house. He calls 911 and fires his gun over their heads. They flee, and he turns over a surveillance videotape to the police (Gurney, 2013). To his astonishment, they arrest him! Why? Where does he live?

A neighborhood watch volunteer notices a stranger, a tall young man wearing a hoody, walking through his gated neighborhood one evening after dark. He calls 911. The operator advises him not to pursue the youth who overhears his call and turns toward him. The youth, who is African American, begins to challenge him, demanding to know where he lives and then punches him. He falls to the ground, pulls out his gun, and shoots the youth. The police arrive, interview him, and let him go (Botelho & Yan, 2013). Why? Where does he live?

In the play *Mother Courage and Her Children* (Brecht, 1939/1980), a sturdy matriarch halts her caravan at an execution site in the European countryside, realizing with horror that the man bound at the stake is her son. He explains, bemusedly, that he doesn't understand what is going on. Last week he had been raiding villages, raping and killing and pillaging, and had been commended by his commanding officers. This week he did the same thing and has been condemned to death. What is going on?

POLITICS RATHER THAN LOGIC AND THE PUBLIC GOOD DETERMINE LEGAL ACTION

In the 1980s, the Special Committee on Pornography and Prostitution (1985) held hearings across Canada regarding the public's attitude toward **pornography**. Representatives of widely varying groups (who ranged in their politics from social and religious conservatives to a group of young female lawyers in British Columbia) enumerated the viciousness of pornography, pronouncing that it "is the theory and rape is the practice" (Morgan, 1980, p. 139), and recommended redefining obscenity as material in the media that was violent and degrading toward women and others (Cossman, Bell, Gotell, & Ross, 1997). When, citing research conducted in Denmark, Sweden, the United States, and West Germany (Kutchinsky, 1991), I pointed out that sexual crimes against women and children had not risen with the legalization of pornography, I was characterized by some of those groups as "anti-woman." Having found the character of a significant proportion of gay and lesbian pornography to contain sadomasochistic elements, I cautioned those opposed to such content not to promote its criminalization, lest it came back to haunt them. My comments were dismissed as preposterous. As I shall point out on more than one topic in this book, very often criminal justice policy is not guided by empirical findings but rather by waves of populist sentiment championed by activists of one stripe or another.

Not too long after, Janine Fuller, purveyor of lesbian and gay literature via her Little Sister's Book and Art Emporium, had to fight Canada
Customs all the way to the Supreme Court of Canada for the right to
order and disseminate such material, material precisely defined by the
law that emerged from those recommendations as sadomasochistic and
degrading to women (Fuller & Blackley, 1995). In 2004, she was granted
an honorary degree by Simon Fraser University and hailed by many as
a champion of women's rights.

THE CHANGING DEFINITION OF A CRIME AGAINST NATURE: SEXUAL MORES

When I ask my students to describe a "crime against nature," they inevitably volunteer acts that pollute or destroy the environment or natural resources. In fact, a book indicting the administration of President
George W. Bush written by environmental attorney Robert Kennedy Jr.
bears that title (Kennedy, 2004). In law, however, the term has referred
(e.g., since 1814 in the United States) to "unnatural sex acts," such as
oral and anal sex, which to this day remain illegal in several states
(whether committed homosexually or heterosexually), although those
laws are increasingly falling into disuse or gradually being removed
from the criminal code of each state. Such acts have long been totally
legalized among consenting adults under the Canadian Criminal Code
(RSC 1985, c.46, s.159[2]), which is federal so criminal statutes do not
differ among provinces. In Canada, that trend began with Minister of
Justice Pierre Trudeau's declaration in 1967 that "There's no place for
the state in the bedrooms of the nation" (Trudeau, 1967).

Perhaps the most famous case actually occurred in Britain in 1895,
when the renowned playwright Oscar Wilde was sentenced to two
years at hard labor for engaging in such "crimes against nature" with
Lord Alfred Douglas, the son of the Marquess of Queensbury (Hyde,
1963). Marquess Douglas, ironically, wrote the rules of boxing.

That injustice continued into more recent times. For instance, Alan
Turing is considered one of the most brilliant mathematicians ever produced in the UK. He was instrumental in cracking the Enigma Code
used to transmit military orders around the world by Germany in
World War II, thereby shortening the war in Europe, some say by several

years. He went on to build a computational machine, basically a pre-cursor to the computer, known as the **Turing machine**. (The acclaimed 2014 film about Turing, *The Imitation Game*, is worth watching.) Despite his unprecedented contributions to the Allies, he was prosecuted for crimes against nature (homosexuality) in the 1950s and to avoid prison submitted to chemical castration. He died by cyanide poisoning when he was 42 years old—some say by his own hand.

In India, parts of Africa, and various Islamic countries, homosexual acts are punishable by life sentences or even death. In fact, on May 29, 2010, the president of Malawi, which is 80 percent Christian, pardoned a gay couple that had been sentenced to a long prison term for getting married. In part, the pardon came thanks to the intervention of the United Nations Secretary-General (BBC, 2010).

Before those of us living in the United States become too smug, it should be noted that Curtis and Gilreath (2008) in the *Wake Forest Law Review* describe how the persistence of the existence of laws regarding crimes against nature were used recently in Georgia to prosecute a 17-year-old boy who had oral sex with his 15-year-old girlfriend though it was consensual and vaginal sex was not regarded as criminal. The young man received 10 years and had to register as a sex criminal. They also cite a similar case in North Carolina that had a less severe outcome.

What is the point of all the case studies described above? Namely, when it comes to sexuality and sexual behavior, laws differ widely in their prosecution not only in the United States, where much of the criminal code is governed by each state, but also in many different countries where religions vary from Christian to Muslim. Not so in Canada where the criminal code is federal, so all jurisdictions are governed by one law. A second point is that, in the course of history, the mores regarding sexuality have evolved from condemning nonreproductive sex of all kinds, including all homosexual and all oral, anal, and masturbatory practices, to varying degrees of acceptance or indifference. Third, the development of laws that adequately represent these changing sexual mores is fraught with difficulty. For example, an academic analysis of the effects of an advocated policy, an assessment based on foresight into how the desired change in law could play out, might be miscast as obstructionist.

Those young female lawyers in British Columbia who demanded that laws change to make the depiction of violent and degrading sex unlawful did not contemplate the use of that law against material intended for lesbians, some of which is violent. So they once again joined a crusade, this time against the law they had themselves perpetrated. The picture in their collective mind was to oppose male violence against women, not violent sex committed by women against women in videos.

One day, several years ago, I attended a meeting of the women's studies department at my university. I was the only man in the room of over a hundred women. That condition of gender isolation brought home to me how lonely it has been to be a woman for centuries in the former almost exclusively male domain of academia. This isolation is experienced not only in academia. My wife, Cristina Martini, describes arriving in North America as a female engineer and experiencing a less than welcoming climate among her fellow engineers, prompting her to return to college to obtain a charter accountancy designation, which she now uses, ironically, as the CFO of an engineering company. In October 2018, Donna Strickland, an associate professor at the University of Waterloo, won the Nobel Prize in physics, putting the lie to the professor at CERN in Switzerland who recently argued that physics was the purview of men.

I realized then how brave those women were. The only time I had ever experienced anything similar was when I attended the initial meeting of the feminist group of the American Psychological Association at a convention in Washington, DC. Why? As a male who had been greatly influenced by both a strong mother and a loving, instructive sister 10 years older than me, I had been tutored to appreciate the female perspective and plight in society. And now I had two daughters in whose upbringing I was deeply involved as my wife was also in graduate school and had the same heavy schedule of work and study. In Washington, I had been warmly welcomed, but in my own university, I wasn't certain of the audience's reaction to my presence, so I chose to remain circumspect.

The speaker, a law professor from the University of New Mexico, was working the crowd, and it was loving her performance. I listened in disbelief when she commented on how she would like to "get into Madonna's pants" and then went on, rejecting completely the even-handed use of the law, to argue that, when it came to pornography, the law should allow an exception for violent lesbian sex.

The crowd ate it up, but as a male, I felt as though I had stumbled into the female equivalent of a football team's locker room or a barroom full of partisan English soccer fans. Human nature in homogeneous groups is clearly not gender specific. I chose what I would call discretion, not wanting to throw cold water on someone else's party; others might have called it cowardice on my part. Off-color remarks don't usually offend me unless they hurt someone's feelings. What I found disturbing, however, was what appeared to be a lack of logico-deductive reasoning displayed by the law professor. She was apparently of some eminence, having been invited to speak so far from home. How does one operationalize an antiviolence law given that, if the content is deemed lesbian, it is exempt from legal action? How, given the predilection for such material by many males, can one deem certain pornography as lesbian? For example, would a picture in *Playboy* of one female whipping another qualify? I could see no solution to the conundrum in that analysis. Thus the discussion, whether held during the Fraser Commission hearings (Special Committee on Pornography and Prostitution, 1985) or in the special lecture in women's studies, is often characterized by two things. The first is a picture in the activists' minds of what they oppose and, narrowly framed, wish changed at all costs. Second, there is a demand for exceptionalism, in other words, exemption from the unexpected consequences of any change in law (once a law has been adopted that targets what the proponents opposed) if those consequences affect the minority groups whom there was no intention to victimize. Perhaps, the old adage—"Be careful what you wish for"—would apply.

COERCIVE CONFORMITY

As a researcher in the area of group **conformity**, I examined the situation and wondered if that influence was at work. In our research (Boyanowsky & Allen, 1973), we found that individuals would change their judgments to go along with the **ingroup** majority even if it espoused opinions diametrically opposed to the individual's private opinion and even if one individual supported those opinions but was perceived to be a member of the disliked **outgroup**. Regardless of the group's composition, or of its previous victimhood, the same powerful ingroup conformity processes prevail and overcome phlegmatic logical analysis.

To turn back to the question of the law professor arguing for the exemption of depictions of violent lesbian sex from pornography laws, although the intention could have been to seek a higher degree of justice by overturning the usual thinking about gender, violence, and sex, the crowd's ethos appeared more apt to be "Now it's our turn." And so, to me, the situation demonstrated why so many laws remain unjust. Perhaps a Marxian analysis is in order here. Karl Marx would argue that all relations, even sexual ones, are based on who has the power (MacKinnon, 1989) rather than on a striving toward **egalitarianism**.

THE VARIETIES OF SEXUAL DESIRE

Even as anal and oral sex and homosexuality have achieved tolerance (a shifting community standard) and even acceptance (approaching normality) in most Western societies, there is one form of sexual desire that remains taboo and abhorred—pedophilia, usually defined as the desire for sexual relations with individuals under the age of 13, although the legal rule varies from one place to another. In Canada, the age is 16, and there must be full consent. In homosexual relations, it is 18 years of age (though the gay community is lobbying to have it reduced to 16 years of age as well). As homosexuality was in the past, pedophilia is most often a dark secret, and like homosexuality, it has proved intransigent to clinical treatment.

In my opinion, invoking Darwin, sexuality, like other characteristics, manifests itself in all the permutations possible, with heterosexuality and preference for attractive mates of reproductive age prevailing as the most reproductively successful manifestation of sexual preference (i.e., strategy) because it enables the survival of the gene pool. I do not preclude the other possibilities that keep reappearing in the population, however. And those variations include lust for members of the same sex and, in addition, lust for young children, those pubescent, those somewhat older than the individual, and even the very old—hence the persistence of all of those forms. That is the growing conclusion of many, most prominent among whom is Dr. Michael Seto, one of the pre-eminent authorities on the subject whose landmark *Archives of Sexual Behavior* article is titled "Is Pedophilia a Sexual Orientation?"(2012).

In Toronto in 2006, Michael Briere, the murderer of 10-year-old Holly Jones, was removed from society for 25 years. He claimed viewing child pornography drove him to his crimes. How then do we deal with the issue of prevention? As an academic working in criminal psychology, I have the privilege—in fact, given my field of study, an obligation—to think about such very difficult issues for more than five minutes.

The facts as reported are apparently pretty straightforward: Briere said he "always" wanted to have sex with a young girl, that he "must have viewed some (pornographic) material beforehand," and, apparently in a frenzy, went out and at random grabbed, tried unsuccessfully to have sex with, and then, pathetically fearful of discovery, killed an innocent child. The self-evident solution is to ban child pornography, that is, explicit material whose intention is to arouse sexual desire in the consumer and that depicts individuals under the age of consent. How could there be any disagreement? Most of us find such material either at least merely irrelevant to our interests or, very often, offensive and even disgusting. We must, however, ask what it is we are trying to achieve. If it is the protection of children from sexual exploitation, that is already a serious crime. It is illegal to have sex with underage children. If it is preventing the production or trafficking in such materials, that too is prohibited. It is illegal to exploit children sexually for commercial purposes in most if not all countries. If it is to prevent the viewing of such materials, the consequences for society become more complex.

Are we as a society in favor of banning the viewing of materials whose content we find offensive or that depict acts that we find repugnant? If so, I believe we do so ill advisedly. For example, in the 1960s, the world watched in horror the US telecasts of the beating of civil rights marchers in the South and of the little Vietnamese girl who was suffering from napalm burns. And in the 1980s, the televised beating by Los Angeles police of Rodney King disgusted and appalled us. We all know what followed: public indignation and positive social and political change aimed at the perceived injustices depicted. In those instances, viewing violence proved a useful if uncomfortable spur to rectify the injustices involved.

Such outcomes notwithstanding, in the United States, Canada, and Britain, recent laws have made access to pornography depicting under-age children in sexual situations illegal. That is, merely looking at a sexualized image of a child on your computer potentially makes you a criminal. Although the laws are usually couched in words apparently intended to deter predators, viewing this pornography has also been outlawed, springing special police units manned by officers sharing the views of the anti-pornography lobby of previous decades, perspectives that have spread very widely. Most notoriously, they enveloped the singer-songwriter Peter Townshend in the United Kingdom among others, but also thousands of offenders in the United States where viewing child pornography is in some jurisdictions now a felony punishable by a minimum of five years. In Canada, dozens of individuals, including surgeons, career soldiers, and most recently a prominent prosecutor, have been charged, none of whom has a record of previous offenses against children.

In addition, the murder of Jane Longhurst by Graham Coutts, who allegedly watched web sites such as Rape Action, inspired her mother to lobby for a law forbidding "violent and extreme" pornography in the United Kingdom, reminiscent of the Canadian law to which I have referred. The upshot of all those efforts is that, in Britain, criminal responsibility has been shifted from producers (targeted by the Obscene Publications Act of 1959) to, in May of 2008, consumers of pornography. And, barring the entreaties of the Baroness Miller of Chilthorne Domer and a few others, this shift has happened with hardly a whimper from the academic community, politicians, and the public. It is, in my opinion, a breach of the rights of individuals of an almost unprecedented magnitude. How can one justify such a truncation of freedom?

Both the sexual exploitation of children and the production and trafficking of such photos and audiovisual materials are already illegal. Does it not follow that, in order to protect our basic freedom to seek any information extant, including images and words, the mere viewing of materials, however offensive, should not be illegal? Perhaps the only remaining compelling reason for criminalization is that the material does cause violently aggressive behavior on the part of most viewers.

To wit, testimony based on laboratory studies and given to the Fraser Commission and under oath in court by some social scientists had convinced the lawmakers that viewing such materials led to antisocial behavior.

But do those findings translate into significant trends in the real world? Is there such evidence? In fact, the research on child pornography reveals a great irony. The first evidence arose in Denmark, where the legalization of all pornography, including child pornography, was followed by a reduction in child molestation (Hessick, 2011). Research on sex offenses in most countries, including Japan, since the legalization of pornography or the liberalization of pornography laws has revealed a similar drop in sexual offense crime rates, including rape (Diamond & Uchiyama, 1999; Kutchinsky, 1973). With the popularization of the Internet in the mid-nineties, there has been an uncontrolled, unprecedented explosion of pornographic materials and of consumer usage of every type, including heterosexual, homosexual, child, and bestial. Pornographic sites are among the most accessed in the world, according to some researchers (Castleman, 2016). A causal link would predict a commensurate huge increase in violent sex crimes such as aggravated rape and child molestation or at least a statistically significant increase. Our research (Boyanowsky & McElveen, 2010) and that of others has revealed no such trend (for a review of findings on both sides of the issue, see Gillespie, 2012). In fact, contrary to some of the claims made by social scientists and members of the public alike, the rate of serious sex crimes has paradoxically declined (Finkelhor, Shattuck, Turner, & Hamby, 2014).

How can that be? The decline is certainly not because in this era of heightened sensitivity to the abuse of children we have become laissez-faire regarding such offenses. On the other hand, a major factor is that, for those with various sexual preferences, exposure to erotic materials of choice, resulting in an appropriate degree of arousal, provokes innocuous outlets, whether social or solitary, consensual sex with a partner or masturbation. For many **pedophiles**, however, clinical studies (Seto, 2018) and my own conversations with clinicians have revealed that there exists a major deficit in arousal in the absence of sexually preferred individuals. Thus exposure to the pornographic material alleviates that chronic deficit. And, of course, viewing such material for arousal purposes is much safer and more immediate than pursuing arousal through the risky behavior involved in hanging around school-yards or serving in a childcare capacity or as a teacher or clergy member and preying upon children.

Once aroused, individuals can then easily achieve release. Thus the irony is that by banning mere viewing, we may be promoting more actual predation in a very repressed sector of the populace who often lead otherwise normal lives. That subsector of the populace appears to be a product of genetic or other constitutional variation and is much wider spread than previously suspected. To wit, Jack Crone, a senior executive with RBC Dominion Securities in Vancouver with a $600,000 salary, a wife and seven children, and no previous record of child abuse or any other crime, was convicted of possessing child pornography on his computer and sentenced to prison (CBC, 2009). On June 6, 2012, Christopher Ingvaldson, a private school teacher with no previous record, was convicted of the same crime (Hager, 2013). Googling child pornography convictions brings up many such cases.

So, did Michael Briere abduct Holly Jones because, in his words, he "must" have been viewing child pornography? Perhaps, but if that is true, it is an exception to any observed trend, long term and short term, and not only the wrong reason for legislative initiative, given recent precedents, but potentially downright dangerous for society in general and for our children in particular. As those earnest young lawyers addressing the Fraser Commission hopefully learned, when we rush to change laws to eliminate those things we find personally offensive, rather than first carefully researching the effects of those changes upon crime rates, we do so, as a society, at our peril. That is why there is an extremely important role to be played by the discipline of scientific criminology—the study of the effects of the law—whenever lawyers and legislators mount a campaign to make a human activity illegal.

CONCLUSIONS

So, as we have shown, in Western jurisdictions (barring the edicts of the Catholic Church), homosexuality and oral and anal sex have segued in the eye of most of the public from crimes against God and abnormal perversions to merely distasteful practices to being almost universally accepted in secular Western European and North American societies as within the range of normal sexuality. Homosexuality has come to be viewed as inborn and very compelling rather than as a lifestyle preference by most of the public, if not by the fundamentalist protestant and Catholic churches. Hence, gay marriage is widely accepted. But the same status has not been accorded pedophilia, largely to protect children, who as minors are under the protection of the state and assumed not able to make their own decisions regarding sexual behavior. Children are thought to need protection from the desires of adults and, in modern times, even from their own parents and custodians.

PROTECTING YOUNG PEOPLE FROM BEHAVIOR THEY MAY ACTUALLY DESIRE

In the past, during more traditional and conservative times, children who perceived themselves to be members of the opposite gender were scoffed at or even punished by their parents, leading these children sometimes to self-mutilation and suicide. Fortunately, that condition is now recognized as part of the same Darwinian random selection lottery, and remedies are available. Kian Olsheski always felt he was a boy trapped in a girl's body. Finally, at age 14, having researched his plight, he wrote a heartrending letter to his parents (Beard, 2019). To their credit, he was able to convince them and now lives as a 17-year-old boy, doing what he always loved: skateboarding, playing in the woods, and hunting. He even has a beard and a girlfriend. But one form of sexual activity remains prohibited.

On Tuesday, March 7, 2017, Jaclyn McLaren, a middle school (sixth to eighth grade) teacher in Belleville, Ontario, pleaded guilty to several charges of having had sex with at least eight of her teenaged male students (Canadian Press, 2017). It may have begun when one student inadvertently found a nude selfie photo of McLaren while using her cellular phone in the classroom for school purposes and began to blackmail her for more, which progressed to her having oral sex with at least two of her students and another teenaged male. From court records, it appears the boys regarded the activity as a source of status and self-aggrandizement and passed the photos around. In other cultures and times previous, society may have concurred. In fact, in many societies

16- or even 14-year-old boys are warriors, armed and dangerous and engaged in killing and sexual assault as the spoils of war (e.g., in North American aboriginal and African tribal societies—though it is true that many boys have been coerced into these roles, especially in Africa). The Belleville boys' reaction of braggadocio notwithstanding, today the criminal justice system declared them victims, saying also that they had been victimized by child pornography, as at least one student sent his teacher a photo of his genitals. McLaren was sentenced to two years in prison followed by two years of probation (CBC, 2017).

The issues in this case are the betrayal of trust in regard to McLaren's position as a teacher. The child pornography charge appears rather moot, as it was the boy who sent her the photo of himself, perhaps voluntarily, but once a law is in place, it works more like a blunt object, more like a hammer than a surgical instrument. A very different attitude toward student-teacher relations was expressed in Mordecai Richler's book *Cocksure*, wherein an older female teacher took over a classroom of obstreperous young boys and turned them into model, well-behaved scholars (Richler, 1968). When asked by a visiting group the secret of her **pedagogical** success, she proudly announces she performed **fellatio** on them when they got out of hand, eliciting shock but also garnering admiration.

The book, seen as harmless and amusing in Canada and the United States when it was published, would almost certainly be condemned in those countries by many if not most for its ethos today. In fact, although it won the Governor-General's Award for literature in 1968, it was banned from stores in the UK, Australia, New Zealand, Ireland, and South Africa. Mr. Richler, however, was not charged with creating child pornography. Given the turn of events, would he be today, and does it make sense to regard such writing, intended to be satirical and humorous, as pornographic? And so norms, laws, and standards of tolerance, though affecting one another, can cycle—often in **dissynchrony** with one another.

THE EVOLUTION VERSUS THE CONSTANCY OF WHAT IS A CRIME

According to my students and Robert Kennedy, however, the idea of crime against nature has evolved into something very different in the minds of the public. What crime? Whose nature?

Do those examples imply that there is no enduring consensus through history and across sociocultural-political boundaries on what is a crime? Not so, say many criminologists such as Graeme Newman (1976) who found considerable agreement in the condemnation of several crimes among people surveyed in countries as widely ranging as India, Indonesia, Iran, Italy, the United States, and Yugoslavia although there was some disagreement about the severity of punishment appropriate for acts such as robbery, appropriation or larceny, incest, and, surprisingly, factory pollution. Homosexuality was perceived as deserving of punishment by a majority of informants in all but the US sample.

If, however, the definition of a crime is the breaking of a law, described by Wilson and Herrnstein (1985) as an identifiable behavior circumscribed in place and in time, then, ironically, states of tyranny imposing horrific treatment on citizenry by despots are not criminal; the oppressive, unjust acts of tyrants are not crimes so long as they do not contravene the criminal code of their country.

Are all laws then purely arbitrary? No, says Sorokin (2002) in his early landmark study. There are laws outlawing acts that are viewed as intrinsically bad by all societies and so criminal. An example would be murder and those identified by Newman (1976) cross-culturally, in other words, acts that are mala in se (bad in themselves). But of course, not all acts are universally abhorred, so some are merely mala prohibita, crimes by virtue of an existing law. Are there some examples one can point to among our opening case studies or are they all mala in se? Perhaps.

Although murder, the intentional killing of another human being, is universally condemned and so categorized as mala in se (bad in itself), the definition of a human being employed and the circumstances in which the act of murder occurs determine whether it is a crime in a society. In our *Mother Courage* (Brecht, 1939/1980) example, her son was being executed because he had killed a peasant in a raid, although such killing was condoned by the state while battles were being waged in the Thirty Years War in Europe. He had obviously not been made aware of an armistice declared while he continued to kill the enemy. Killing in peacetime was punishable by death. Here is an instance when cell phones might have saved his life.

LIFE VERSUS CHOICE AND THE INTENTION TO KILL

Driving through the Mt. Currie Indian Reserve recently, I noticed a sign on a church that read "Respect All Life From Conception to Natural Death." Clearly, the sentiment communicated was that a fetus from its earliest form was a human being and should not be aborted. That is the position of the Roman Catholic Church and many other religions and was the official view for many years in Canada and the United States. After a century or more of back-alley abortions, deaths of young girls and women, and the misery of unwanted children, laws were passed in both the United States and Canada allowing legalized abortions under specific conditions (Criminal Law Amendment Act, 1968–69) or restrictions were declared unconstitutional (as in *Roe v. Wade*, 1973).

Nevertheless, because individual hospital boards, some of them Catholic, refused to provide any abortions and there was a lack of facilities in other locations; because some women were reluctant to submit their case to any public body; and, in the end, because of the belief that a woman should have ultimate decision-making power over her own body, Dr. Henry Morgentaler, a Canadian physician, established freestanding women's abortion clinics, in direct contravention of the law (Pelrine, 1983). Morgentaler was repeatedly charged and tried by jury—and repeatedly set free by those juries of his peers (Martin, 2008). That created a conflict between the written law and the will of the people, which led to the law being challenged as violating the Charter of Rights in the Canadian Constitution. As a result, the law was struck down as unconstitutional (*R. v. Morgentaler*, 1988)—another manifestation or outcome largely produced by what we have referred to as community standards, a very important concept referring to what the public will tolerate or not tolerate or what the public refuses to act on, despite the actual existence of the law.

Community standards and public will are the mechanisms that govern the legal system. They operate analogously to Darwin's theory of natural selection that accounts for what life forms will survive and thrive (Darwin, 1859/2005). In similar fashion, they determine what laws will actually be enforced regardless of the efforts of government in a democracy to spell things out in legislation. For example, blasphemous libel was a Canadian law based on the precept that the constitution operates under God, making it a crime to verbalize harsh criticisms of any religion (Criminal Code RSC, 1985, c.46, s.296). This law was repealed only in December 2018. Whether the statute would have survived a constitutional challenge in modern times is debatable, but the last time it led to a conviction (of an Anglican priest for posting a criticism of the Catholic Church in Quebec) was way back in 1935. A similar law exists in Ireland, but another was recently wiped from the books in the UK. So the ultimate crime historically in those countries where the Catholic Church ruled all aspects of life was a crime against "God." This sort of crime remains paramount in some fundamentalist Muslim countries (e.g., Saudi Arabia and Iran), but elsewhere it is now receding in importance through being ignored, even as deviance (or apostasy) is tolerated and ultimately as the public will slackens and the law falls into disuse. In the United States, **blasphemy** laws in individual states have a colorful history dating from the seventeenth century. There is a blasphemy law still on the books in the Massachusetts General Laws based on one dating from 1697:

> Whoever willfully blasphemes the holy name of God by denying, cursing or contumeliously reproaching God, his creation, government or final judging of the world, or by cursing or contumeliously reproaching Jesus Christ or the Holy Ghost, or by cursing or contumeliously reproaching or exposing to contempt and ridicule, the holy word of God contained in the holy scriptures shall be punished by imprisonment in jail for not more than one year or by a fine of not more than three hundred dollars, and may also be bound to good behavior. (MGL c.272 § 36)

That law leaves little room for many standup comics or Monty Python movies such as 1979's *The Life of Brian*, called blasphemy by the Archdiocese of New York and condemned by the Rabbinical Alliance as a vicious attack on Judaism and the Bible. Fortunately, New York apparently had no blasphemy law in place, and the director Terry Jones and the cast got away scot-free.

But more surprisingly, given its recent date, is a twenty-first-century blasphemy case in Pennsylvania. That state had enacted a law against blasphemy in 1977. In the fall of 2007, George Kalman, an enterprising businessman and producer, applied to the Pennsylvania Department of State to incorporate a film company called I Choose Hell Productions LLC. The Pennsylvania Department of State informed him that his application could not be accepted because a business name "may not contain words that constitute blasphemy, profane cursing or swearing or that profane the Lord's name." In February 2009, Kalman filed suit to have the provision against blasphemy struck down as unconstitutional. On June 30, 2010, US District Judge Michael M. Bayslon of the Eastern District of Pennsylvania, in a 68-page opinion, ruled in favor of Kalman, finding that the Pennsylvania blasphemy statute violated both the Establishment Clause and the Free Exercise Clause of the First Amendment to the United States Constitution.

In fact, no one has been convicted of violating a blasphemy law in the United States since atheist activist Charles Smith of Little Rock, Arkansas. In 1928, he rented a storefront and gave out free atheist literature there:

> The sign in the window read: "Evolution Is True. The Bible's a Lie. God's a Ghost." For this, he was charged with violating the city ordinance against blasphemy. Because he was an atheist, and therefore, wouldn't swear the court's religious oath to tell the truth, he wasn't permitted to testify in his own defense. The judge then dismissed the original charge, replacing it with one of distributing obscene, slanderous, or scurrilous literature. Smith was convicted, fined $25, and served most of a twenty-six-day jail sentence. His high-profile fast while behind bars drew national media attention.
>
> Upon his release, he immediately resumed his atheistic activities, was again charged with blasphemy, and this time convicted. In his trial he was once more denied the right to testify and was sentenced to ninety days in jail and a fine of $100. Released on $1,000 bail, Smith appealed the verdict. The case then dragged on for several years, until it was finally dismissed. ("Charles Lee Smith," 2018)

Like civil rights statutes, blasphemy laws in the United States are an example of the conflict and tension that exist between the statutes of individual states and the First Amendment of the American Constitution: "Congress shall make no law respecting an establishment of religion, or prohibiting the free exercise thereof; or abridging the freedom of speech, or of the press...."

The First Amendment, then, invokes a community standard of tolerance (for deviance, the abnormal, the minority) that may fly in the face of existing community norms. Community norms, unlike community standards, represent the average or modal (most common) way of thinking or behaving in a community. A "norm," then, is a very different concept and one that people wishing to punish "deviants" often invoke, saying, for example, "Most decent people don't behave that way." Americans can be grateful that the authors of the Constitution in their intellectual brilliance appreciated the difference and created a bill of rights to protect those "different" ways of thinking and behaving.

Those case studies of the history of blasphemy laws demonstrate how laws once deemed the highest priority when offenses against the deity were unanimously perceived to be paramount in gravity and to be enforced rigidly as a deterrent to the people slowly eroded in importance with the advent of new information like Darwin's theories. Those new paradigms created division in beliefs among the populace. What was once self-evident truth for the country was now being challenged. There were competing norms, so community standards of tolerance for deviance increased. Eventually, even for Christian citizens, secular authorities and the judiciary replaced the august position of the Church.

LAWS AGAINST IMBIBING, INGESTING, AND INHALING SUBSTANCES BASED ON HARM DONE VERSUS HARM REDUCTION

Perhaps one of the most fascinating areas of criminality is ingestion of substances. Christianity historically supports drinking wine, whether turning water into wine as a miracle wrought by Jesus Christ or wine's representation as the blood of Christ in communion. So drinking wine could hardly be regarded as mala in se, though in fundamentalist Muslim countries it is strictly illegal (and for being involved in bootlegging, even punishable by death or by up to 150 lashes in some states such as Saudi Arabia). Drinking alcohol is also forbidden in Mormon society. And, in fact, groups led by the Women's Christian Temperance Union, despite the politically disadvantaged position of women in early-twentieth-century US and Canadian society, were able to push through the laws prohibiting alcohol that prevailed in both countries. **Prohibition** was first enacted on a provincial basis in Canada in 1901 in Prince Edward Island. Eventually other provinces followed. It lasted well into the 1920s when temperance laws started to be repealed, province by province.

With the passing of the **Volstead Act**, the United States followed suit from 1920 to 1933. That allowed Sam Bronfman, the notorious Montreal liquor producer, to amass his fortune running booze to the States (Faith, 2007). Some say the Kennedy family of Boston made its fortune the same way (Marrus, 1992). Obviously, the bootleggers' opportunistic behavior was regarded as merely mala prohibita or it would have been much more difficult for those families to achieve the status and respectability they eventually did after Prohibition was repealed. In a similar vein in 2014, Marc Emery, a Vancouver entrepreneur who made a fortune selling marijuana seeds to US buyers on the Internet, was released after serving a five-year sentence in the United States (Hayward, 2010). It remains to be seen what his place in history will be as California, and many other states, have recently decriminalized or outright legalized the possession of marijuana. The Prime Minister of Canada, Justin Trudeau, has followed suit, and marijuana was officially legalized in Canada on October 17, 2018.

Prohibition triggered one of the largest outbreaks of gang violence in US history as various mobs fought for their piece of the action in illegal sales (Boyanowsky, 2009), and the current prohibition on recreational drugs has spawned the same type of gang violence in normally peaceful Canada. So the issue does indeed involve relative harm done on a much larger scale. The HBO TV series *Boardwalk Empire* is a brilliant depiction of that violent 1920s era in American history.

It is not that the advocates of the ban had no basis for their enmity toward alcohol. Anecdotal evidence and scientific study to the present day can point to the effect of alcohol on human health (alcohol, unlike other drugs, distributes itself throughout every water-containing cell in the body—hence the characterization "pickled" is valid; National Institutes of Health, 2007). Other effects include reduced economic productivity, domestic dysfunction, and abuse of women and children, not to mention physical and verbal aggression against men, traffic accidents, and deaths and disease and general public disorder. For those reasons, a case was made for the consumption of alcohol being mala in se.

Defenders of alcohol argue for its positive effects as a social lubricant, disinhibitor, and relaxant—and, especially with red wine, even as a reducer of strokes. They often also point to it as the least of evils compared to recreational drugs, especially **narcotics** such as heroin and amphetamines such as crystal methamphetamine. In the thirties and forties, marijuana was vilified as a demon drug (the now cult film originally produced as a public deterrent, *Reefer Madness*, is worth watching, if only for a chuckle). By the 1970s, marijuana was paired with alcohol in the public eye as a mild drug, probably little more dangerous than tobacco. The demon drug then was heroin as laboratory studies had shown that rats made physically dependent on heroin or its similar counterpart, morphine, would keep taking it and abstain from food until they died (Beck & O'Brien, 1980).

Professor Bruce Alexander, a psychologist at Simon Fraser University, noted how similar the lives of those woebegone rats captive in bleak wire cages were to the desolate lives of heroin addicts. So he set up an experiment wherein all rats were made physically dependent on morphine, a medically dispensed form of heroin (because heroin is illegal to prescribe—another quirk of lawmaking that makes no sense since morphine is reputedly even harder to stop taking once addicted). Half of the subjects were left in the single wire cages and kept taking morphine. The other half was placed in Rat Park, a large enclosure where they could fight, procreate, build nests, and establish social networks. Those rats, by and large, stopped taking morphine despite its continued availability and went "cold turkey," demonstrating how social circumstances and opportunities can trump physical addiction and dependency (Alexander, Coambs, & Hadaway, 1978).

Dr. Alexander related in guest lectures to my class in the 1980s that they had extreme difficulty publishing their startlingly dramatic results since they flew in the face of conventional medical wisdom. All the research published previously on the topic found that addicted rats would take heroin or morphine and neglect taking food and water until they died. For Alexander, his finding was a testament to the salutary power of a rich social life in defiance of merely "feeding the monkey"—the addiction—to the importance of not living alone in a wire cage devoid of stimulation, a situation comparable to the bleak solitude opiate addicts retreat to even on the street.

Obviously, much of the drug issue for humans is more complex. Witness the number of deaths among wealthy artists and actors at the top of their game, perhaps most poignantly Philip Seymour Hoffman (who had recently won an Academy Award for best actor), Heath Ledger, Amy Winehouse, and too many others. But it does bode well for rehabilitation programs that promote a rich social life, physical exertion, and immersion in the natural world, which all combine to overcome the sterility of a lonely room with only the needle and the drug to anesthetize the pain and loneliness of despair.

Now the research shows that tobacco is exceedingly dangerous to one's health (Physicians for a Smoke-Free Canada, 2003). And even marijuana, in its most recent, extremely potent iteration, is dangerous and can trigger psychosis in some young people (Fergussen, Poulten, Smith, & Boden, 2006). Nevertheless, "crystal-meth" has somehow pre-empted first heroin and then cocaine as the most demonic drug, one that is regarded as so addictive and violence-causing that it must be prohibited at all costs (National Institute on Drug Abuse, 2002, 2007). What has precipitated that change?

Heroin (actually its precursor, opium) was resisted by the Chinese who were forced by the British in two conflicts in the mid-1800s to allow its importation from British India (Moulder, 1977). Heroin was also lauded as a replacement for morphine. Heroin was the latest thing: a nonaddictive wonder drug marketed as **Bayer's H** in North America and used widely by society matrons (our great- and great-great-grandmothers) to eliminate the vapors, a state of melancholy, and to reduce "hysteria" (Askwith, 1998). Then, in Canada, Prime Minister Mackenzie King had it brought to his attention that not only Chinese "coolies" (workers) were using it regularly but white Anglo-Saxon citizens as well, so he introduced legislation making it illegal (Carstairs, 2006). So too, in 1919, the US courts ruled that doctors could not prescribe heroin to heroin-dependent people (Davenport-Hines, 2004). As mentioned earlier, the criminalization of heroin and then marijuana and other drugs has fueled the second major crime wave in North

America, spanning Canada, the United States, and, most virulently, Mexico (Carstairs, 2006).

The history of criminalization has tracked first alcohol, then heroin, then marijuana, then cocaine, and then amphetamines. Finally, tobacco is now making its run to be declared illegal (Bailey, 2010) based on the principle that it is mala in se, that is, intrinsically evil or bad. In many places, including Vancouver, British Columbia, it is now illegal to smoke tobacco indoors in gathering places or even in parks and other public places outdoors. I think the actual lesson to be gleaned from such events, as illustrated by HBO TV's *Boardwalk Empire* regarding North America's historically most serious crime wave, is that prohibiting dangerous drugs promotes more crime than it prevents. That is, this prohibition creates harm. So if society can somehow manage for most of its citizens to regulate the use of alcohol, that most dangerous drug (based on its effects on society, physically and socially), decriminalizing other drugs should follow and should lead to less crime in general. Let us now examine the evidence.

To begin, people don't usually kill one another over alcohol, except where it is illegal, such as on certain Native American reservations and in other places with large indigenous populations, such as **Nunavut** in Northern Canada. Those constituencies made it illegal to possess alcoholic beverages without a permit in hopes of reducing alcohol's epidemiological effects, and that prohibition has, once again, made bootlegging remarkably profitable with the attendant criminal gangs proliferating (Canadian Press, 2010). In summary, our analysis suggests that drugs, wherever illegal, are rendered mere mala prohibita.

Some disagree, claiming decriminalizing all drugs will trigger huge increases in use, thereby increasing harm done (Weatherburn & Jones, 2001). Yet the one bold decriminalization experiment undertaken so far, by Portugal in 2001, has demonstrated that, contrary to common sense and moralistic analyses, there has been a decrease in the use of drugs by its young people—as well as a drop in **HIV-AIDS** and in injection drug use (Greenwald, 2009) and a decrease in the rate of violence associated with the drug trade. This finding parallels the trend that occurred when Prohibition was revoked and the consumption of alcohol became legal. Hence, significant harm reduction has ensued.

MALA IN SE BASED ON RELIGIOUS SCRIPTURE

The other basis for mala in se is religion. That is, God's or Mohammed's or Christ's word is that the activity in question is against his will and so should not only be declared a sin but a crime. Thus, devotees turn to their holy scriptures to align themselves against a certain behavior or group.

In her radio show, Dr. Laura Schlesinger allegedly said that, because she is an observant Orthodox Jew, she views homosexuality as an abomination according to Leviticus 18:22, so it cannot be condoned under any circumstance. The following response is an open letter to Dr. Laura ("Fact Check: Letter to Dr. Laura," 2004), written by an unknown person though apocryphally attributed to Dr. J. F. Kaufmann (whom he claims it falsely made famous) and posted anonymously on the Internet:

Dear Dr. Laura:
Thank you for doing so much to educate people regarding God's Law. I have learned a great deal from your show, and I try to share that knowledge with as many people as I can. When someone tries to defend the homosexual lifestyle, for example, I simply remind him that Leviticus 18:22 clearly states it to be an abomination. End of debate.

I do need some advice from you, however, regarding some of the specific laws and how to best follow them.
a) When I burn a bull on the altar as a sacrifice, I know it creates a pleasing odor for the Lord (Lev 1:9). The problem is my neighbors. They claim the odor is not pleasing to them. Should I smite them?
b) I would like to sell my daughter into slavery, as sanctioned in Exodus 21:7. In this day and age, what do you think would be a fair price for her?
c) I know that I am allowed no contact with a woman while she is in her period of menstrual uncleanliness (Lev 15:19–24). The problem is, how do I tell? I have tried asking, but most women take offense.
d) Lev. 25:44 states that I may indeed possess slaves, both male and female, provided they are purchased from neighboring nations. A friend of mine claims that this applies to Mexicans, but not Canadians. Can you clarify? Why can't I own Canadians?
e) I have a neighbor who insists on working on the Sabbath. Exodus 35:2 clearly states he should be put to death. Am I morally obligated to kill him myself?

f) A friend of mine feels that even though eating shellfish is an Abomination (Lev 11:10), it is a lesser abomination than homosexuality. I don't agree. Can you settle this?

g) Lev 21:20 states that I may not approach the altar of God if I have a defect in my sight. I have to admit that I wear reading glasses. Does my vision have to be 20/20, or is there some wiggle room here?

h) Most of my male friends get their hair trimmed, including the hair around their temples, even though this is expressly forbidden by Lev 19:27. How should they die?

i) I know from Lev 11:6–8 that touching the skin of a dead pig makes me unclean, but may I still play football if I wear gloves?

j) My uncle has a farm. He violates Lev 19:19 by planting two different crops in the same field, as does his wife by wearing garments made of two different kinds of thread (cotton/polyester blend). He also tends to curse and blaspheme a lot. Is it really necessary that we go to all the trouble of getting the whole town together to stone them? (Lev 24:10–16) Couldn't we just burn them to death at a private family affair like we do with people who sleep with their in-laws? (Lev. 20:14)

I know you have studied these things extensively, so I am confident you can help.

Thank you again for reminding us that God's word is eternal and unchanging.

Your devoted disciple and adoring fan.

Clearly, whether the letter is from Dr. Kaufman or an anonymous impostor, the point it makes so eloquently (the author's disingenuousness notwithstanding) is that, if you use the scriptures to determine what a crime is, you must abide by all scriptural dictates rather than picking and choosing because they are the unassailable word of God.

CRIMINAL JUSTICE SYSTEMS

Thanks to TV shows such as *Law & Order*, internationally, many people know some elements of the US criminal justice system better than they do their own systems. For instance, in Canada, judges are all appointed by the provincial government for provincial courts or by the federal government for superior and supreme court positions. In the United States, however, many state judges are elected or have to stand for reelection after being initially appointed. On the other hand, nominees to the Supreme Court (one chief justice and eight associates) and to other federal superior courts are chosen by the president and ratified by the Senate based on their conception of the individual's merit. Therefore, although a mix of methods exists, many American judges gain office through the will of the people. That is incomprehensible to the rest of the world because only two other nations have judicial elections. In some small Swiss cantons, judges are elected; and in Japan, supreme court justices may have to run for reelection, but it is largely a formality (Liptak, 2008).

The argument is that, in a democracy, the people must decide who becomes a judge. The opposing, Canadian view is that judges voted in by the people can be swayed by public opinion (community norms, as we discussed) in what is basically a popularity contest, making it more difficult for them to remain impartial, especially in cases involving unpopular defendants or victims. Hence the killings of civil rights activists in Alabama during the 1960s by members of the **Ku Klux Klan** were not prosecuted as murder (a state crime) due to the objections by the community and state government to the civil rights activism of those murdered (community norms favored segregation). They were prosecuted as a conspiracy to commit murder (a federal crime and a lesser offense) and adjudicated over by appointed federal justices selected on the basis of merit. Once again the power of community standards is demonstrated, even in the face of the law. To reiterate, community standards are what the citizens will tolerate other people doing. These standards are unlike community norms, which represent what most people think, do, expect, or epitomize. Thus, the community norm just about anywhere in the world is heterosexuality, but community standards regarding whether a city or country accepts or at least tolerates homosexuality vary widely. Consider the similarities and differences between San Francisco and Malawi, for example. In those two jurisdictions, community norms may be identical (heterosexual couples), but community standards (acceptance of gay and lesbian relationships) could not be more different.

Also, in Canada the Criminal Code is federal and so uniform across the country. In the United States, each state has its own criminal code. That is why certain sex acts, such as oral sex, anal sex, and masturbation, are still illegal in certain states (decreasingly so, though the laws, like those of blasphemy, may remain on the books). Also illegal in some states is abortion (under certain circumstances) as well as gay marriage. All are legal in Canada.

Some Canadians as well as all Americans are startled when the Crown (prosecution) in a Canadian court appeals a verdict of not guilty. They cite double jeopardy, the principle that a member of the public cannot be tried twice for the same crime. That principle exists only in the United States. In Canada but not in the United States, defendants can be tried again. Thus there are some significant differences between the two apparently similar criminal justice systems, though they are both based on English common law.

In Italy, procedures can be even more convoluted, as Amanda Knox, the young American student from Seattle, discovered. After being denigrated in the press, she was convicted of murdering a roommate during a "sex orgy" and sentenced to 26 years of imprisonment in 2007. But she was found not guilty upon appeal, at which point the prosecution appealed that verdict and won a new guilty verdict. In the meantime, however, she had returned to the United States after already serving four years in prison. She did not return to Italy and, in 2015, was finally exonerated in absentia by Italy's Supreme Court. No more prosecution would thus be allowed on the charge of murder. Her hopes were not high when the tortuous process dragged on, but apparently justice finally prevailed (Knox, 2013)—though not through a procedure any American or Canadian woman would have anticipated.

To allow the reader a quick snapshot of how countries and their criminal justice systems differ, I have included schematic comparisons in table form of a few that are of most potential interest to North American readers (see tables 1.1, 1.2, and 1.3). I find it useful to refer to these comparisons from time to time as I read case studies and criminal reports from different countries.

IN SUMMARY

1) Although we all believe we know what appropriate behavior is in regards to self-defense or fighting the enemy, the consequences of killing someone can vary from imprisonment to death or, by

contrast, to receiving a hero's accolades, depending on the circumstances, the law, and the community.

2) Crimes are often responded to based on community standards rather than community norms, especially when sex crimes are involved, including the viewing of sexual acts in the media.

3) There is considerable consensus across countries regarding what acts are crimes, but when it comes to sexual preference, ingesting or drinking substances, or insulting God, societies vary widely in their standards of tolerance if not norms.

4) The effort to differentiate between crimes intrinsically bad and those that are crimes merely because a statute exists has led to the terms mala in se and mala prohibita. Trying to differentiate between them has proven extremely challenging and will be addressed in the next chapter.

Table 1.1. Japan, China, Australia, and Germany: Geographic, Demographic, and Legal System Facts

	JAPAN	CHINA	AUSTRALIA	GERMANY
POPULATION	127,078,679 (July 2009 est.) 127,103,388 (July 2014 est.) 126,168,156 (July 2018 est.)	1,338,612,968 (July 2009 est.) 1,355,692,576 (July 2014 est.) 1,384,688,986 (July 2018 est.)	21,262,641 (July 2009 est.) 22,507,617 (July 2014 est.) 23,470,145 (July 2018 est.)	82,329,758 (July 2009 est.) 80,996,685 (July 2014 est.) 80,457,737 (July 2018 est.)
GEOGRAPHIC SIZE	total: 377,915 sq km land: 364,485 sq km water: 13,430 sq km Note: Area includes Bonin Islands (Ogasawara-gunto), Daito-shoto, Minami-jima, Oki-no-tori-shima, Ryukyu Islands (Nansei-shoto), and Volcano Islands (Kazan-retto)	total: 9,596,960 sq km land: 9,326,410 sq km water: 270,550 sq km	total: 7,741,220 sq km land: 7,682,300 sq km water: 58,920 sq km Note: Area includes Lord Howe Island and Macquarie Island	total: 357,022 sq km land: 348,672 sq km water: 8,350 sq km
ETHNICITY	— Japanese 98.5% — Koreans 0.5% — Chinese 0.4% — Other 0.6% (2002 census) — Japanese 98.1% — Chinese 0.5% — Korean 0.4% — Other 1% (includes Filipino, Vietnamese, and Brazilian) (2016 est.)	— Han Chinese 91.6%, Zhuang 1.3% — Other 7.1% (includes Hui, Manchu, Uighur, Miao, Yi, Tujia, Tibetan, Mongol, Dong, Buyei, Yao, Bai, Korean, Hani, Li, Kazakh, Dai and other nationalities) (2010 est.) Note: The Chinese government officially recognizes 56 ethnic groups.	— English 25.9%, Australian 25.4%, Irish 7.5%, Scottish 6.4%, Italian 3.3%, German 3.2%, Chinese 3.1%, Indian 1.4%, Greek 1.4%, Dutch 1.2% — Other 15.8% (includes Australian aboriginal 0.5%) — Unspecified 5.4% (2011 est.)	— German 87.2% — Turkish 1.8% — Polish 1% — Syrian 1% — Other 9% (2017 est.)

Continued

Table 1.1. Continued

	JAPAN	CHINA	AUSTRALIA	GERMANY
CRIMINAL JUSTICE SYSTEM	— Modeled after German civil law system with English-American influence — Judicial review of legislative acts in the Supreme Court — Accepts compulsory ICJ jurisdiction with reservations; accepts ICCt jurisdiction	— Based on civil law system — Derived from Soviet and continental European civil code legal principles — Legislature retains power to interpret statutes — Constitution ambiguous on judicial review of legislation — Has not submitted an ICJ jurisdiction declaration; non-party state to the ICCt	— Based on English common law — Accepts compulsory ICJ jurisdiction with reservations; accepts ICCt jurisdiction	— Civil law system with indigenous concepts — Judicial review of legislative acts in the Federal Constitutional Court — Accepts compulsory ICJ jurisdiction with reservations; accepts ICCt jurisdiction
HOW JUDGES ARE MADE & APPOINTED	— Judges in Japan are formally appointed by the prime minister and the cabinet. — The Japanese judiciary is unitary, unlike the systems of judicial federalism of countries such as the United States and Australia. — The appointment of judges in Japan is largely determined by the recruitment, training, and promotion of career judges admitted into the Legal Training and Research Institute (LTRI) and overseen by the chief justice and the general secretariat.	— The judge system, a major component of the judiciary, refers to all the rules and institutions related to the election and qualification of judges, forms of election, tenures, rewards and penalties, and salary and compensation of judges. — Constitution and laws provide for the powers and procedures for appointing and removing judges. — Presidents of courts at local levels are elected and removed by the National People's Congress at the same level. — The president nominates the vice president, members of the Judicial Committee, presiding judges, deputy presiding judges, and judges for appointment and removal by the Standing Committee of the People's Congress at the same level.	— The High Court consists of the chief justice and six other justices, who are appointed by the governor general. — The appointment of a federal judge is first considered by the cabinet; after the cabinet has agreed on its nominee, the attorney general then formally recommends the appointment to the governor general.	— Judges in the German Federal Court of Justice are appointed by the federal president after they have been selected by a committee whose specific job is to select judges for the federal courts. — Judges in the state (Land) courts are appointed by the Land government or the Land minister after they are selected by a committee constituted for selecting judges for the Land.

	Japan	China	Australia	Germany
	— Most judges begin their careers in their mid-twenties and serve until about 65 years of age. — Supreme Court chief justice designated by the cabinet and appointed by the monarch; associate justices appointed by the cabinet and confirmed by the monarch; all justices are reviewed in a popular referendum at the first general election of the House of Representatives following each judge's appointment and every 10 years afterward.	— Assistant judges of a court are appointed and removed by the president of the court. — Judges sitting at special courts are elected and removed with procedures separately set forth by the Standing Committee of the National People's Congress — Chief justice appointed by the People's National Congress; term limited to two consecutive 5-year terms; other justices and judges indirectly elected by municipal, regional, and provincial people's congresses from candidates nominated by the chief justice; these judges appointed by the Standing Committee of the People's National Congress.	— Most judges are appointed from a pool of legal practitioners who have had many years of experience in appearing before the courts and thus have a familiarity with the judicial practices and procedures. — Mandatory retirement at age 70.	— Judges are appointed for life, for 12-year terms, or until they reach 68 years for the federal courts and 65 years in the higher and lower administrative courts.
LEVELS OF POLICE	— Law enforcement in Japan is provided by the Prefectural Police under the oversight of the National Police Agency (NPA). — The NPA is headed by the National Public Safety	— The national security system is made up of the Ministry of State Security and the Ministry of Public Security (MPS), the People's Armed Police, the People's Liberation Army (PLA), and the state judicial, procuratorial, and penal systems.	— Law enforcement in Australia is facilitated by police, sheriffs, and bailiffs under the control of state, territorial, and federal governments.	— Law enforcement in Germany is divided between the different levels of federalism: the federal level (Bund), the state level (Land), and the local level (Kommunen).

Continued

Table 1.1. Continued

	JAPAN	CHINA	AUSTRALIA	GERMANY
LEVELS OF POLICE (continued)	Commission (NPSC), ensuring that Japan's police are an apolitical body and free of direct central government executive control. — Police are checked by an independent judiciary and monitored by a free and active press. ***National Police Agency*** NPA supervises and controls the police activities of 47 Prefectural Police departments and the Tokyo Metropolitan Police Department. The NPA is composed of 7,800 officials, comprising 2,100 police officers, 900 Imperial Guards, and 4,800 civilians. The NPA is headed by a commissioner general who, with the approval of the prime minister, is appointed by the NPSC, a state body that holds the rank of a ministry of state; it	— MPS oversees all domestic police activity in China, including the People's Armed Police Force. ***Ministry of Public Security*** Responsible for public security, MPS is part of the State Council, China's chief administrative body and the principal police and security authority. Law enforcement services in China are provided by public security bureaus, the provincial and municipal public security counterparts that, under the leadership of local government, operate in the main towns, cities, and counties of China. These bureaus in conjunction with MPS are active in — Crime prevention, suppression, and investigation; — Ensuring law and order; — Preventing extremism, violence, and terrorism; — Maintaining state security; — Administering registration duties (identification documents, birth certificates, exit-and-entry permits, stay and travel permits for visitors to China); — Riot and public demonstration control; and — Public information network security.	A number of specialist agencies also administer a wide variety of legislation related to white-collar crime. — In Australia there are two distinct but similar levels of police force, the various state police forces and the Australian Federal Police (AFP). State police services are responsible for enforcing state law within their own states (including cities within the states) while the AFP is responsible for the investigation of crimes against the Commonwealth of Australia and that occur throughout the nation. ***Australian Federal Police*** The AFP is the Australian government's leading law enforcement agency. Its four core functions are prevention, deterrence,sss	— There are two federal police agencies in Germany: the BPOL, responsible for nationwide policing, and the Bundeskriminalamat (BKA), responsible for international policing. Both fall under the federal Ministry of the Interior. — The German states are responsible for managing the bulk of Germany's police forces. Each state of the 16 making up the Federal Republic of Germany has its own police force known as the Landespolizei (state police). Each state has a code that lays down the organization and duties of its police (Landespolizeigesetz or Sicherheits—und Ordnungsgesetz). German law enforcement services are provided by a combination of different forces that have either

guarantees the neutrality of the police and administers the NPA.

NPA duties include

— Dealing with natural disasters, emergencies, and civil unrest;
— Tackling organized crime;
— Vehicle and road administration;
— Assisting in international crime investigations;
— Protecting the Japanese Imperial families (the role of the Imperial Guard);
— Police training;
— Police communications;
— Criminal identification; and
— Inspection.

MPS is made up of several agencies that deal with operational and administrative aspects of national policing. Essential operational agencies include

— National security;
— Economic crime investigation;
— Border control;
— Criminal investigation;
— Fire control;
— Prison security;
— Traffic control;
— International police cooperation;
— Drug control; and
— Counterterrorism.

partnership, and innovation. It is responsible for investigating offenses against the Commonwealth of Australia and advising on the national security framework.

At the national level, the AFP works with Australian government departments, state and territory law enforcement agencies, and other partner agencies to disrupt, deter, and defeat criminal activity.

At the global level, the AFP operates within a large network of international law enforcement agencies, industry partners, and foreign governments to identify and disrupt transnational serious and organized crime.

state, national, or international mandates.

Bundespolizei

With 40,000 employees—more than 30,000 of them fully trained police officers—BPOL is a countrywide operational police force responsible for domestic security. As part of Germany's Ministry of Interior, it is Germany's uniformed police responsible for

— Border security, including passport control;
— Coast guard services, which comprise the surveillance of land borders and national sea borders;
— Protection of federal buildings and foreign embassies;
— Reserve forces to deal with demonstrations, disturbances, or emergencies;

Continued

Table 1.1. Continued

	JAPAN	CHINA	AUSTRALIA	GERMANY
LEVELS OF POLICE (continued)			Through its International Deployment Group, the AFP also provides a range of capacity development initiatives and peacekeeping and stability operations. The group contributes to the development, maintenance, or restoration of the rule of law in countries that seek Australia's support. The AFP is responsive to a rapidly changing criminal environment and has eight key investigative priorities: — Serious and organized crime; — Crime operations; — High tech crime operations; — Intelligence; — Protection; — Aviation; — International Deployment Group; and — Counterterrorism.	— Transportation and passenger security at international airports and on German railways; and — Rescue helicopter service.

Source: Interpol (2019); CIA (2010, 2014, 2019); International Court of Justice (2019)
Note: Terminology for ethnic groups come from the sources.
ICJ = International Court of Justice; ICCt = International Criminal Court

Table 1.2. Canada, United Kingdom, France, and Russia: Geographic, Demographic, and Legal System Facts

	CANADA	UNITED KINGDOM	FRANCE	RUSSIA
POPULATION	33,487,208 (July 2009 est.) 34,834,841 (July 2014 est.) 35,881,659 (July 2018 est.)	61,113,205 (July 2009 est.) 63,742,977 (July 2014 est.) 65,105,246 (July 2018 est.)	64,057,792 (July 2009 est.) 66,259,012 (July 2014 est.) 67,364,357 (July 2018 est.) Note: The above figures are for metropolitan France and five overseas regions; the metropolitan France population was as follows: 62,150,775 (July 2009 est.) 62,814,233 (July 2014 and July 2018 est.)	140,041,247 (July 2009 est.) 142,470,272 (July 2014 est.) 142,122,776 (July 2018 est.)
GEOGRAPHIC SIZE	total: 9,984,670 sq km land: 9,093,507 sq km water: 891,163 sq km	total: 243,610 sq km land: 241,930 sq km water: 1,680 sq km Note: Includes Rockall and Shetland Islands	total: 643,801 sq km land: 640,427 sq km water: 3,374 sq km Note: These totals include the overseas regions of French Guiana, Guadeloupe, Martinique, Mayotte, and Reunion. Numbers for metropolitan France follow: 551,500 sq km total: 551,500 sq km land: 549,970 sq km water: 1,530 sq km	total: 17,098,242 sq km land: 16,377,742 sq km water: 720,500 sq km

Continued

Table 1.2. Continued

	CANADA	UNITED KINGDOM	FRANCE	RUSSIA
ETHNICITY	— Canadian 32.2% — English 19.8% — French 15.5% — Scottish 14.4% — Irish 13.8% — German 9.8% — Italian 4.5% — Chinese 4.5% — North American Indian 4.2% — Other 50.9% (2011 est.) — Canadian 32.3% — English 18.3% — Scottish 13.9% — French 13.6% — Irish 13.4% — German 9.6% — Chinese 5.1% — Italian 4.6% — North American Indian 4.4% — East Indian 4% — Other 51.6% (2016 est.) Note: Percentages may add up to more than 100% because respondents were able to identify more than one ethnic origin.	— White 92.1% (of which English 83.6%, Scottish 8.6%, Welsh 4.9%, and Northern Irish 2.9%) — Black 2% — Indian 1.8% — Pakistani 1.3% — Mixed 1.2% — Other 1.6% (2001 census) — White 87.2% — Black/African/Caribbean/ Black British 3% — Asian/Asian British: Indian 2.3% — Asian/Asian British: Pakistani 1.9% — Mixed 2% — Other 3.7% (2011 est.)	— Celtic and Latin with — Teutonic — Slavic — North African — Indochinese — Basque minorities Overseas departments: — Black — White — Mixed-race — East Indian — Chinese — Amerindian Note: Specific data not available.	— Russian 79.8% — Tatar 3.8% — Ukrainian 2% — Bashkir 1.2% — Chuvash 1.1% — Other or unspecified 12.1% (2002 census) — Russian 77.7% — Tatar 3.7% — Ukrainian 1.4% — Bashkir 1.1% — Chuvash 1% — Chechen 1% — Other 10.2% — Unspecified 3.9% (2010 est.)

CRIMINAL JUSTICE SYSTEM	— Based on English common law, except in Quebec, where a civil law system based on French law prevails — Accepts compulsory ICJ jurisdiction with reservations; accepts ICCt jurisdiction	— Based on common law tradition with early Roman and modern continental influences — Has nonbinding judicial review of Acts of Parliament under the Human Rights Act of 1998 — Accepts compulsory ICJ jurisdiction with reservations; accepts ICCt jurisdiction	— Civil law system with indigenous concepts — Review of administrative but not legislative acts — Has not accepted compulsory ICJ jurisdiction — Has not submitted an ICJ jurisdiction declaration; accepts ICCt jurisdiction	— Based on civil law system — Judicial review of legislative acts — Has not accepted compulsory ICJ jurisdiction — Has not submitted an ICJ jurisdiction declaration; non-party state to the ICCt
HOW JUDGES ARE MADE & APPOINTED	— Judges of the Supreme Court of Canada, the federal courts, the appellate courts, and the superior-level courts are appointed and not elected by the federal government. — Judicial appointments to judicial posts in the so-called "inferior" or "provincial" courts are made by the local provincial governments. — Because judicial independence is seen by Canadian law to be essential to a functioning democracy, the regulating of Canadian judges requires the involvement of the judges themselves. — Chief justice and judges appointed by the prime minister in council; all judges appointed for life with mandatory retirement at age 75.	— The United Kingdom does not have a single unified judicial system. — England and Wales has one system, Scotland another, and Northern Ireland a third. — Only a barrister can pursue the rank of judge. — A barrister is usually recommended to judgeship based on her or his rank in law school. — The Supreme Court was established by the Constitutional Reform Act 2005 and implemented in October 2009, replacing the Appellate Committee of the House of Lords as the highest court in the United Kingdom. — Most judicial appointments are organized by the Judicial Appointments Commission, designed to make sure candidates are appointed on merit.	— The highest court of appeal is the Cours de Cassation (judges are appointed by the president from nominations of the High Council of the Judiciary). — The Constitutional Council or Conseil Constitutionnel has three members appointed by the president, three appointed by the president of the National Assembly, and three appointed by the president of the Senate. — The Council of State or Conseil d'Etat is the final arbiter of cases relating to executive power, local authorities, independent public authorities, public administration agencies, or any other agency invested with public authority.	— The Constitutional Court and the Supreme Court of the Russian Federation are the highest courts. (Note: In February 2014, Russia's Superior Court of Arbitration was abolished and its former authorities transferred to the Supreme Court, which in addition is the country's highest judicial authority for appeals, civil, criminal, administrative, and military cases, and the disciplinary judicial board, which has jurisdiction over economic disputes.) — Judges are appointed by the Federation Council of Russia on the recommendation of the president of Russia, whereas other judges for all federal courts are appointed simply by the president. — According to the Constitution, judges are independent and subject only to the law.

Continued

Table 1.2. Continued

	CANADA	UNITED KINGDOM	FRANCE	RUSSIA
LEVELS OF POLICE	— In Canada, there are three levels of police forces: municipal, provincial, and federal. — Constitutionally, law enforcement is a provincial responsibility, and most urban areas have been given the authority by the provinces to maintain their own police force. — All but three provinces in turn contract out their provincial law enforcement responsibilities to the Royal Canadian Mounted Police, the federal police force.	— The United Kingdom, which is made up of England, Northern Ireland, Scotland, and Wales, does not have a national police force. Instead, there are 44 geographic forces in England and Wales and a single force in Scotland and in Northern Ireland. — Each force is led by a chief constable, who is accountable to law, to the Home Secretary, and to local democratic oversight. Democratic oversight is provided by elected police and crime commissioners (PCCs) in most areas and by the Mayor's Office in London.	— Law enforcement in France is conducted at the national and municipal level, and is the responsibility of a variety of law enforcement agencies. — Three agencies operate at the national level, and at the local level, each commune is able to maintain its own municipal police. — The three national law enforcement agencies are 1) Police nationale, formerly called the Sûreté; 2) Gendarmerie nationale; and 3) Direction générale des douanes et droits indirects.	— Law enforcement services in the Russian Federation are provided by several different departments of the Ministry of the Interior: Criminal Investigation; Economic Security and Corruption Counteraction; Extremism Counteraction; Transport; Public Order and Coordination of Interaction with Executive Authorities of the regions of the Russian Federation; Traffic Safety; Private and Public Property Protection; Witness Protection; Safety of International Major Events;

— Territorial police forces carry out the majority of policing. These are police forces covering a "police area" (a particular region) and having an independent police authority.
— Special police forces are national police forces that have a specific, non-regional jurisdiction, such as the British Transport Police. The Serious Organised Crime and Police Act of 2005 refers to these as "special police forces."
— Non-police law enforcement agencies also exist; their officers are not police constables, but they still enforce laws.
— Miscellaneous police forces, mostly having their foundations in older legislation or Common Law, also exist.

— French municipalities may also have a local police called the police municipale, garde municipale, or garde champetre, with restricted powers.

Support for Specialized Aviation Units;
Inquiries;
Investigation;
Internal Troops; and
Internal Affairs.

Source: Interpol (2019); CIA (2010, 2014, 2019); International Court of Justice (2019); *Find Fun Facts* (2013)
Note: Terminology for ethnic groups come from the sources.
ICJ = International Court of Justice; ICCt = International Criminal Court

Table 1.3. The United States: Geographic, Demographic, and Legal System Facts

	United States
POPULATION	307,212,123 (July 2009 est.) 329,256,465 (July 2018 est.)
GEOGRAPHIC SIZE	9,833,517 sq km total: 9,833,517 sq km land: 9,147,593 sq km water: 685,924 sq km
	Note: Includes only the 50 states and District of Columbia, no overseas territories.
ETHNICITY	White 79.96%, Black 12.85%, Asian 4.43%, Amerindian and Alaska native 0.97%, native Hawaiian and other Pacific islander 0.18%, two or more races 1.61% (July 2007 estimate) White 72.4%, Black 12.6%, Asian 4.8%, Amerindian and Alaska native 0.9%, native Hawaiian and other Pacific islander 0.2%, other 6.2%, two or more races 2.9% (2010 est.)
	Note: A separate listing for Hispanic is not included because the US Census Bureau considers Hispanic to mean persons of Spanish/Hispanic/Latino origin including those of Mexican, Cuban, Puerto Rican, Dominican Republic, Spanish, and Central or South American origin living in the United States who may be of any race or ethnic group (white, black, Asian, etc.); an estimated 16.3% of the total US population is Hispanic as of 2010.
CRIMINAL JUSTICE SYSTEM	— The federal court system is based on English common law. — Each state has its own unique legal system, of which all but one is based on English common law (Louisiana is still influenced by the Napoleonic Code). — Legislative acts undergo judicial review. — The United States does not accept compulsory ICJ jurisdiction and withdrew acceptance of ICCt jurisdiction in 2002.
HOW ARE JUDGES MADE & APPOINTED	— Supreme Court justices, court of appeals judges, and district court judges are nominated by the president and confirmed by the United States Senate, as stated in the Constitution. — Article III judges are appointed for life, and they can only be removed through the impeachment process. — One is not nominated or appointed to the position of chief judge (except for the Chief Justice of the United States); the position is assumed based on seniority. — Although there are no special qualifications to become a judge of these courts, those who are nominated are typically very accomplished private or government attorneys, judges in state courts, magistrate judges or bankruptcy judges, or law professors. The judiciary plays no role in the nomination or confirmation process. Some judges are voted in by the public.

	United States
LEVELS OF POLICE	— Policing in the United States is conducted by numerous types of agencies at many different levels. Every state has its own nomenclature for agencies, and their powers, responsibilities, and funding varies from state to state.
	— Federal police possess full federal authority as given to them under United States Code. Federal law enforcement officers are authorized to enforce various laws not only at the federal level but also at the state, county, and local levels in many circumstances.
	— Most states operate statewide government agencies that provide law enforcement duties, including investigations and state patrols. They may be called "State Police," "State Patrol," or "Highway Patrol" and are normally part of the state's Department of Public Safety.
	— County police tend to exist only in metropolitan counties and have countywide jurisdiction. In some areas, there is a sheriff's department that handles only minor issues, such as the service of papers (as a constable would do in other areas), along with security for the local courthouse.
	— Municipal police range from one-officer agencies (sometimes still called the town marshal) to the 40,000 men and women of the New York City Police Department. Most municipal agencies take the form (Municipality Name) Police Department.
	— There are other types of specialist police departments with varying jurisdictions. Most of these serve special-purpose districts and are special district police. In some states, they serve as little more than security police, but in states such as California, special district forces are composed of fully sworn peace officers with statewide authority.

Source: Interpol (2019); CIA (2010, 2014, 2019); International Court of Justice (2019)
ICJ = International Court of Justice; ICCt = International Criminal Court

CHAPTER TWO

A MULTIDIMENSIONAL MODEL OF CRIME

This chapter examines the shortcomings of dividing crime into merely mala in se and mala prohibita and how the courts evaluate gravity or seriousness of crime. Postmodern theorists argue that all crime is a **social construction**, that is, made up by society. Postmodern theory derived from the symbolic interaction theory of G. H. Mead (1913) argues that there is no independent reality and so truth is whatever the particular cultural group decides it is. This concept is derived from a branch of philosophy known as **phenomenology** in which reality is not really accessible. By contrast, this chapter argues that violence is a physical phenomenon naturally existing in the real world and is separate and independent from aggression, which infers motivation and so is a product of social construction. It proposes a multidimensional model of crime that demonstrates the relationship between violence and aggression and how the seriousness of different types of crimes can be calculated. The intended result is to allow the reader and the courts to consider, compare, and assess the relative gravity of crimes as diverse as murder and pollution.

The struggle to differentiate between **mala in se** and **mala prohibita** has plagued the law since William Blackstone described the difference in his great work *Commentaries on the Laws of England* in 1766. Blackstone also eventually invoked his religious beliefs to describe those crimes that were mala in se as violating the precepts of God and religion, as we discussed in chapter 1. Davis (2006) reviews the various usages of those terms since Blackstone's time and concludes a different criterion must apply. He suggests, alternatively, the social psychological concepts of equity theory. That is, when people conclude that their outcomes do not measure up to their input, they feel unfairly treated.

A THREE-DIMENSIONAL DYNAMIC MODEL FOR ANALYZING CRIME

Given the fragmented efforts of society toward the understanding and social control of the seemingly extremely heterogeneous phenomena discussed in chapter 1, this chapter develops a systematic three-dimensional model for identifying the gravity of all crime. It is an ecological three-dimensional system that identifies acts, first, according to the violence they involve but cautions that violence, unlike the multiplicity of negative characteristics attributed to it in social construction, is an independent entity existing in the physical world and is defined as the amount of energy or force released or exerted. Violence is not necessarily malevolent or even negative or intentional. The intensity on this dimension, as on all three, may vary from 0 to 10 for computational purposes.

VIOLENCE AS AN INDEPENDENT PHYSICAL ENTITY

We speak of a storm, earthquake, or volcano as being violent and destructive, but unless we believe in the god Pele or Vulcan or in the wrath of at least some deity (the Christian god or Gaia), we cannot rationally impute intention to those often awe-inspiring and destructive events. The philosopher Immanuel Kant, however, pointed out, referring to the Lisbon earthquake of 1755, that the human tendency is to impute intention. Yet **violence** is not always associated with destruction. Giving birth is violent, producing pain and even injury or death to mother or child at times, but its purpose is to produce life rather than to destroy it. And, as demonstrated in the Canadian experience with pornography discussed in the previous chapter, sex, too, can be violent—that is, it can involve considerable force expended, without necessarily harming the participants. In fact, by the late 1990s, the attempt to socially reconstruct bondage and other **sadomasochistic sex** had evolved to the point that a mainstream television channel, Showtime, had a regular program called *Kink* at 10 pm on Friday nights (not that I ever watched it) featuring the elaborate bondage and other rituals of ordinary citizens (with safe words, intended to alert the perpetrator of the violence that his or her consensual "victim" had had enough). Again, this type of subculture underlines that violence is only negative when overlaid with attribution (e.g., he is using it to hurt me). But stripped of those connotations, violence is merely the use or presence of force or an expenditure of energy.

VIOLENCE IN SPORT

Following the same line of reasoning, is it a paradox that relatively peaceful people, such as the Canadians or Swedes who embrace hockey so passionately, make a strong distinction between the exhilaration of a violent body check that knocks someone into the boards and the so-called "Bertuzzing" of someone? For those unfamiliar with hockey, "Bertuzzing" is driving someone from behind into the ice with the intention of inflicting pain and even injury, as Todd Bertuzzi of the Vancouver Canucks appeared to do against Steve Moore in an NHL hockey game. That action provoked an aggravated assault charge against Bertuzzi and a subsequent civil suit on the part of Moore whose neck was broken and hockey career ended (Shoalts, 2006). Thus an act can involve anywhere from zero to the maximum amount of violence possible, plotted as 0 to 10 on a 10-point scale, independently of harm or intention.

Ironically, although Canada purports to disdain violence and especially the street violence characterizing American street crime, Canadians defend the phenomenon of hockey fights for which the combatants are given offsetting five minute penalties so that neither team is put at a disadvantage. In every other North American sport, engaging in or even behaving as if you plan to engage in a physical fight leads to ejection from the game. Witness the automatic suspension of the Phoenix Suns' Boris Diaw and Amar'e Stoudemire who merely left their team's bench and rushed to the aid of Steve Nash but made no contact with anyone. Nash had been intentionally decked by San

Antonio's Robert Horry. With Diaw and Stoudemire out, San Antonio won the playoff series and went on to the 2007 NBA championship.

THE DIMENSION OF INTENTION

The mere presence of violence, then, is not what causes us to call something a crime, just as the dimension of violence alone does not adequately account for the general condemnation of the behavior of Robert Horry. Had he accidentally bumped into Nash, no major incident would have occurred. Accordingly, a second dimension—intention—is crucial to any analysis of the structure of crime. Thus if violence is high but intention to cause harm is low, no crime is attributed. For example, one could hardly make a person having a grand mal seizure criminally responsible for any injury or damage resulting from the convulsion. So too children or especially adults who have tantrums by throwing themselves on the floor and pounding it with their fists or more probably slamming doors and shouting can be quite intimidating, but they could only be regarded as aggressive if they pounded another person or damaged property, hence the legal term mens rea, or guilty in the mind. Sometimes, having a guilty mind means having an intention to harm; sometimes it means a certain kind of knowledge, for example, that received property was stolen. If the angry adults had "lost their mind" (i.e., became insane), they similarly could not be held criminally responsible. Consider the case of Vincent Li, who murdered, decapitated, and ate parts of his innocent victim, Tim Maclean, on a Greyhound bus crossing the Canadian prairies. Despite the bitterness of the victim's family and the outrage of the general populace (White, 2009), which invoked both community standards and norms, Li was found not criminally responsible. In other words, even when behavior is highly abnormal and by community standards not the least tolerable, it can be considered not criminal. The perpetrator is not drawn and quartered or summarily shot as might happen to a rabid dog although, inevitably, the horrendous act has infuriated those closest to the brutalized victim.

On the other hand, someone who shoots at another person or someone's property or runs a car at either is using force and intention to harm, so the combination of violence AND intention is identified as an aggressive act and a violent crime, which could be labeled assault or even attempted murder. But things are often not quite as clear if the intention is to harm but no or little violence accompanies it. A poignant example is a story from the early twentieth century. A Vancouver woman was venerated because she took in older boarders and took care of them, feeding them well and inspiring their adoration of her. She was paid from their pension checks. Then it was discovered that she had insidiously poisoned her boarders over time, slipping a little cumulative arsenic into their delicious meals and causing their deaths, with no pain or discomfort, in order to keep collecting their checks and to take in even more boarders in the same regimen. Here we have a crime of no or little violence but a maximum of intent.

In the case study at the beginning of chapter 1, I describe strange intruders being discovered throwing Molotov cocktails at a homeowner's property and the frightened occupant's shooting at the thrower. In most US jurisdictions, the occupant would go free, as initially did the neighborhood watch volunteer in Florida who shot and killed Trayvon Martin, thanks to the "stand your ground law in that state." In Canada, however, the outcome would be very different: the test is that the law permits just enough force to halt the intrusion. Thus, if the intruder carried a gun, shooting would be more likely to be sanctioned. Interestingly, according to case law, the use of such violence as a response would also be more likely deemed appropriate if the intruder had a past record of violence in similar circumstances, even if the occupant was not aware of it, an odd, counterintuitive finding of the court (*R. v. Yaeck*, 1991), but exactly why we avoid people with past records of violence. Here, the emphasis is on the concept of violence once again, with the degree of violence standing alone in the second example to determine whether a crime has been committed. But something is missing in this analysis.

THE DIMENSION OF HARM DONE

The third factor to consider in the model is the dimension of harm done. Logically, a shooter who fires into a crowd but harms no one gets a lesser sentence in law than one who manages to hit one or more people. But consider a gun bearer whose firearm discharges accidentally (as did the rifle of Canadian General Daniel Menard in Afghanistan in 2010; Chase, 2010). Though the result is also violent, perhaps 10 on the force release–violence dimension, it is zero on the intention dimension; so even if Menard had killed someone, he would not have been held responsible for murder in a court of law. Perhaps he would be charged with manslaughter if any possibility of intending harm could be divined. Or, in other circumstances, an accidental shooter could be held liable for merely carrying the gun or more so for not being sufficiently diligent in firearm care.

Still, I was startled to discover that coincidentally in both Red Lake, my hometown in Northern Ontario, and Madison, Wisconsin, my graduate school hometown, where many locals engaged in hunting, it is often flippantly suggested that one take an intended victim hunting if one wishes to escape prosecution for murder. How easily that could happen was demonstrated in the now infamous quail-hunting accident when former Vice President Dick Cheney shot his companion, who escaped relatively unscathed as they were using very small birdshot rather than goose loads or even slugs (Wallsten & Riccardi, 2006). And yet the German singer Nadja Benaissa of the band No Angels was recently charged with causing grievous bodily harm for having had sex with three men though she knew she was HIV positive (Agence France-Presse, 2010). One developed AIDS. Although intention to infect them was difficult to prove, the balance of probabilities suggested she cared little for the welfare of her sexual partners, not even caring whether she gave them a life-threatening disease. Thus her score would be relatively low if she were merely reckless or, like the murderous boarding-house lady, high if she intended to kill. Thus determining degree of intention is vital. The courts must make the decision where to mark her based on the evidence provided.

THE SCHEMA OF THREE DIMENSIONS FOR COMPARING DIVERSE CRIMES

This system of locating the act in a multidimensional space in order to evaluate its seriousness also demonstrates why the law finds it so hard to grapple with the newest iteration of "crimes against nature" or against the environment, e.g., pollution. Not only is there very often no violence involved, but the degree of intention or even negligence is very difficult to measure. Thus, like the slow poisoning of retired boarders, the crime of polluting the environment is often difficult not only to detect but also to prove mens rea, that is, to prove the degree of deliberate **culpability** in the incident's occurrence. Of course, detection is not a problem in the case of a violent event, for instance, the explosion and burning of the BP *Deepwater Horizon* oil platform in the Gulf of Mexico in the spring of 2010 (Agrell, 2010). But how culpable is the company for the accident? Did the company overlook warning signs that led to the deaths of several workers and to near death for the whole ecosystem, the Gulf of Mexico, that millions rely on not only for a livelihood but for actual survival? Was BP recklessly taking risks to maximize profit, or was the spill merely an unforeseeable catastrophe, like the hurricane that destroyed New Orleans, referred to in court proceedings as an "Act of God"?

To illustrate the three-dimensionality of the system, as part of a larger study of the effects of seasonal temperature on violent crime using archival data, Yasayko (2010) and I laid out the differences among 1) purely verbal threats against bus drivers, which do not involve an intention to do physical harm; 2) spitting at someone where the intention to harm is higher; and three other categories—3) spitting on the face, 4) physical assault, and 5) assault with a weapon—in which both intention and harm increase incrementally. As an aside, it is interesting that assault with a weapon, which embodies all three components— intention, harm done, and force exerted—is not only the most serious crime but also the one that was most highly correlated with seasonal temperature.

The general ecological models presented in figures 2.1 and 2.2, by using three dimensions, underline the differences in ecological space occupied by different acts and why different people and institutions take such different stands on what they feel should be society's appropriate reactions. For example, murder by firearm would be recorded in space as Force = 10, Intent = 10, Harm = 10; but murder by poison would be Force = 0, Intent = 10, Harm = 10. Thus an equally harmful, intentional act may sometimes garner lesser sentences, perhaps because it is not so visibly disturbing to public order (i.e., violent).

Figure 2.1. An ecological representation of violence and aggression against
bus drivers

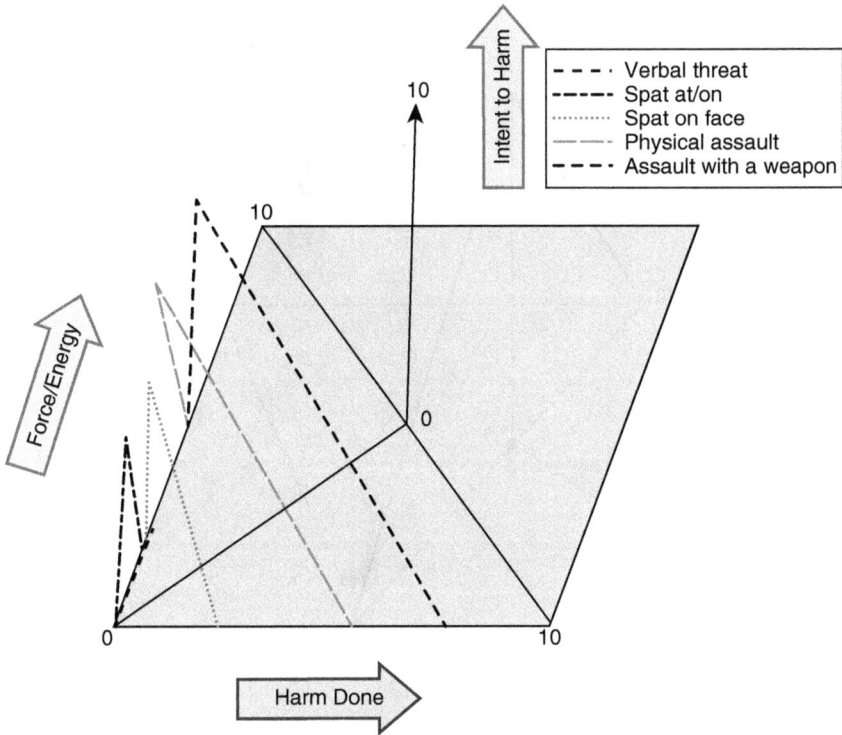

Source: Boyanowsky (2011); adapted from research the author conducted
with Yasayko (2010)

Death by pollution, which never attracts the same severity of pen-
alty, is better understood in this multidimensional space, for there is
usually very little force employed and even though harm done may be
high, intention becomes very difficult to define, translating by default
into "intentional" or criminal negligence or recklessness and liability,
a much softer parameter. Thus, within the criminal justice systems of
Canada and the United States, all three elements or dimensions (force,
intent, and harm) must exist for a crime to be regarded as true aggression, that most feared and abhorred category of "violent crime." These
crimes involve willfully harming someone in the most blatant manner

Figure 2.2. A general ecological model of violence and aggression

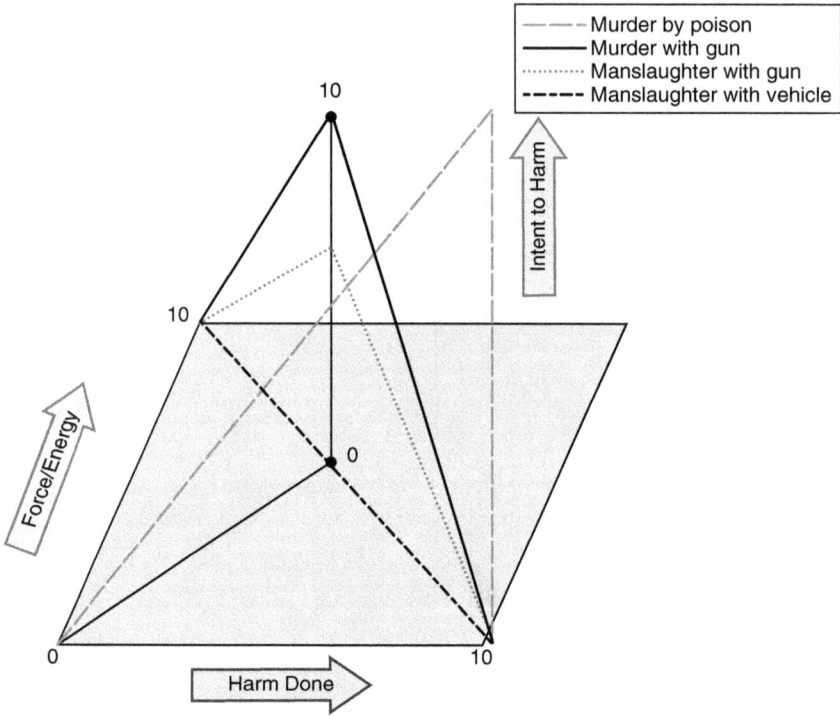

Source: Boyanowsky (2011); adapted from research the author conducted with Yasayko (2010)

(e.g., murder), shooting someone with a gun, or hacking a person to death with a machete or hoe, which, as we shall see, was the most common way to kill hundreds of thousands in Rwanda (chapter 8).

By contrast, in the social science literature, aggression and violence are often used interchangeably, leading not only to theoretical misconceptions but to demands for social and legal policies that may in fact be misguided if not downright damaging. To wit, I had a research assistant, using definitions derived from the general ecological model, code 100 published studies on violence and aggression. Most of the articles were found to be studying aggression, although they usually referred only to violence. Perhaps more insidiously, a significant number identified acts as aggression although the acts by our definition were merely violent. This misidentification was especially evident in studies of the social behavior of young boys (e.g., rough and tumble play characterized as aggressive).

Abortion, in the view of pro-choice supporters who advocate for legal access to it, would be equally intentional and almost as forceful as murder by firearm but would be viewed as doing zero harm (0 H) because the fetus is not considered a person. By contrast, anti-abortion supporters would view the death of the "unborn child" as murder and allocate a "harm done" score of 10 (10 H), emphasizing the violence of the act in the manner of the pro-life students at the University of Calgary, who were censured by the administration for their display of dead aborted fetuses (Canadian Constitution Foundation, 2010). Those anti-abortionists reflected the sentiment seen on the church sign in Mt. Currie, referred to earlier. Some pro-choice supporters might admit harm done in late term abortion but argue a superordinate consideration: the right of women to govern their bodies trumping the right to life. That debate then morphs into the debate about capital punishment and war, both also with superordinate sanctions imposed upon the act by the state, rendering it, as discussed in the introduction, noncriminal.

That is, the model clarifies the debate between capital punishment advocates and those opposed to capital punishment and between those who approve of engaging in war versus so-called pacifists: there is no difference. The argument is merely whether one approves of or opposes a higher power's—the government's—engaging in intentional homicide: murder for a superordinate purpose.

Accepting that caveat, with those three dimensions, we can plot the severity of crime and the appropriate response, both of which are determined by society's differentiating between aggression (intention and harm) and mere violence (force expended or applied with no target or intention to harm). There is, however, a fourth dimension to which we allude repeatedly in our examples. It is the element of knowledge or conscious awareness.

In the eyes of the law, one is incapable of knowledge or conscious awareness (of causing harm or breaking the law) if suffering from a mental illness. So the horror of his crime notwithstanding, Vincent Li was found "not criminally responsible" and so not convicted of murder. On the other hand, Nadja Benaissa, although not resorting to violence, confessed to being aware of her HIV condition, though she expressed no intention to infect her sexual partners. So she was charged with aggravated assault. Should the young Manitoba woman who, despite using alcohol, drugs, and sniffing glue, repeatedly carries children to term be charged similarly as she is aware of the grievous bodily harm she is inflicting upon her children (Tait, 2001/2002)? If one takes the position that the right of a woman to make decisions regarding her body trumps the rights of the unborn or the right of society to decide for her, does it follow that she must bear the criminal responsibility for damaging her children repeatedly and be treated by society as a criminal? That has not been society's recourse to date. Knowledge is clearly important here as well.

The leniency of society's responses to the "unfit mother" in the previous example or to crimes committed by those judged "not criminally responsible," such as Vincent Li, often provokes outrage from the public. In the same way, manslaughter with a vehicle is often seen as garnering a sentence that is too mild. In all three cases, intention may be 0 or minimal, and it is difficult to argue it is more than that unless the person, like the intruder in the opening example, has a history of violence. Knowledge (conscious awareness) of the potential effect of one's actions usually is anywhere from 0 to minimal (1 to 3) but not high.

Adding that fourth dimension of knowledge completes the model, for one can now calculate the degree of culpability of polluters in cases such as the Union Carbide explosion in Bhopal, India, which led to the immediate deaths of 3,000 people in 1984 and many more since (Press Trust of India, 2010). It is also possible to calculate the degree of responsibility that British Petroleum bears for the Deepwater Horizon explosion and the horrendous oil spill in the Gulf of Mexico in 2010.

To determine degree of culpability (C) theoretically, one can assign a numeric value from 0 to 10 to the dimensions outlined and multiply knowledge (K) x [force (F) + intention (I) + harm done (H)] to arrive at this result for Vincent Li:

$$C = (K = 0) \times [(F = 10) + (I = 10) + (H = 10)]$$

In other words, Li would score 0 without the formula's denying, as the victim's family protested, that he fully intended to kill his victim

(Sinclair, 2010). Those with merely diminished intellectual responsibility (children, the mentally challenged) would compute, but score low. But Nadja Benaissa would score about 50 or 70 because her knowledge was complete, both the force she used and her intention were at the lower limit, and the harm she did was at least midway between minimal harm and death:

$$C = (K = 10) \times [(F = 1) + (I = 1) + (H{\sim}5)]$$

For the gentle, caring poisoner, the culpability score would be about 200:

$$C = (K = 10) \times [(F = 0) + (I = 10) + (H = 10)]$$

For the homicidal shooter scoring 10 on all dimensions, C would equal 300, thereby reflecting the greater distress to society created by the use of graphic violence. And yet the polluter's knowledge score (K) would be between 0 for a true accident to 5–10 if there were a significant degree of knowledge of the potential for disaster, as many claim existed in our two examples. Although force (F) would be at 10 and intention (I) minimal at 1, harm done (H) should be set not only at 10 but at a multiple of 10 to account for the range of **dissemination** (D). So the calculation for harm would be [$H = 10 \times D$] with D ranging from 1 to infinity based on the perceived widespread effects on people, the environment, and the economy, a weighting factor yet to be determined but one with which judges and juries struggle in civil damage suits as well. Thus, the final formula for gravity of crime or culpability can be expressed as follows:

$$C = K [F + I + (H \times D)]$$

In a moralistic or religious society, abortion would score very high (e.g., ~250). In a feminist society, it is not computed at all, being legal as is capital punishment and waging war when dictated by the state. That analysis suggests the son in the play described in chapter 1, *Mother Courage*, was wrongfully executed, as he had no knowledge of the ceasefire that had been declared. As for abortion, it is interesting that in Canada, since the original law allowing abortions under strict conditions was struck down as unconstitutional, no one has attempted to replace it, even the Conservative government in power from 2006 to 2015 that had promised to do so. The formula suggests that politically it would be difficult to justify, analyzing the components involved.

IN SUMMARY

The approach outlined here allows acts normally attracting the attention of the criminal justice system to be analyzed in multidimensional space for their gravity and for comparison purposes, and it may perhaps contribute not only to the efforts of investigators of such phenomena but also, given the implications, to the efforts of society's policymakers, as well. This model does not replace or deny the idea that crime is a social construction. Rather it points out the confusion and even injustice that can prevail if social construction is alone applied to define violence, harm, and intention. The eclecticism of the model proposed will hopefully inform the efforts of theoreticians, jurists, legislators, and the general public trying to make sense not only of crime but of the punishment or lack thereof meted out by the courts.

Key concepts are those comprising the multidimensional space: 1) force/energy, 2) intent to harm, 3) harm done, 4) conscious knowledge, and 5) dissemination of the effect of the act (i.e., how widespread among people and the environment are the effects).

Two important concepts that have been used in my analysis are social construction, a notion taken from G. H. Mead who along with C. W. Morris devised symbolic interaction theory in *Mind, Self and Society* (1934). Social construction argues that reality exists only from the shared perspective of those who communicate with each other, so our conception of mental illness, aggression, violence, and harm done, for example, are based on consensus. I would argue that violence alone is distinct when stripped of its overburden of modern meaning, that it is an independently existing phenomenon not just a social construction. Hence my analysis is eclectic—an amalgam of argument for an objective independent reality regarding the existence of violence and social construction when we imbue violence with intention and declare its harm to people or the environment. Then, we proceed to prosecute its perpetrators under the aegis of law.

CHAPTER THREE

EXPLANATIONS OF CRIMINALITY

WHAT IS CRIMINALITY?

This chapter delves into the nature of criminality. Why do some people become criminals, not just committing one crime but several, perhaps throughout life? It begins with a letter to the *New York Times* that could have been written today but was written over 105 years ago, arguing that explanations based on genetics or biology in general are merely letting the guilty relieve themselves of responsibility, that wrongdoers must take the rap for what they perpetrate rather than passing the buck (by saying "The devil or my genes or my family made me do it").

Four different case studies of criminality purportedly derived from different causes are described. There follows a discussion of the constitutionality of criminality: what the constitution of the individual criminal comprises in its various manifestations. The point is to consider whether criminality can be found entirely within the individual person or just when the situation is factored in as well.

This indignant letter was published in the *New York Times*:

AGAINST LOMBROSO'S THEORY.
Thinks the Law Should Not Recognize the "Born Criminal."
To the Editor of The New York Times:
The forthcoming edition of the late Cesare Lombroso's work on "Criminal Man" is announced to contain "certain simple but sure rules for

discriminating between the born or incorrigible criminal, the irresponsible lunatic, and the occasional criminal."

The trouble with this eminent Italian's work is that he built from a wrong foundation. The sooner his ideas as to "the born criminal" are totally discredited in the popular mind (as they are already with genuinely accurate observers) the sooner a false system of dealing with crime will be brought to an end.

There are no "born criminals": every man is a potential criminal, and every criminal is a man who has in some particular refused to observe the rights of others, rights which are in the main expressed in statutes. He should be held responsible for his acts, unless it can be shown that he is not in mental condition to be responsible for anything, in which case he should no longer be allowed to walk abroad a free man.

When the courts get rid of the Lombrosan habit of finding a thousand excuses for the criminal and get back to the principle of holding all men to a just responsibility for all their deeds, the increase in crime may be checked. When the current twaddle about "heredity" and "environment" is silenced, as it should be, the damage done to civilization by this brilliant but mistaken Italian scientist will begin to be repaired.

W. C. Taylor

Brooklyn, July 18, 1910

Notice the date, 1910, but more than 108 years later, the debate rages on. Are some people born criminals and so not responsible for their penchant for breaking the law, or does the environment create the conditions and shape the attitudes and behavior of humans so that most are law-abiding most of the time whereas others become criminals in response to environmental stressors and social influences? Or most simply, are all people potential criminals but some are of lower moral functioning and so, by default, become criminals because they don't know the difference between right and wrong? Of course, a few are just mentally ill, out of touch with reality, and so cannot be held responsible or allowed to move freely in society.

FOUR CASE STUDIES

Let's take four cases that appear to be based in distinctly different causal factors. I will describe them in some detail, and then I will review the main theories that account for their occurrence. In the conclusion to this chapter and in the next, I will review the factors that apply.

The first, to be discussed further in chapter 5, was related to me in Prince Rupert, British Columbia, by a man on a magnificent yacht parked next door to the one my son was skippering to Alaska for a family from Chicago for which I was serving as crew. The man obviously was quite wealthy but had very sad eyes and a defeated air about him even though he was living the dream in retirement: cruising the West Coast, fishing, and taking it easy. I noticed he had taken a shine to Alexei, and though appearing naturally somewhat gruff in manner, was very friendly, chatty, and solicitous toward him. I soon found out why. It took only two minutes after he found out I was a criminologist specializing in violent and aggressive behavior for him to start to tell me his sad tale.

He too had a son, of a similar age, who was in jail for taking a man hostage and beating and robbing him. It was his son's second identical offense, but the young man had also had a lengthy record of criminal offenses involving robbery, extortion, and violence that began in preadolescence. He had been a very willful, unmanageable child with a hair-trigger temper if frustrated, who would try to sweet talk anyone but would explode if that didn't work. He'd been thrown out of kindergarten on the first day, and out of several schools, despite being very good looking and possessing a gift of verbal facility that his father said could "sell icebergs to Eskimos." Though he had a private school education and never lacked for anything, including the love of his parents, lying, cheating, and stealing were chronic behaviors until as a young adult, he was no longer allowed in the house, having threatened his parents and stolen many articles to support his growing drug habit. The sad father, with a sigh and a shrug, allowed that he no longer had anything to do with his son, though his wife kept in touch.

I was feeling a little concerned that he would ask me for a diagnosis because his son's story read like a textbook entry, but I was spared that painful necessity when he concluded by saying: "His psychiatrist says he is a psychopath." And true to form for that personality type, he had wreaked almost as much havoc on his family as he had on society in general. The man ended by saying he and his wife had gone through extensive therapy to deal with parental issues of guilt.

I shall discuss this case further in chapter 4, which focuses on psychopathy.

The second case involves a polite, quiet little man who was a model patient in a state mental hospital in Wisconsin when I was a graduate student in social and clinical psychology in Madison. His name was Ed Gein. He looked like the cartoon character Elmer Fudd of Bugs Bunny fame, and had been regarded by his neighbors in Plainfield as an odd but harmless fellow who lived by himself in a ramshackle farmhouse. He did handyman jobs, brought them venison roasts, and even babysat their children on occasion until a police investigation into the disappearance of the owner of the local hardware store (horrifyingly led by her son, the sheriff) found her in his barn strung up and eviscerated like a deer. His house, which reeked of foul smells and was littered with junk and garbage, contained lampshades made of human skin, an armchair made of human arms, and drawers of nipples, jars of vaginas, and other gruesome keepsakes. It was a scene so horrendous that the story inspired the films *The Texas Chainsaw Massacre* and *Psycho*, among many lesser productions. Only Gein's dead mother's sealed-off bedroom, preserved shrine-like, retained any semblance of a normal residence.

The third case is that of Vincent Li, a Chinese immigrant and computer technologist whose behavior while working at a menial job became increasingly bizarre until his wife left him and he left his job, gave away his possessions, and started on a cross-country bus trip that culminated in his stabbing to death, decapitating, and devouring body parts of an unsuspecting young man, a fellow passenger on board unknown to him. Internal voices urged Li that the man must be killed before he killed Li himself.

And finally the fourth case: Nagatomi Hakudo, a doctor in Japan, built a shrine of remorse in his waiting room where patients could watch videotapes of his war crime trial and confession. He said, "Few know that soldiers impaled babies on bayonets and tossed them still alive into pots of boiling water. They gang raped women from the ages of twelve to eighty and killed them when they no longer satisfied their sexual requirements. I beheaded people, starved them to death, burned them, and buried them alive, over two hundred in all. It is terrible that I could turn into an animal and do these things. There are really no words to explain what I was doing. I was truly a devil" (Chang, 1997, p. 59). Hakudo was referring to the slaughter of an estimated 250,000 Chinese by invading Japanese soldiers in a few short weeks beginning in December 1937, known now as the Rape of Nanking (Chang, 1997). Those monstrous Japanese soldiers, who survived by and large, returned to mundane lives after World War II rather than continuing as savage mass murderers back home in Japan, which traditionally has had a much lower homicide rate than most other countries (Dutton, Boyanowsky, & Bond, 2005). Hakudo's extreme remorse and self-imposed penance are a case in point.

Given these diverse case studies, how does one account for human criminality and violent aggression? One approach is to attribute it to the universal human condition, as did W. C. Taylor, the 1910 letter writer to the *New York Times*. The argument is that we are all criminals at some level, but some of us choose not to act out, probably out of a personal moral standard or, if not, out of fear of punishment by the law—known in academic circles as general deterrence. Most people of such an opinion regard legal punishment as too lax. That we are all potential criminals is the basic idea behind what is known as the classical school of criminology, which is most associated with Cesare Beccaria (1764/1985), who argued that punishment should be keyed to the severity of the crime.

By contrast, the psychoanalyst Sigmund Freud's (1940/1949) thesis was that as infant humans before socialization, we are merely vehicles possessing two reservoirs of energy or instinct: **Thanatos**, or the death instinct that underlies aggression and violence, and **Eros**, the life or love instinct that drives sex, love, and compassion. What is manifested is dependent upon how the child is socialized and overcomes crises at crucial stages of psychosexual development from the **birth trauma** through to punishment for sexual curiosity as a small child (Freud, 1940/1949). Although as a student, I found Freud's scheme fanciful at best, after many years of study, I now realize he actually created the conceptual foundation for all developmental theories, the colorful metaphors Eros and Thanatos, id, ego, and superego notwithstanding. Freud's theories will be discussed in greater depth in chapters 5 and 6.

Taylor, the letter writer, a mere member of the public was, however, objecting to theorizing on an entirely different level: he rejected Lombroso's notion that some people are just born "that way" and so, the implication is, can't really help themselves. What does Taylor's approach really mean? It means that people have free will, a notion descended from religion and the justification for differentiating between those good people who will go to heaven or paradise and those who will for eternity burn in hell. In postmodern theorizing, free will is also referred to as "human agency." It also forms the basis of all criminal justice systems (Norrie, 1983).

This concept of human agency is essential because, to be guilty of a crime, a person must be capable of forming the intent to commit the crime and proceed rationally. That notion, as discussed in an earlier chapter, is also known in many countries as the idea of guilt in the mind or **mens rea**. The issue can be elaborated by recognizing that a person may intentionally commit a crime (e.g., kill someone), but because of mental illness or lowered or impaired mental capacity (emotionally or intellectually) not be completely knowledgeable or aware of the context and consequences of the act. But the opposing view, one that forms the basis of scientific inquiry, is known as **determinism**, originally biological determinism. The determinist argues that if we could reveal all the factors that led to a person's behavior, beginning with that person's origins and examining all the factors affecting him or her along the way, we could anticipate all that individual's actions (Vanyukov, 2004). To put it another way, if we had the equivalent of an infinitely powerful computer that could factor in every necessary precursor to every action a person makes in life, we could create an algorithm that perfectly predicts that individual's behavior in every instance.

That position implies that biogenetic forces preempt the notion of Freud and other developmental theorists that we are all the same at birth and that how our caregivers deal with the unfolding drama of the growing child determines how he or she will turn out psychologically and behaviorally. How could that be? There are several possibilities.

BIOLOGICAL AND DEVELOPMENTAL APPROACHES TO THE EXPLANATION OF CONSTITUTIONAL CRIMINALITY

GENETIC AND INHERITED

A person's *constitution* refers to the elements, structure, forces, predilections, and characteristics, mental and physical, that make up the way that individual is constructed and functions in an enduring way. How people are constituted affects what they bring to any situation regardless of the time or place. Some examples of those characteristics are clearly genetic and inherited, such as eye color and body morphology (build). More recently, low activity of an inherited mutation of the gene **monoamine oxidase A (MAO-A)** has been found to be related to delinquent behavior (Nilsson et al., 2006).

GENETIC BUT NOT INHERITED

Other things are genetic but not inherited. Genes can mutate or be altered by environmental factors, as has been suggested for some cases of cerebral hemisphere dominance resulting from in utero traumatic experiences, toxins, or other stresses that, at an early stage, alter a developing embryo (Ishikawa & Raine, 2003; Kandel & Mednick, 1991). An early discovery was the effect of x-rays (Kandel & Mednick, 1991). Exposure to a significant amount of x-rays can alter the chromosomal/ genetic structure of the person experiencing them. Similarly, the effect of thalidomide is another example. This anti-nausea drug was given to pregnant Canadian women in the 1960s but not approved for use in the United States, and its use resulted in appendage deformities in their children (Lenz, 1988). The effect of alcohol leading to fetal alcohol spectrum disorder is a third (Randall, 2001). The damaged chromosomes will not be passed on, however, so despite the devastating effects for the individual, mercifully, the consequence is not hereditary. Also not inherited is the XYY, or supermale, chromosomal configuration associated with criminality in some men (Jacobs, Brunton, Melville, Brittain, & McLemont, 1965).

NEITHER GENETIC NOR INHERITED

Some of the most important constitutional characteristics are neither genetic nor inherited but socially derived and developmental. Our characteristics are influenced by our caregivers' treatment of us in early childhood (see the research of Harry Harlow in chapter 4) or by the type of school we attend: military, permissive, or religious. (Ignatius Loyola, founder of the Jesuit schools, apparently said, "Give me the child until he is seven, and I will give you the man.") There is timing involved, however, according to Freud (1940/1949) and others, wherein specific rules and attitudes and values must be internalized during critical periods or windows of development. For example, Freud theorized that seven years of age marked the beginning of the latency period when aggression and violence for the normal child, who has passed through the early unsocialized phases of aggression, lie dormant until puberty.

IN SUMMARY

The controversy regarding whether criminality is voluntary or determined, in fact "caused" by our constitutions, still rages over 150 years after Lombroso's theorizing.

Four case studies were presented of very different kinds of individuals: a prodigal son of a well-to-do family who repeatedly commits crimes; a person of marginal intelligence raised in an isolated, extremely antisocial backwoods family by a tyrannical mother; an immigrant with poor linguistic skills who develops paranoid schizophrenia; and a Japanese soldier who committed horrendous war crimes and then suffered a life of guilt.

Varieties of constitutional approaches ranging from hereditary to social learning are described.

BIOGENETIC EXPLANATIONS OF CRIME

This section follows the historical development of **biogenetic constitutional theories**, beginning with Lombroso. It then traces their decline over the years and their unexpected resurgence with the discovery of the relationship between multiple physical and/or physiological anomalies and aggressive criminal behavior. The case studies presented earlier are discussed and analyzed for main probable causal factors. Recent research using modern brain-imaging technology has established connections among genes, the brain, and offending, connections that support constitutional theories posited 150 years ago.

Cesare Lombroso was an extraordinary individual whose interests spanned art, medicine, and criminology; hence, he was what is known as a **polymath**. He lived in an amazing time when gathering examples, specimens, and data was a passion. This enthusiasm for science was perhaps best exemplified by Charles Darwin (1871/1981) who 20 some years after his voyage to the Galapagos produced his theory of **natural selection**, arguing that there is no grand design in nature only myriad variations produced by evolutionary forces and that those that function well in their environment—eat, compete, breed, thrive—survive. That view suggests that nature throws DNA around like mud against a wall and that some sticks, and does okay, but most doesn't, based on what works in that environment.

Lombroso (1876/2006) gives the impression of suffering from attention deficit hyperactivity disorder (ADHD) in the way he thrust about almost bobbleheadedly taking in the frenzy of discoveries and theories that exploded upon the world in the mid-1850s, from Auguste Comte's notion that the object of science is to gather as many positive examples as possible to Lombroso's own observations as a medical officer of fractious soldiers who were characterized by tattoos, physical, and physiognomic (facial) and physiological anomalies that suggested to him they were throwbacks to more primitive members of more savage races on the evolutionary scale. Because of his flamboyant style and almost frenzied attempts to unify all his ideas in one theory, which was, nevertheless, constantly evolving, he has been dismissed by many modern criminologists as ludicrous.

But as Mary Gibson and Nicole Hahn Rafter (Lombroso, 1876/2006), who were initially among the disdainers of his work, proclaim in the introduction to their landmark English translation of his theory, in the context of his times, he was a giant intellect and, ironically, a liberal turned socialist who worked to better the lot of women, criminals, immigrants, and the generally downtrodden of that time in history. As they admit in their study of him, his theories are extremely complex and have been oversimplified by hostile reportage (Lombroso, 1876/2006). Nevertheless, here they are reduced to a few essential concepts: he believed a significant portion of criminals (about 33 percent) was born with inherited cognitive-emotional deficits that doom them to engage in violent and antisocial behavior and that a significant portion of those can be identified through physiognomic (facial) features (Lombroso, 1876/2006).

He admitted, however, that most criminals are merely occasional offenders who engage in illegal behavior due to circumstance or situational factors; passion (elevated emotional outbursts) or insanity (not being able to distinguish between reality and delusion, as we have discussed); or, finally, moral insanity. Those who suffer from moral insanity, he argued, are otherwise rational human beings who feel no compunctions about lying, cheating, harming other human beings, or breaking any laws (Lombroso, 1876/2006)—a type that sounds strikingly similar to more modern conceptions of the psychopath (chapter 4). Modern critics of Lombroso, especially those with a Marxist bent, do not comment on the full breadth of his theorizing, choosing to dismiss him for suggesting that physiognomy is a marker of criminality. Yet this first attempt at discovering a biological indicator of criminality is ultimately proving to have considerable validity.

ONTOGENY RECAPITULATES PHYLOGENY

In the 1850s, one of the most influential German biologists, Ernst Haeckel, coined this phrase: **"Ontogeny recapitulates phylogeny"** (Nelson, 2009, p. 246). The phrase proclaims that the development of an individual reproduces the course of evolution so that we begin as simple amoeba-like embryos, then aquatic animals in the womb, then amphibians, and then air-breathing four-legged land creatures, and finally two-legged primates and progress from there. Lombroso (1876/2006) eagerly adopted this unifying principle, using it to explain how some people have not evolved as much, especially children (more savage, unsocialized, less developed) and women (who are nevertheless normally protected from criminality by the maternal instinct, perhaps fueled by estrogen, the female hormone). It also allowed for accidents of nature that resulted in throwbacks to earlier human forms and so a propensity for less socialized general behavior, a concept referred to as atavism. Finally, the perspective allowed for degeneracy, that is, antisocial behavior caused by pathology in the genes or protoplasm—"diseased ancestral elements"—that affects neuropsychological functioning and is often manifested as epilepsy (Lombroso, 1876/2006).

THE EMPIRICAL RECORD

How have those concepts fared a hundred years later? If you ask most sociologists, especially Marxist or critical criminologists, they inevitably dismiss the notion that "born criminals exist" or that one could recognize their propensity for criminality through physiognomy. And, in fact, in two major early studies, the first conducted by Charles Goring in 1913 titled *The English Convict* and the second by E. A. Hooton in 1939 titled *The American Criminal*, the results were mixed at best and not very supportive. Goring (1913) found violent criminals were larger, stronger, and bad tempered. Makes common sense. There was a high correlation (.655) between criminality and defective IQ, epilepsy, insanity, and venereal diseases as well (Goring, 1913). Lombroso would regard those findings as support for his theory, but Hooton (1939) claims that criminals, in fact, showed more anthropologically advanced facial features than noncriminals. Of course, multiple physical anomalies cannot be rated on a primitive to advanced scale. Nevertheless, certain of these anomalies have been shown to have some correlation to criminality. With the rising tide of sociological criminology, especially Marxist sociology, that swept academia cresting in the 1980s, most criminologists had dismissed Lombroso as a dinosaur to be relegated to the trashcan of historical theory.

Then a funny thing happened. First, there persisted among the public a belief (apocryphal or not) that one could distinguish a criminal face from a noncriminal face, as demonstrated by Bull and Green, who showed students and police officers 10 photos of men and asked them what 11 crimes they had committed. There was significant agreement in both groups regarding the looks of muggers, violent robbers, those committing company fraud, drug possession, and gross indecency (Bull & Green, 1980). But the irony was that the photos were merely of friends of the researchers, none of whom had a criminal record. Does that study show that the idea that there is a physiognomy of criminals is all based on stereotypes? Not really. It merely shows that, given a task, ordinary, bright people and professionals will do their best and that appears to invoke consensual beliefs, some of which are, admittedly, stereotypes. Or is it possible that those individuals had the criminal propensities attributed to them but had not actualized them or been detected?

In fact, when actual criminals are shown in photos, Thornton (1939) found students identified them and their offenses at better than chance. Most startlingly, Kozeny (1962), who distilled composite photos of 730 criminals into 16 offense categories, found statistically significant accuracy in the identification of which composites had committed specific crimes. So is it merely stereotype operating or is something more Lombrosian perhaps going on here?

Two studies suggest stereotypes and what Charles Horton Cooley (1902) called "the looking glass self" have a significant hand in it. Cooley's theory was that our identities and personalities are formed by the way we see ourselves, for example, in the mirror and as a reflection, also, of the way others see and respond to us. One study was conducted by a Vancouver otolaryngologist (eyes, ears, nose, and throat specialist) named Lewison (1965), the other by a group of researchers in the New York City area (Kurtzberg, Mandell, Levin, Lipton, & Shuster, 1978).

Lewison (1965) selected 100 convicts at Oakalla Prison in Burnaby, British Columbia, for cosmetic surgery for the types of physical deviations Lombroso described and followed them for two years postoperatively to measure their rate of **recidivism** (reconviction). Another 100 candidates had nothing done to them. Lewison (1965) found substantially lower recidivism among the postsurgical group than the controls, 53 percent versus 75 percent, once drug addicts and those assessed to be **psychopaths** were factored out. Interestingly, the facially enhanced psychopathic group, though not showing less recidivism, moved on to white-collar crime from their more blue-collar assaults and robberies, assumedly from the new opportunities afforded them by their improved looks.

In a much larger study of 600 candidates for surgery at New York's Ryker's Island Prison by Kurtzberg et al. (1978), recidivism rates among inmates receiving surgery alone was 30 percent; surgery with counseling, 33 percent; those receiving no treatment, 56 percent; and, surprisingly, among those receiving counseling alone, 89 percent! It appears that counseling was not only a useless, extra expense but counterproductive and that having your facial features improved will reduce your chances of reconviction and, so we presume, of reoffending as well. Do those studies suggest, as Cooley would argue, that it is all in the eye of the beholder? Do self-regard and stereotyping by others create criminality?

Not necessarily so. An ingenious study by Marnie Rice of 500 inmates over 20 years argues that something else is operating as well. Although prison records had suggested that treatment had had little beneficial effect, when those retrospectively assessed to be psychopathic were separated from the nonpsychopathic, a very different picture appeared (Rice, 1997). Psychopaths who received treatment actually increased their recidivism, whereas nonpsychopaths responded very positively to treatment (counseling) with lower recidivism rates, supporting both Lewison's (1965) and Kurtzberg et al.'s (1978) findings. Obviously, the psychopaths who learn through imitating others developed a better repertoire for their cons (scams for taking advantage of others) by interacting in the therapy groups.

MULTIPLE MINOR PHYSICAL ANOMALIES

As it turns out, we cannot attribute those results merely to stereotyping. According to Peter Hammond et al. (2004), who until 2015 was a professor of computational biology at the UCL (University College London) Institute of Child Health in the UK, three-dimensional facial analysis can detect fragile x syndrome, a genetic condition leading to specific mental disorders. It can also suggest the presence of other conditions, including Hans Eysenck's personality factor, psychoticism. So too is fetal alcohol syndrome (FAS) flagged by multiple physical anomalies, as is Down syndrome, which is reflected in lowered mental functioning. But unlike Down syndrome, FAS is associated with increases in the propensity for aggression as well as reduced mental, especially executive, functioning and intolerance for **frustration**, among other potential behavioral problems (Niccols, 2007). But does the existence of a genetically based propensity for a certain behavior, added to a physical marker of that propensity that might encourage a particular societal attitude, always mean antisocial behavior or criminality?

THE BAD NEWS BEARS II

I once had an 11-year-old boy with FAS, now often called fetal alcohol spectrum disorder, join the Little League baseball team I was coaching. He had just come out of 30 days of psychiatric observation for viciously beating up his adoptive mother and older, more athletic brother. I made him the catcher and the captain, which forced him to focus constantly or get hit on the head. Also on the team were bullies, who were told they could not bad mouth anyone on our or any other team; the ADHD dreamers, who were seated if they missed noticing a fly ball land near them; and a few exceptional athletes. We won the championship, but it required constant supervision and instruction and encouragement. At the end of the season, many parents of the problematic boys came to me, practically with tears in their eyes, claiming it was the first time their sons had managed to finish a season on a team. Hence the name, derived from a Disney film, the league gave our team—the Bad News Bears.

What does this example tell us? Even individuals biologically disposed to misbehaving can function well—under very specific environmental demands, namely, structure, supervision, and dictates—in an interdependent group like a team. The classic 1967 war film, *The Dirty Dozen*, based on a true story about 13 American soldiers convicted of crimes who embark on a suicide mission in World War II, purports to show that even the most scurrilous of individuals, under the right leadership within an all-encompassing mission, can be a successful team. The psychologist Robert Hare, who created the most common assessment tool for detecting psychopathy (*The Psychopathy Checklist*), disagrees (Hare, 2003). Although he obviously did not assess the members of the mission, he argues that were they "true" psychopaths, they would not have been able to form a reliable, interdependent team. Considering that they did form such a team, this is a moot point, but perhaps they were criminally inclined not purely by nature.

THE EFFECTS OF EPILEPSY

Because there do seem to be biological factors contributing to certain behavioral propensities, the second hypothesis Lombroso (1876/2006) put forth for criminality, degenerate or diseased genes, also appears to have some credence, although he used epilepsy as his main indicator and in fact unifying concept. Is there evidence that epilepsy, or more specifically epileptic fits, are associated with increased violence and aggression? After the notion had been dismissed for several decades, research now strongly supports that hypothesis. Mark, Ervin, and Sweet (1972) describe a young girl whose violent episode—the stabbing of another girl in a cinema washroom—could be triggered in the laboratory by deep cranial electrical stimulation that was similar to her ictal (midseizure) attack, and Lewis, Shanok, Grant, and Ritvo (1983) in a large study of adolescents discovered a strong relationship between severity of violent and aggressive behavior and epileptic seizures. So, as Lombroso (1876/2006) conjectured, there is a higher incidence of epilepsy among convicted individuals, and the more serious and wide-ranging the crimes, the greater the presence of epileptic symptomology.

Thus, according to Lombroso (1876/2006) and others (e.g., Raine, 2014), about 33–35 percent of criminals can be accounted for by heredity and degenerate genes. But is there any evidence for criminality's being transmitted through the genes? Studies done in Scandinavia where there are meticulous records for the last 200 years have supported the theory using adoption studies of siblings raised apart, in some cases identical twins (Lichtenstein et al., 2000). Although some reviewers have tried to attribute the results of those studies to bad methodology or have argued that, at best, they have produced weak relationships, others argue that the weight of findings from so many studies is overwhelming when put together.

Ellis (1982) and others have concluded that, given the distillation of findings from family studies, twin studies, adoption studies, karyotype studies, and studies on the genetic influences on correlates of criminality (e.g., ADHD, academic achievement, alcoholism, impulsivity, intelligence, learning disabilities, manic depression and **schizophrenia**, and low MAO-A activity), inheritability of the predilection to offending cannot be dismissed or denied. Nevertheless, biological factors are neither exclusive nor straightforward causes of criminality.

For instance, my friend Sacha Tolstoi, great grandson of the writer Leo Tolstoi, has not only a sister but a twin brother who is schizophrenic. Sacha, however, is completely the opposite: outgoing, charming, well spoken, full of joie de vivre, and a good but, in his own judgment, not "great" writer. It is understandable that he may not have entirely inherited the genius of Leo, who is regarded by many as one of the greatest novelists of all time, but given the fate of his siblings, how did he escape the serious mental illness of the brother with whom he shared his mother's womb and parental genes, not to mention his sister's schizophrenia? That mystery geneticists have yet to unravel, but in criminality studies monozygotic (single egg) twins show significantly greater concordance (i.e., similar probability) for criminality than do dizygotic twins who share the environment of the womb and very similar, but not totally identical, genes (Raine, 1993). Fortunately for Sacha, he is a dizygotic twin. We may also conjecture that youngsters inheriting some genetic disposition to misbehavior may need to experience specific toxic environmental events to potentiate, or even trigger, their criminality.

CONCLUSIONS REGARDING HERITABILITY AND CRIMINALITY

The case of Vincent Li is clearest. He committed his horrendous murder in response to voices increasingly urging him to defend himself against the innocent and unsuspecting Tim McLean on that Greyhound bus. Of all the mental illnesses, **paranoid schizophrenia** is the one most prominently associated with aggressive behavior and violent crime. Yet this illness would hardly qualify as born criminality. Nevertheless, according to Short, Thomas, Mullen, and Ogloff (2013), who studied a sample of more than 4,000 schizophrenics, even those not suffering from substance addiction were about twice as likely to be convicted of a violent crime as people matched with them for various characteristics but not suffering from the condition. That is a dramatic difference not found very often in research on different populations.

What then of Ed Gein? He was always odd and obviously strongly influenced by a domineering and fanatical mother who created ambivalence about his increasing interest in sex through her abhorrence of women, especially those in the nearby town of Plainfield ("they are all shameless whores"), while abusing his hapless father. Finding him masturbating to anatomical images in *Grey's Anatomy*, she allegedly professed that that was better than consorting with women. But his brother did not share that disposition. The mother's death and the presumed ensuing trauma to Ed of her loss triggered Ed's transformation of her room into a shrine while his own living quarters increasingly assumed the metaphorical filth and disorder of his conflicted mind until his obsession with the taboo of sex led to grave robbing, the ritualistic adornment of human female skin, perhaps the consumption of sexual organs, and, eventually, the murder and disembowelment of women.

Some theoreticians, especially orthodox Freudians, would argue that his bizarre relationship with his mother was a sufficient cause of Ed's criminality. I would contend that it might have been necessary but that his criminality required a biological precursor, perhaps a combination of lower intelligence and a disposition to deviance characterized by primitive urges. I think some predisposition set him apart from millions of other boys, including his brother, who died earlier, perhaps killed by Ed for criticizing his mother. Other boys have similar mothers and face bereavement upon their deaths without setting out on a course of necrophilia, the physical mimicking of womanhood (dressing in human skin), cannibalism, and murder. As you can see, whether IQ or psychological conflict is invoked in explanation, the causal factors of this crime are not very far removed from the ancient hypotheses of Lombroso.

By contrast, the case of Nagatomi Hakudo, the Japanese doctor, underlines the power of socialization and the effects of situations of maximum coercive conformity pressure. Hakudo committed horrible atrocities against the Chinese in Nanking during the massacre only to repent and seek redemption—even at the risk of condemnation from his fellow Japanese. His socialization began with the cultural values he absorbed from childhood that regard non-Japanese as subhumans and surrendering soldiers as below contempt (according to the training and values inculcated by Bushido, the Japanese military code, in actuality invented and popularized by an American).

One must note that offending Japanese soldiers, upon returning to Japan, rather than behaving like the monsters they resembled in China and elsewhere, reconstituted a society that is among the most law-abiding and violence free in the world even while characterized by a great interest in violent media, especially violent pornography. (Perhaps these soldiers became obedient citizens because of their similarly strict conformity to society's mores and laws—just as their absolute conformity to the military code made them vicious monsters.) Lombroso would regard Hakudo as an occasional criminal overwhelmed by circumstance, which he regarded as the most common type of criminality but not necessarily requiring instigating conditions as extreme as war, merely social conditions characterized by deviant norms.

Scholars from Gustave LeBon to Vernon Allen and Philip Zimbardo (of the Stanford prison experiment) have noted the power of situational factors, especially the coercive pressure of the majority to inundate and overwhelm individual predilections. And so in Hakudo's case, we observe the flipside: the norm was to behave monstrously toward the Chinese and the community standard of tolerance was very low in the Army of the Rising Sun, for any offense. So the rule for those mindless subjects was to engage in the horrifying slaughter or be perceived as a dissident or even a traitor. Apparently not much prompting was required, so well "socialized" and adhering to the ingroup norm were those Japanese soldiers, especially the officers who arranged competitions to see how many heads they could cut off in the shortest time.

In a long series of studies, Vernon Allen (1975) and his colleagues tried to inculcate independence in the face of group conformity pressure, one of the most dictatorial and insidious phenomena discovered by social psychologists. Even in the relatively benign and transitory circumstances of the behavioral laboratory, they were stymied. As soon as social support, that is, the presence of an agreeing partner, was withdrawn, conformity slavishly returned to previous levels in the face of a continuing unanimous majority. (With an agreeing partner, most subjects did not conform.) After many attempts to inculcate independence from the unanimous majority, finally in a series of studies (reported by Allen, 1975), I was able to instill continuing solitary independence by having subjects who were male members of the Canadian Armed Forces respond independently if first they were primed by a supporter agreeing with them unknown to the rest of the group who remained in silent surveillance of the subject for the second half of the experiment. Thus, as far as the subject was concerned, he had acted alone in the group, and he believed the pressure group perceived him to be acting alone and consistently resisting group pressure. And so his role in the group—as the outlier—hadn't changed. Clearly, the role in the group was the instrumental factor in producing continued independence. Once more Cooley's looking glass self hypothesis proved predictive of behavior.

OTHER CONCLUSIONS

MODERN CONCEPTIONS OF THE BIOLOGICAL BASES OF CRIMINALITY

The most encompassing theory I have encountered, dubbed **evolutionary neuroandrogenic theory** by Lee Ellis (1982), hypothesizes that certain genes and prenatal environments promote high testosterone regimes in the fetus. Their effects include a susceptibility to seizures in and around the limbic system (see figure 6.1), tendencies toward lowered central nervous system arousal, and a rightward shift in hemisphere functioning. Seizures are associated with wide emotional instability producing anger and frustration in situations where others might be more sanguine. Coupling those reactions with lower sensitivity to pain and ever encroaching boredom and a lesser ability to pick up nuances of language along with fewer positive emotions leads to a litany of unfortunate outcomes: epilepsy, ADHD, poor school performance, recreational drug use, thrill seeking, and generally haywire behavior.

A less spectacular but perhaps even more common sequence of emergent criminality tracks poor genes and poor prenatal environments (i.e., in the womb) that retard brain development (e.g., in the neocortex). The results are smaller brains, lowered prefrontal functioning, and the morbid combination of low intelligence and diminished cognitive functioning, which means less efficient executive control and monitoring of the limbic system and so poor school achievement, a bad work record, and defective long term planning (Ivanovic et al., 2004). In other words, these poor beginnings leave people at great risk to fall into criminality unless a welfare state softens their fall with food and shelter and social guidance, or at least individual counseling.

In conclusion, what Lombroso and others noticed 150 years ago and, somewhat primitively, characterized as criminal man is still being studied. In other words, being born with defective genes or corrupt neurological processes is still being touted as the principal developmental cause of many chronic criminals. The idea is not simply that certain people are born as criminals, which makes no sense, but that they are at extremely high risk to become criminals due to a combination of genes and prenatal environmental events. These factors make a minority of troublesome individuals unstable or, for the majority of career criminals, just functionally not very attractive or bright and so incapable of high achievement in society.

In hindsight, the atavistic hypothesis inspired by Darwin (1871/1981) and the related incomplete development theory of Haeckel (ontogeny recapitulates phylogeny; Nelson, 2009) appear to be superfluous mechanisms, but probably the best guesses available to those brilliant observers in the late nineteenth century. Now, however, we can observe the living brain with all of its functioning through the window of magnetic resonance imaging. And what we find are brains of some criminals that do not activate normally to stimuli intended to elicit emotion and in fact do contain anatomical anomalies. As Lombroso wrote somewhat colorfully when he inspected the brain of the executed bandit Villella,

> At the sight of that skull, I seemed to see all of a sudden, lighted
> up as a vast plain under a flaming sky, the problem of the nature
> of the criminal—an atavistic being who reproduces in his person
> the ferocious instincts of primitive humanity and the inferior

animals. Thus were explained anatomically the enormous jaws, high cheek-bones, prominent superciliary arches, solitary lines in the palms, extreme size of the orbits, handle-shaped or sessile ears found in criminals, savages, and apes, insensibility to pain, extreme acute sight, tattooing, excessive idleness, love of orgies, and the irresistible craving for evil for its own sake, the desire not only to extinguish life in the victim, but to mutilate the corpse, tear its flesh, and drink its blood. (Lombroso, 1911, p. xv)

This description could be of a character straight out of *The Texas Chainsaw Massacre* or some other slasher movie. Sifting through this collection of characteristics, many plausible, some fanciful, one realizes, given my examples above, that Lombroso wasn't as completely far off as we had originally come to believe based on his critics, though the sources of his descriptors range from the biogenetic to the sociocultural.

THE STRUCTURE AND FUNCTIONING OF THE BRAIN

Today, we have added insight because of **functional magnetic resonance imaging (fMRI)** that reveals the degree of activity in various parts of the brain and coaxial tomography (**CT scan**) that creates a three-dimensional picture of brain structures. This technology shows us that the structure of the brains of violent criminals and their functioning is significantly different from those who have not committed extremely violent acts. As Raine (2013) reported, murderers from good homes had a 14.2 percent reduction in right orbitofrontal functioning—"a brain area of particular relevance to violence."

Raine's "blueprint" begins with genes that segue into brain structure and ultimately influence neurotransmitter functioning (MAO-A). Low MAO-A has been linked to antisocial behavior much in the same way that low **serotonin** (when, for instance, depleted by use of cocaine or stress) is associated with irascibility and tendencies to violent outbursts. Raine connects those effects to brain structure in the limbic system associated with abnormal emotional reactions and to the frontal cortex associated with making judgments—individuals afflicted with this brain structure often make poor decisions and engage in impulsive actions. He points out that males with the low MAO-A genetic condition have an accompanying reduction in the volume of the **amygdala**, the anterior cingulate, and the orbitofrontal cortex. This cascade of neural deficits is found in criminals, completing the sequence "from genes to brain to offending" (Raine, 2013, p. 260).

Raine points out that his phrase, quoted above, is an oversimplification, and reviewing research in the area, he lays out a schema of brain processes under three headings—**cognitive, affective**, and **motor**—and aligns them with the related brain structures. Any dysfunction in those regions complicates the outcomes in thoughts, feelings, and actions—and potentiates violent behavior. So he is not talking about direct outcomes but about effects that can lead to antisocial behavior and violence.

At the cognitive (thinking) level, the various structures implicated include the ventromedial prefrontal cortex, the medial polar-prefrontal regions, the angular gyrus, and the anterior and posterior cingulate. Diminished function within those regions leads to "poor planning, impaired attention, the inability to shift response strategies, poor cognitive appraisal of emotion, poor decision making, impaired self reflection and reduced capacity to adequately process rewards and punishments" (p. 260). The effects create the social elements that lead to crime—poor occupational and social functioning, breaking social rules, not noticing punishment cues that provide a compass for behavior, bad decisions, and poor cognitive control over aggressive thoughts and feelings.

The affective (emotional) level factors are centered in the neural structures of the amygdala/hippocampus, the insula, the anterior cingulate, and the superior temporal gyrus. Damage in those areas results in an inability to read emotions in others, impaired memory and learning ability, lack of disgust, impaired moral decision making, lack of guilt and embarrassment, lack of empathy, poor fear conditioning, poor emotion regulation, and reduced discomfort at the commission of moral transgressions. The consequence is a greater ability to commit horrendous crimes against others, poor conscience development, and overall, a greater probability of committing violent crimes against other people.

The third motor group includes the dorsolateral prefrontal cortex, orbitofrontal cortex, and inferior frontal cortex. The results of impairment include response perseveration (continuing repetition regardless), no ability to inhibit inappropriate responses, and impulsivity. So, in general, there is an inability to change one's response set, for example, in order to resolve a conflict and to avoid punishment.

IN SUMMARY

The theoretical parameters "roughed out" by Lombroso over 150 years ago appear to have some credence. Modern research has found that multiple physical anomalies can be symptomatic of underlying neurological conditions and deficits.

Inherited tendencies toward criminality have been born out in studies of families; for example, those with criminal biological fathers have a greater likelihood of themselves being convicted of crimes. However, not all genetic tendencies to crime are inherited, and, as discussed in the previous chapter, some in fact exist due to physiological traumas or toxic substances ingested or imposed upon the mother or experienced by the offending individual him or herself.

Genetic tendencies are not mandatory for committing horrendous acts, however. Many of the most barbaric crimes have been committed by people adhering to a group norm when community standards allow little tolerance for deviance, as was found in the highly conforming Japanese troops during World War II who followed the code of the Imperial Japanese Army. But now neuroscience has established a link among neural functioning, brain structure, and crime, perhaps not as flamboyantly as Lombroso exclaimed on seeing Villella's brain, but of comparable importance.

CHAPTER FOUR

PSYCHOPATHY: DIONYSIUS AND THE ANTIHERO IN SOCIETY

This chapter covers the phenomenon of psychopathy and psychopaths. From a historical chronicling of the disorder to the modern identification of it and its pernicious effects on society, the chapter describes various individuals who have been identified as psychopathic and then delves into their psychophysiological anomalies perhaps causally implicated in their lack of empathy, lack of fear, and their inability to anticipate the consequences of their actions. Several case studies are examined in the light of recent research.

DIONYSUS: ESCAPE FROM HUMAN REASON

Dionysus is the god of winemaking, ritual madness, ecstasy, and those who do not belong to conventional society. He symbolizes the chaotic, the unexpected, and the dangerous—everything that can be attributed only to the unforeseeable actions of gods. Many heroes and antiheroes are Dionysian.

The man, handsome, strong, and debonair, sneaks into the enemy base, sets bombs, fights off several security guards, and escapes in a state-of-the-art aircraft he apparently can fly, just as the base explodes in a ball of flame. He lands in Monaco and, doffing his flying suit for a tux, wins thousands of euros at the casino and ends up bedding the beautiful enemy agent who is intent on killing him—all apparently without breaking into a sweat from either effort or fear. Who is he? James Bond, of course, the longest running film franchise in history. It is clear we the audience (men and women) can't ever get enough of that Dionysian character. The only sign that he is also a "problem" involves meeting with his superior officer in the British secret service, a matronly woman (in films between 1995 and 2015) who is continually either suspending him for insubordination (not following orders) or grudgingly rewarding him for outstanding success in his operations.

The model for Bond was an actual person, the original professional spy, Sidney Reilly (born Zigmund Rozenblum). The name change notwithstanding, Reilly was a Ukrainian from Odessa who worked for the British against the Germans and Turks during World War I and went on to oppose the communist takeover of Russia, coming within a hair's breadth of pulling off a counterrevolution that would have changed the course of history, had the British not broken their promise to supply a relatively small number of troops for an invasion. Along the way, he charmed several women and may have been involved in the death of one husband; he certainly shared in the widow's inheritance. The brilliant British TV series, *Reilly, Ace of Spies*, made clear the profound ambivalence the British War Office felt toward its prime operative.

Closer to home during the same period in history, a handsome, daring young man was troubled. He had attempted to pass exams at the Royal Military College in Kingston, Ontario, by cheating and was found out. He was about to be expelled, to the enduring shame of his well-placed family for whom he had been a burden since childhood. Luckily for him, if tragically for Europe and North America, World War I broke out and an "accommodation" was reached wherein he enlisted in the army and was shipped overseas. Fighting the "Bosh" wasn't as romantic as the recruitment posters had promised: trenches filled with sewage, rats, typhoid, foot rot, and unrelenting rain punctuated by brief forays over the top during which men were mowed down like wheat facing an army of reapers armed with German machine guns.

Then he looked skyward and against the brilliant blue of a rare sunny day saw the world's first combat fighter planes engaging each other in exhilarating maneuvers, some crashing and burning but most surviving, saluting each other, and returning to their respective bases where the pilots were greeted by "batmen" (valets) and billeted in

French chateaux. Now that was the way to fight a war, he decided, and presented himself to the Royal Flying Corps. There are different versions of what transpired. Some suggest that he claimed experience in aircraft in Canada and that he was a "graduate" of the Royal Military College in Kingston, Ontario. In any case, he was welcomed. Because the average life span of a Royal Flying Corps fighter pilot was only 45 days during some periods of the war, and as only upper-middle-class young men need apply (aged 18 to 20), they were in short supply, and this "colonial" seemed to have the right background and capability.

Billy Bishop advanced quickly from being an observer to a fighter pilot. Though he never became an outstanding flier, he had one thing going for him: he was a dead shot and fearless killer. In their vastly superior aircraft, the Germans, after engaging and usually outdueling the British and then running low on petrol, would wave goodbye and begin returning to their bases on the other side of No Man's Land. Suddenly, a British plane, with guns blazing, was hot on their tails and shooting down fleeing Germans until it ran out of gas and landed on a road. Then the pilot, Bishop, hitched a ride back while someone fetched his aircraft. Clearly, for this assassin, "All's fair in love and war" was the rule in effect rather than upper-class notions of "noblesse oblige" regarding the sporting way to engage in aerial dogfights. But he killed Germans in many different situations, as he often roamed alone far behind enemy lines.

One recollection has Bishop and his close friend, Captain Albert Ball, planning the first ever airborne raid: they were to load their aircraft with handheld bombs and attack a German air base. Unfortunately, just days before the assault, Ball, then the ranking "ace" (most kills in the British Air Corps), was himself shot down and killed. On one occasion, a disconsolate Bishop, apparently having drowned his sorrow in alcohol at dawn, instructed his batman to load his plane with all of the bombs it could carry and, despite his "fragile" condition, took off. Hours later, he returned triumphantly reporting that he had flown over the base and, while the aircraft were still on the ground, hurtled bombs at them by hand, destroying them all, as well as the airdrome itself.

Bishop became an instant celebrity in London, receiving medals, even the highest award possible, the Victoria Cross, from the king and adulation from high society. He ended up shooting down more

German planes (72) than any Allied pilot in World War I, though it was George "Roy" Brown, another Canadian pilot, who shot down Manfred von Richthofen, the Red Baron, the greatest ace of that war (80 kills). Unfortunately, Bishop's drinking and general misbehavior became increasingly difficult for the authorities to deal with, and as the Americans entered the war and resources increased dramatically, he was sent home, over his protests, to embark on a lecture tour to "encourage" more recruits. He returned for a final combat tour, shooting down 25 aircraft in 12 days of patrols, an almost incredible number.

The last chapter of Billy's story remains controversial. Although he was lionized in the brilliant off-Broadway Canadian musical *Billy Bishop Goes to War*, when the National Film Board of Canada was making a film about him (*The Kid Who Couldn't Miss*, by Paul Cowan [1982]), researchers could find no evidence of the air raid in German records. Perhaps they had been destroyed in bombing during World War II or …? While most of Billy Bishop's "kills" were witnessed, scores were accepted on a gentleman's honor system, including the amazing multiple kills he reported, as many as three to five in one or two patrols.

Captain Eddie Rickenbacker, America's top ace, was a study in contrasts to Bishop. Although sharing Bishop's love of speed and adventure, Rickenbacker (who changed the spelling of his name from Richenbacher due to wartime anti-German sentiment) pursued his career by the book, promoting the transition of racecar drivers like himself to pilots and not being involved in any disputed kills. He went on to found Eastern Airlines and Rickenbacker Motors, which, alas, went bankrupt.

Cristophe Rocancourt was a worldwide phenomenon two decades ago. He had posed as the son of Nelson Rockefeller to bilk New Yorkers of hundreds of thousands of dollars after arriving in the United States as a fugitive from Switzerland. When the heat from investigators got too intense, he migrated to California where the name Rockefeller had insufficient cache, so he assumed an identity as the illegitimate son of famed movie producer Dino De Laurentis and started working people on the "B-list who aspired to the A." As a result, he took in even more money fraudulently until, once again, the atmosphere got too risky, and he moved on to Whistler, British Columbia. There, he told me, people were so unsophisticated and eager to rub elbows with the nearly famous, "It was like taking candy from babies." Soon he was on the cover of *Vanity Fair* and the subject of a *60 Minutes* TV profile.

When I requested an interview with him, he was being held for extradition in the North Fraser Pretrial Centre (NFPC) in Coquitlam, British Columbia. He scores a "39 out of 40 on the psychopathy scale," sources told me. "He'll see you, he is very bored." The man whom I spent many hours with separated by glass was, in the bright orange prison outfit, not very prepossessing: a weasel-faced, thirty-something Frenchman of slight stature who, to me, resembled the evil dwarflike gangster depicted in one of my favorite movies, *Chinatown*, directed by the famed and disgraced Roman Polanski. But Rocancourt was amazingly well spoken and agreeable.

Rocancourt told me he had been born to a teenaged prostitute who had dumped him on his young, longshoreman father's doorstep and left. The man, in turn, gave his mother the child. She was a destitute countrywoman with whom Rocancourt would, at a very young age, sneak into fields at night to steal potatoes. She finally could not take care of him and brought him to an orphanage where, he said, the Catholic brothers treated him very well and he became a celebrity among the residents because he could tell enthralling stories. It was then he realized that people loved stories, the more outlandish the better, and that skilled raconteurs gained status and power.

Rocancourt eventually escaped from the orphanage and somehow survived in the Paris subway. When I asked him whether he had ever been frightened, he said, "If you live as a child in the Paris subway, nothing after that scares you." Over some time, he began to make the acquaintance of a young university student who eventually took him home and introduced him, as a curiosity, to his peer group of Parisian intellectuals. Rocancourt absorbed everything from them like a sponge: the vocabulary, ideas, accent, manners, and customs, and they were quite happy to help an "enfant sauvage" in the best tradition of the philosopher Rousseau. Once he was properly equipped, and they introduced him to the right people, he began his grifting, getting people to invest in his get-rich-quick schemes. However, he was eventually implicated (falsely, he claimed) in a Swiss bank robbery in which someone was killed, so he had to flee to North America.

In my interviews with him, Rocancourt emphasized how much he admired education and how much he loved his son born in a marriage to a *Playboy* centerfold. He said that once out of prison (in three years he estimated—he actually got five), he would attend university so he could help young people in need. True? Or as a true psychopath, was he merely telling me what he thought I would find most sympathetic? The last I heard from him he was at the Cannes Film Festival on the arm of supermodel Naomi Campbell, having starred in an allegedly pornographic film with her. I suppose she would have qualified as a young(ish) person, but a "young person in need"?

Moving toward the darker side, I once had a very bright, attractive research assistant helping me with an environmental psychology project wherein we studied how the layouts of various halfway houses (transition residences for persons coming out of prison) affected social interaction among the residents. At one point, she asked me whether I was familiar with a well-known local gangster whose name sounded vaguely familiar. She told me that despite being yet another weaselly, small-statured fellow, he was extremely charismatic and had intimidated everyone in the halfway house she was visiting to study, running drugs and getting everyone to do his bidding. In a paternal way, I cautioned her not to get too close to him. She replied indignantly, "What do you think I am, an idiot? I wouldn't touch him with a 10-foot pole."

I thought no more of it, and we finished the project. Twelve months later, I heard from the Royal Canadian Mounted Police that he had been stopped and apprehended for violation of parole. Turns out he was driving her car and had been living with her and beating her regularly. She was a very intelligent, independent woman with a bright future, but due to her having consorted with a known felon, she was blackballed from employment within the criminal justice system in British Columbia and had to move away to the neighboring province of Alberta. After her "friend" got out of jail, he and two cohorts, on contract, showed up at a residence to execute a target in the underworld, but since he wasn't home, ended up shooting his wife. That time he got 25 years.

To summarize: we have a larger than life spy whose keepers were ambivalent about him, but who is romanticized in wildly popular films; a real-life war hero with serious issues of honesty and personal deportment; a charismatic though physically unattractive grifter; and a cold-hearted killer. What to make of them? Psychologists and psychiatrists have been trying to understand similar characters for more than 150 years. Let us examine the potential causal factors of their behaviors, keeping in mind the differences among these case studies. We will return to the specific cases at the end of the chapter

Over 200 years ago, Philippe Pinel (1806/1962) identified an odd mental disorder as *"manie sans délire"* (Raine, 2014) in which individuals without the classic symptoms of insanity constantly engaged in antisocial acts. As we discussed in the last two chapters, Lombroso (1876/2006), who examined hundreds of delinquent Italian soldiers, claimed there was a born criminal type, comprising about 25 to 30 percent of the recidivistic criminal population, who could be identified through multiple physiognomic and neurological anomalies. In 1904, Kraepelin (1904/1968) described a type of antisocial personality that was constantly flouting convention, was cruel and manipulative, and often ran afoul of the law. Freud (1927) proposed that some people do not proceed through the stages of development from id-based behavior to proper ego development and so do not develop a fully functioning superego or conscience. Also, some followers of psychoanalysis claim that individuals who receive improper socialization by caregivers retain "lacunae" (empty spaces) in their superegos that promote deviant behavior. Franz Alexander's (1931/1962) conclusion from studying many prisoners and troubled citizens was that they suffered from "a constitutional inferiority" that resulted in "moral imbecility."

Most modern research and theory, according to Robert Hare (Hare & Neumann, 2007), the preeminent researcher in the field, owe an intellectual debt to Hervey Cleckley's 1941 book, *The Mask of Sanity*, republished in 1976. Cleckley's purpose was to narrow and define more specifically a psychiatric category that had grown diffuse. In rich descriptions of 15 case studies, Cleckley (1976) described psychopaths who were "unsuccessful" (imprisoned or hospitalized) and "successful" (political leaders, businessmen, academics, and physicians). Both types were characterized, first, by superficial charm, good intelligence, absence of delusional or irrational thinking, and lack of nervousness or psychoneurosis. As well, they often threatened, but rarely carried out, suicide threats.

Second, they were marked by chronic behavioral deviance, including inadequately motivated but antisocial behavior; poor judgment and failure to learn from experience; unreliability; fantastic and uninviting behavior, especially when drinking; impersonal, disjointed sex lives; and failure to follow a life plan.

Third, psychopaths could be identified by emotional-personal deficits: untruthfulness and insincerity, lack of remorse or shame, usually poor emotional reactions, pathological egocentricity and incapacity for love, lack of insight, and unresponsiveness in most interpersonal relations.

Surprisingly, among their many crimes, none of Cleckley's "classic" psychopaths had committed murder, robbery, or rape, categories of offense prominent in the public's view of psychopaths and with which high scores on Hare's more recent diagnostic tool, the **Psychopathy Checklist (PCL-R)**, appear to be associated. But what was the origin of that condition? Cleckley seemed to favor, as did Lombroso, some genetic condition, as very often no obvious pathological cause—organic, environmental, or familial—was uncovered.

Coincidentally, in the same year, the prominent forensic psychiatrist Benjamin Karpman (1941) published a treatise in which he argued that confusion regarding and, indeed, opposition to the concept of psychopathy stemmed from the fact that it actually comprised two types: the **primary psychopath**, whose origins were difficult to ascertain but were, perhaps, genetic, and the **secondary psychopath** or **sociopath**, whose seemingly identical reactions and maladjustment to the world were caused by social factors such as severe mistreatment, abandonment, and the absence of prosocial role models and regimens during the crucial first four to five years of childhood. Thus, the blunted emotions and pathological egocentrism and mistreatment of others that the second type manifested were actually successful strategies for these damaged survivors, as predicted by Freud in his theory and confirmed by Bowlby in his study of children. Bowlby (1951) expanded that notion in his widely accepted attachment theory of development. He claimed that severe mistreatment in infancy resulted in irreversible damage to a person's ability to relate kindly and lovingly to others.

Obviously one cannot do the definitive experiment on humans to test Bowlby's hypothesis, but Harry Harlow, a former professor of mine at the University of Wisconsin–Madison, had conducted a series of brilliant if somewhat brutal studies on baby rhesus monkeys who experienced social isolation. Within six months, this isolation had totally debilitated them (Harlow & Suomi, 1971). That is, to test the relative effect of maturing normally versus in total isolation from others of their peer group or even from elders, babies were raised alone for anywhere from three to nine months. By six months, the most serious effects had taken place, and once reintroduced to their peers, the monkeys raised in social isolation appeared overcome by fear and anxiety. The effects were most debilitating for males who proved unable to have sexual relations or compete in their peer group. Females, however, experienced some degree of rehabilitation by putting them in touch with a skillful, normal male.

However, once having given birth to an infant, the "rehabilitated" female subjects of the experiment treated it miserably, ignoring it, rejecting it, and even sitting on it or using it as an instrument to bang on the cage. Harlow noticed the abused infants kept trying to make contact with their uncaring mothers, so he created a series of experiments to find out how persistent infants would be in making tactile contact. He created surrogate mothers made of cloth or even wire, yet the infants persisted in trying to connect, even if the surrogate provided no milk to them. The only form of sadistic mother that worked completely was one that had spikes project or blew air when the child got close. Harlow's conclusion was that contact comfort was the most indispensable experience a mother could provide. Clearly, Bowlby's hypothesis that brutal treatment in infancy makes an individual unable to relate lovingly to another, to bond, is central to the dysfunction so many individuals who are survivors of abuse and neglect manifest.

One study that inadvertently approximated the brutal treatment of Harlow's monkeys was conducted by the psychiatrist René Spitz (1965). He observed and measured the development of infants in an orphanage (foundling home) who were cared for by professional nurses and compared them with infants in a women's prison cared for by their own mothers. Even though the children in the orphanage began their stay developmentally superior to those in the prison, within two years, 37 percent had died (only two from disease) whereas the children in the prison were all alive and doing well. The difference was that the children raised in prison received unlimited care and contact with their mothers, whereas the orphans received only formal custodial care with minimal human contact. Moreover, many children in the foundling home (or, in separate cases, other babies who were hospitalized for more than five months) developed severe psychological disorders, including very shallow affect and irreversible **anaclitic depression**, and some even lost the ability to learn to speak. Obviously severe damage to their neurobiological systems had occurred.

A sad outcome of the Communist Romanian dictator Nicolae Ceauşescu's policy of enforced high birthrate was that tens of thousands of children were abandoned in orphanages by impoverished parents and condemned to conditions similar to those noted by Spitz or even to those approximating the isolation Harlow imposed in his own experiments. My wife, Cristina Martini, although one of those children labeled after the "decree" as "*decreţei*," was fortunately raised in a loving extended family of not only grandparents and parents but neighboring parents as well. Others less fortunate were placed as infants in virtual warehousing where they received no contact comfort, very little food, and a great deal of abuse, physical and sexual. She remembers visiting an orphanage in her neighborhood as a young girl and even then being infuriated at how badly the children were neglected—listlessly vegetating naked, soaked in their own urine—and beaten or isolated.

Izidor Ruckel (Bahrampour & Horn, 2014), one of those children who was rescued, perhaps in the nick of time, recalls that beatings were almost welcome, as they at least constituted some contact. Even after he was adopted by loving American parents, he eschewed prolonged hugs, and beatings remained a lingering need. Still, he attributes his less damaged cognitive-emotional neural system to the fact that a specific woman worker in the orphanage fortuitously "adopted" him, giving him special physical and emotional care that the less fortunate did not receive. Nevertheless, he said he was sufficiently damaged so that he ultimately fled his middle-class home in the United States to live on the street, but some modicum of ability to experience affection remained, and he returned when he heard his family had been in a serious car crash. He now works with survivors of those orphanages.

One of the most disturbing individuals I ever encountered did not turn out like Izidor. A dark-haired, exotic-looking young woman, she was a student in my criminology class on violence and aggression and told me she wished to do her class presentation on Allen Legere, a serial killer dubbed the Monster of the Miramichi, to whom she "was related." I was taken aback, as she was from northern British Columbia, not New Brunswick. Then she disappeared. As it turned out, she had confided in a roommate in her residence dorm that she planned to kill a homeless person just to see how it would feel. That frightened young woman reported her to the authorities, and my student was detained under the Mental Health Act. Police conducted a search of her room that revealed a mask and a bag containing razors, a knife, rope and garbage bags, and gruesome videos (Keller, 2013). The videos showed her as a teenager standing naked by the family dog that she had hanged and disembow-eled and decapitated, having impaled the head on a stick. She had done the same to the family cat. She had written a violent story in high school and when interrogated by counselors revealed she was planning to kill a schoolmate. Once placed in a psychiatric facility, she tried to recruit two other patients to kill a 12-year-old in the hospital.

Apparently, she told her psychologist that she was studying crim-inology and psychology at Simon Fraser University in order to learn how to get away with violent crimes. The assessing psychologist at her trial described her as an "affectionless antisocial personality with psychopathic tendencies" who showed no remorse for her sadistic crimes and concluded that she would require lifetime supervision. She was given the maximum sentence for what she had done to the pets, which amounted to only eight months' incarceration and two years' probation with a long list of restrictions, including no access to the Internet unsupervised, no fraternizing with children, no pets for life, and the requirement that she inform any friends or lovers of her past.

> "She is a sexual sadist who becomes extremely aroused at thoughts of aggression and torture particularly towards younger children or other vulnerable potential victims," the psychologist wrote (Keller, 2013).

Although she broke probation by accessing the Internet, she has been recently awarded unsupervised access to the public once a week until 11 pm.

She had been adopted from one of those horrendous Romanian facilities at age eight months. As you may recall, Harlow and Spitz found that longer than five months of comparable contact comfort deprivation led to severe emotional and behavioral and social deficits. She appears almost bereft of empathy and focuses only on fulfilling her fantasies. Again, recall the deficits outlined in the previous chapter.

Neuroscientists from Harvard and UCLA studied the Romanian orphans long term and found they had massively underresponsive amygdalae (Tottenham et al., 2010), whereas Nelson and his colleagues (Humphreys et al., 2015) found that those who were put into foster care versus those remaining in the usual deprived-care condition showed, at age 12 years, much less of the **callous-unemotional syndrome (CU)** that is a childhood precursor to psychopathy, suggesting foster care intervention at an early age could mitigate many of the toxic effects if provided early enough.

RECENT DEVELOPMENTS IN PSYCHOPATHY RESEARCH

Research and conceptual notions in psychopathy have followed two broad vectors. The first encompasses the notion that there are one or two types of psychopaths whose characteristic behaviors pose a significant problem for society. The second, in contrast, views psychopathy as a dimensional, not strictly typological, phenomenon. It argues that certain neural and behavioral deficits, when present in sufficient intensity, produce an individual with the configuration of characteristics we label as psychopathy. Of course, role theorists such as Theodore Sarbin and sociologists, especially symbolic interactionists such as Bartusch and Matsueda (1996), argue that the labeling process itself, not an actual distinct pathology, creates the psychopath both in the mind of society and in the mind of the individual psychopath, who, once labeled, is engulfed in a downward spiral of stigmatization. (That the social attribution of deviant identities to individuals or groups leads to the amplification of deviance is often referred to as **labeling theory**.) On the other hand, the psychological and neurological evidence favoring the existence of psychopaths is becoming overwhelming. Raine and

Yang (2006) review the evidence that psychopaths suffer deficits in the areas associated with executive functioning and control of aggression, including a reduced amount of gray matter in the prefrontal cortex and asymmetry in the hippocampus and other structures, findings supported by Oliveira-Souza et al. (2008).

Development of Hare's PCL-R (2003) has done a great deal to reify the concept of psychopathy. Indeed, the *Diagnostic and Statistical Manual of the American Psychiatric Association* only recognized psychopathy as a "specifier" of clinical antisocial personality disorder for the first time in its fifth edition, DSM-5, published in 2013, although psychopathy is still not an officially accepted clinical diagnosis. Nevertheless, Hare's instrument, unlike much differing clinical judgment by assessors, has proved extremely reliable to administer. That is, the PCL-R more reliably obtains similar scores when a subject is tested more than one time, even by more than one person, once testers have been properly trained, and it has proven able not only to reflect basic personality structures such as emotional deficits and superficiality but also to predict a spectrum of antisocial behavioral adaptations to the environment, including tendencies to impulsive aggression and sexual aggression.

Harris and Rice (2007) have argued those antisocial behaviors have evolutionary origins. That is, the successful warrior gets first dibs on resources, food, property, and sex, and consequently his gene pool proliferates. Not surprisingly, many in society find the contemplation of such explanations unpalatable and unacceptable. Sidney Reilly and Billy Bishop might not have. Both Reilly and Bishop demonstrated great courage and risk taking but ultimately had great difficulty fitting in with conventional society and played loose and fast with society's mores, laws, and criteria for success. In a way, their personalities, somewhat deviant, were appropriate for the times. Reilly's charm, thrill seeking, and cold-blooded killing or manipulation of both men and women fit well with the high-risk, deceptive life of a spy, a life requiring absolute cold-bloodedness during war and revolution. So too Billy Bishop's bravery and thrill seeking and lust for killing were assuaged by the most dangerous activity available—fighter pilot— although he played fast and loose with rules of engagement, orders, and chalking up scores. These parameters characterized by integrity were of little interest to him. We may presume that Bishop, Reilly, and the yachtsman's son (whose additional burden of addiction promoted violent crime) were *primary* psychopaths, not having been created by early, massively deprived or abused infancy and childhood. And so, by process of elimination, their psychopathy was genetic in origin.

Not so Rocancourt, who almost starved to death as an infant, who may have suffered prenatal consequences from the alcoholism and drug taking of both his young prostitute mother and longshoreman father, and who did suffer the deprivations of the orphanage. Nor does he seem to have the same predilection for violence as the primary psychopaths previously described.

Hare now believes there are four, highly correlated dimensions to psychopathy:

- **Interpersonal**: glibness, grandiose self-worth, pathological lying, conning, manipulativeness;
- **Lifestyle**: stimulus seeking, impulsive, irresponsible, parasitic, lacking realistic goals;
- **Affective**: lacking remorse or guilt, shallow affect, callousness, lack of empathy, failing to accept responsibility; and
- **Antisocial**: poor behavior controls, early behavior problems, juvenile delinquency, revocation of early release, criminal versatility.

The assessor interviews the subject and reads his or her record, assigning a 0, 1, or 2 score to each of the parameters describing the four dimensions, for example, to "juvenile delinquency." A total score of 30 or more is usually regarded as the threshold indicative of psychopathy.

According to Lykken (2007), who conducted the seminal experiment and reviewed recent research, primary psychopaths do not "condition" well. That is, they do not learn as easily as normal persons through associating a disapproved behavior with an anticipated punishment (e.g., meted out by a caregiver or parent), as they don't experience the same degree of anxiety or fear, which is the mediating physiological state. Nor do they respond as well to positive social rewards for doing the right thing, again because they are inadequately motivated. Thus they do not internalize the mores and rules of society. Eysenck, in his book *Crime and Personality*, hypothesized that psychopathy comprises three dimensions: **extraversion**, which is characterized by low central nervous system arousal, so the individual during the normal course of the day is continually getting bored or even sleepy while others are still alert; **neuroticism**, which makes the nervous system unstable and less able to focus in a learning situation; and **psychoticism**, a confusingly named dimension that actually has less to do with classic psychosis than with a mean-spirited, irascible, contrary, disagreeable attitude to interpersonal relations. (For examples of these attitudes, consult the description in chapter 3 of those suffering deficits in MAO-A.). Those who score high on all three dimensions manifest psychopathy.

Now recall the story of the son of the sad yachtsman to whom I referred in chapter 3. There is always the possibility that he had been severely mistreated in childhood or suffered brain damage, but given the degree of involvement of his parents and their continued suffering during his horrendous adulthood crime career, it wouldn't be out of line to conclude that the source of the son's psychopathy is not only constitutional but also genetic. Or perhaps it originated in some traumatic events in the womb or in the birth canal during the actual act of being born or was the consequence of a lengthy stay in hospital as an infant. The consequences were severe for him, his family, and for his victims.

There is growing evidence that individuals high in psychopathy have a lower state of central nervous system arousal. As Quay (1986) posited, when they are children, such persons sometimes suffer from severe **attention deficit hyperactivity disorder (ADHD)** and so they compensate for an unpleasantly low constant level of internal arousal by continually trying to change the environment or by engaging in constant physical activity.

One young girl whom I observed when I was a psychology student years ago entered her home after school by first scattering her books, clothes, and shoes; then, in order, turning on the stove elements, all the lights, and the stereo full blast; knocking over lamps; grabbing the cat's tail; and trying to whip the goldfish out of the aquarium—all within a couple of minutes. I felt deep compassion for the parents and wondered how they survived many hours with her. Perhaps they relied on the amphetamine Ritalin, whose administration is controversial but which appears to have reduced future offending by young people so afflicted, though many claim the drug is vastly overprescribed. However, in a major study, Fletcher and Wolfe (2009) show that ADHD children are much more involved in crime as adults if left untreated.

According to Quay (1986), such parents cope with great difficulty. His model of the development of psychopathy follows two parallel vectors. In one, constant misbehavior due to ever-encroaching boredom leads to excessive punishment to which, as a result of its severity, the child develops resistance. Consequently, the intensity of physical punishment increases and even leads to abuse and harm when the parents are ill equipped to cope. In response, the child increases his or her antisocial behavior and is often rejected by socializing agents such as schools. Simultaneously, the parents proceed from agitation and increased attempts to control the child to surrender and withdrawal, ultimately. They may even ignore the child when he or she misbehaves in public, leading to the child's further rejection by and isolation from other family members and society. Soon the child is out of the loop of schools and ordinary counseling and may even be on the street or, if the parents have the resources, institutionalized in a "boot camp" type of special education facility. The child may flee and pursue various thrill-seeking or analgesic remedies, such as drug taking, or he or she may join other unfortunate exiles from society, returning home only to ask for money or to abscond with the resources to keep functioning.

Although Hare estimates psychopaths comprise only about 1 or 2 percent of the general population, assessment has revealed that they make up a highly recidivistic 25 to 30 percent of prison populations (a figure fascinatingly similar to Lombroso's observation of more than 100 years ago). As discussed previously, Marnie Rice found that counseling in prison actually reduces recidivism once you factor out the psychopaths for whom group counseling only provides greater opportunity to learn the foibles of others in order to apply them in future criminal undertakings upon release. That is, group counseling enlarges their repertoire of dissembling (faking) behavior or emotions. But since they do not learn from past experience, most inevitably end up back in the slammer. Check out the BBC documentary "Behind the Mask of Sanity: Psychopathy," the second part of the television series *Mind of a Murderer* (BBC, 2002).

According to the studies reviewed in Patrick's (2007) landmark volume to which researchers from around the world contributed, psychopaths apparently have a strong genetic marker in their constitution, have a hypoactive central nervous system with an abnormally functioning amygdala that reduces their central nervous system operation and ability to experience emotional responses, and are much more likely to come from extremely dysfunctional families. Perhaps most pessimistically, many suffer from comorbid psychological disorders, stemming from ill treatment, as did Perry Smith, the superficially sweet, kind, artistic killer of Truman Capote's documentary novel and the film based on it: *In Cold Blood* (Capote, 1966; Brooks, 1967). Smith suffered horrendous abuse and witnessed abuse within his family, which left him not only sometimes delusional (although not dangerous in that fugue state, as Kernberg (1998) notes of other psychopaths) but also triggered homicidal rage when he associated his first victim with his father whom he hated … and loved. That is perhaps the most dangerous type of conflict to experience. As Smith said in the film, "I thought he was a very nice man, right down to the time I slit his throat."

Clifford Olson, born in 1940 in Vancouver, British Columbia, was a difficult child who was filled with bravado. He was a nonstop talker who tormented cats, killed two bunnies, and, at an early age, engaged in petty crimes and misdemeanors such as selling expired lottery tickets and stealing milk money from front door stoops or buying beer from a bootlegger, watering it down, and reselling it to other minors. He left school at 16 and was always in trouble with the law. By the time he was 41, he had spent only four years out of prison during adulthood. Olson displayed all the classic symptoms of the primary psychopath, including attention deficit hyperactivity disorder, lying, stealing, drinking, taking drugs, and constantly looking for excitement and trouble. It was clear that he suffered from low central nervous system arousal and a lack of anxiety (Worthington, 2012).

How then did he become a sadistic serial killer, given his psychological deficit regarding the normal classical conditioning process? Arguably, this transformation would be difficult because in order for an obsession with violence and aggression to form, powerful conditioning is required. That is, to internalize the rules and norms of prosocial behavior, one must be conditionable (physiologically connecting a fear reaction with an anticipated punishment), but on the dark side, to associate sexual arousal with violence and torture, which creates an obsessive personality that becomes increasingly sadistic, one must also be conditionable. Eysenck (1990) and others have argued that, lacking the right amount of anxiety to promote fear associated with the punishment or the right amount of positive affect to associate a neutral event with the reward, psychopaths are poor conditioners.

It is my conclusion that special stimulus conditions must come into play to transform a scatty, irritating motor mouth and liar into an obsessed and increasingly violent and sadistic predator. And, unfortunately, Canada's penal system provided the perfect conditions. While in segregation for ratting on others (he had already been stabbed once for it), Olson was placed in a cell in the British Columbia Penitentiary next to Gary Marcoux. Now imagine being easily bored, dying for stimulation in those practically sensory-deprivation conditions of incarceration, and having the guy next door confide in you how he abducted, tortured, assaulted, and murdered Jeanna Doove, a young girl. Olson would have Marcoux repeat his sordid tale with increasing detail many times while, in the absence of any other stimulation, he used the story for arousal while masturbating.

Despite his conditioning deficit, given the special stimulus-enhancing circumstances created by the lack of environmental distraction, the psychic structure was established for him to obsess over sex with youths. And so he turned Crown evidence, telling his story about Marcoux's confession in exchange for early release. Then, primed for sex with youths, he set out upon a horrendous campaign of picking up adolescent girls and boys and at first seducing, then assaulting, then both torturing and assaulting, and ultimately killing them—until 11 children and youths were dead over the course of a year and a few months. Some killings apparently occurred even when he was under surveillance by the police, so to prevent any more tragedies officers picked him up even in the absence of strong evidence. To the outrage of the public, he was paid several thousand dollars for each body to which he led the authorities. The money was to go to his wife, but the outcry was so great that the attorney general tried to renege on the agreement. To everyone's dismay, Olson's wife was allowed to keep the money. He died in prison in 2011 (Mulgrew, 2011).

The very special circumstances, such as sensory deprivation, that are required for an obsession with violence and inflicting pain to be established psychophysiologically in psychopaths as a conditioned response—in other words, in individuals who have the perquisite lack of empathy required to commit vile and violent acts (note the deficit discussed above in the section on Raine's scholarship)—may explain why, mercifully, serial lust killing remains a rare phenomenon.

IN SUMMARY

The Dionysian character has long fascinated society and even when captured and imprisoned remains a source of attraction: many women write to such monsters asking to visit and spend time with or even marry them.

Psychopathy has a neural basis that is either genetic (primary psychopathy) or the product of a horrendous early infancy or childhood, one that involves conditions similar to the isolation and abuse experienced by Harlow's monkeys or by children warehoused in orphanages (secondary psychopathy). Neither appears amenable to change through talk or other therapy.

Among other deficits, psychopaths have a defective amygdala, a callous and unemotional attitude, and low central nervous system arousal that makes them less empathic and easily bored.

The reason there are so few serial sex killers is that psychopaths do not condition well except in special situations involving extreme sensory deprivation.

CHAPTER FIVE

HOW CRIMINALITY DEVELOPS

This chapter identifies crucial stages wherein trauma and disruptive events interfere with normal development and investigates how criminality emerges as part of the emotional developmental process of the individual. It uses the overall theoretical scheme of Freud as a basic framework for stage progression. Case studies to illustrate the traumas and other theories such as learning theory are discussed.

So far, we have examined in detail the myriad theories (and the research flowing from those hypotheses) that posit there is something inherent in the germplasm of a newborn that increases the probability she or, more often, he will become deviant, delinquent, and even criminal in relationships with family and society. Other theories we will discuss later adopt a "blank slate" premise. That is, the newborn child is perceived to have all the psychophysiological machinery but is awaiting the constant imprint (in modern terms, programming) of experience in the family, in school, and in other institutions (religious, military, business) that will result in the adult human being.

Among these "blank slate" theories, **Marxism** practiced as communism is the best known for its twentieth-century experiments in indoctrination, especially in Russia, China, Cuba, Cambodia, and Vietnam. Fundamentalist Islam is a venerable religion, but more recent prominent examples of that philosophy in various constituencies, such as Iran, have theocracies (rule by religious leaders) that take "central planning" to the extreme. Assuming the system produces the individual, they undertake massive social engineering schemes—often sacrificing thousands, even millions of lives in the service of producing the ideal citizen and a society free from sin, corruption, and crime as willed by God and taught by Muhammad, the Prophet.

Oddly enough, Christianity doesn't fit into that paradigm, as its assumption is that humans are conceived in original sin and must be saved, although the Church, in its heyday, assumed that since God was all knowing, he already knew who would make the cut, and each individual's job was to behave as if part of that heaven-bound cohort. These attitudes explain the reaction to deviance in medieval times that prescribed torture for those who committed "crimes" such as witchcraft, in order to drive out the devil who possessed them.

Nevertheless, when a brilliant young neurologist named Sigmund Freud told Viennese society in the late nineteenth century that its adorable-looking, sweet, innocent newborns were merely so many crucibles for sexual and aggressive energy, it gave them pause. Not satisfied with their bemusement, he went on to explain that all of those lovely lambikins were "**polymorphously perverse**" and would soon be seething with sexual desire in any way available, for example, through sucking the mother's nipple and eventually even lusting after the opposite-sex parent. Having been schooled in psychology during the era of the "blank slate," perhaps best represented by the radical learning theorist, B. F. Skinner, I found Freud's theory amusing at best, a target for scorn and derision at worst, though, as an aspiring writer, I admired the richness of the metaphors. I recalled that the renowned criminal psychologist Hans Eysenck is reputed to have claimed that Freud set psychology back a hundred years. Now, so many years later, I beg to differ.

Rather, I now believe Freud laid out the overall framework for just about every developmental theory of crime that has followed, though perhaps those others have adopted less colorful terms.

THE PSYCHODYNAMIC THEORY OF SIGMUND FREUD

Freud's premise is that criminality stems from disturbances during the normal stages of development of the child from infancy through adolescence, stages that everyone must pass through. In the beginning, there are two instinctual (inherited) types of energy or drives present in the newborn infant: sex and aggression, or life and death.

The sexual or life force is striving to survive, to reproduce. Freud referred to it as libido, whereas Wilhelm Stekel, a follower and not Freud himself, dubbed it Eros and, similarly, labeled the other energy Thanatos. That second energy or drive is aggression or the death force that will strike out during the organism's striving for survival. I find the conceptions of E. O. Wilson's (1975) sociobiology and those of evolutionary psychology to be updated versions of Freud's basic notions, as does the psychoanalyst Otto Kernberg (1998), in that they reason all forms of behavior persist over time in order to perpetuate the gene pool. I suspect, however, that proponents of those theories (e.g., Richard Dawkins, author of *The Selfish Gene*) would take umbrage with being tarred with the Freudian brush. Dawkins (1976) states that the human (and every other organism) is dedicated to perpetuating its gene pool. According to Freud, at birth, along with all the physiological machinery sustaining life, in the psyche of the child there exists only the id, a reservoir containing those life and death forces. The id is governed by the pleasure principle. Consequently, the id seeks pleasure, avoids pain, and is dedicated to fulfilling the desires of the individual, namely sex and aggression, in the service of survival. Hence the newborn infant is purely a hedonistic entity.

It is interesting to note that this conception of the id allows for the theory of Ivan Pavlov (Olson & Hergenhahn, 2009), Freud's brilliant Russian physiologist contemporary. Pavlov argued that even simple organisms have the capacity to learn through **classical conditioning**: that is, through associating certain stimuli in the environment with reward or pleasure, even coming to associate neutral stimuli (e.g., a bell or light) with food or other pleasures to follow. So the stimuli associated with reward or pleasure reinforce and encourage behaviors engaged in, including physiological reactions (like Pavlov's dog salivating to the sound of a bell that is followed by food). But other behaviors engaged in that become associated with pain or punishment have repetition discouraged and even produce a cessation of those behaviors, more formally referred to as extinction. All these responses happen in the service of the survival of the individual (according to Freud) or of the gene (according to Dawkins).

THE ID

Governed by the pleasure principle, the **id** within the child seeks immediate gratification. And so sex exists to reproduce itself and aggression to promote survival (including, by extension, of the gene pool) in the struggle for required resources, regardless of the survival of the individual organism. Thus, in evolutionary psychology (which I argue is a modern form of Freudian psychodynamics), altruism exists in service to, or sacrifice of, oneself for the group that shares one's gene pool at the expense of those who probably don't share any genes. Psychopaths are an exception; perhaps they are nature's way of assuring that at least a few supremely egocentric members will save themselves when the group, as a whole, faces extinction. As an example, consider a character in *The Game of Thrones*, the extremely compelling HBO drama of a mythical prehistoric England. The gigantic Sandor Clegane, King's Landing's most fearsome warrior who claims to love killing above all else and is purportedly devoted to the false boy-king Joffrey, startles his master when the city is overwhelmed by invaders by announcing rather coarsely and disrespectfully, "Fuck the king's guard, fuck the city, fuck the king." He leaves his king and followers to their fate so he can survive to kill another day.

In Darwinian terms, that explanation accounts for why psychopaths comprise only 1 to 2 percent of the general population. The other 98 percent follow the altruistic course of self-sacrifice (and its prosocial mechanisms, cooperation and exchange) because that course enables the natural selection strategy, which works best for survival of the group in ordinary circumstances. That is, for survival of the gene pool at least, if not the survival of every individual, a balance of apparent conflicting interests seems to have been successfully worked out, since we are still here as a species (at least for the moment). But the downside is that in ordinary times we are plagued by such occasionally recurring antisocial specimens of our species as Clifford Olson or the yachtsman's son or Billy Bishop and Sidney Reilly. And we are especially puzzled by what to do about them in peacetime. In previous times, the British sent off their troublesome younger sons to the colonies, financing their exclusion from the homeland as "remittance men."

Furthermore, the phenomenon of altruism accounts for the origins of xenophobia (fear of strangers) and **ethnocentrism**. It is why tribalism is the basis of so much hatred and conflict as humankind "naturally" tends to favor those in its extended family (i.e., those whom Darwin and Dawkins would point out as sharing the same gene pool), especially when resources are scarce. The best known example of that phenomenon in the twentieth century was the Nazi Party, which touted not only racial purity in Germany, calling up memories of an ancient Germanic tribe, but also the need to expand into other parts of Europe (for *Lebensraum* or living room) at the expense of "*Untermenchen*" (less than "true" humans, such as the Slavic peoples or evil forces such as the Jews). During the same period of history, Japanese tribalism and ethnocentric pride of culture enabled Japan, with the same rationalization, to justify the invasion of China and the slaughter of its citizens by the millions, perhaps described most poignantly in the book *The Rape of Nanking* by Iris Chang (1997). The history she records was related to her by the repentant Japanese doctor, Nagatomi Hakudo, whose story I described earlier.

THE EGO

In infancy, the child develops an **ego**, or sense of self, separate from the rest of the world—that part of the self that is in closest touch with the social and physical world. In Freudian theory, then, the ego is essential in the development of the reality principle, the ability to assess and respond to the reality of the world outside of self. Prior to that, its experience—what it perceived—was all part of an undifferentiated world that included the intimate interaction with the mother in cuddling (contact comfort) and breastfeeding. As Bowlby (1951) and Harlow and Suomi (1971) point out (see the previous chapter), disruption of that experience can be devastating to the development of the infant.

In living out the reality principle through the developing ego, the child directs behavior that is consistent with the development of social and physical reality (i.e., with its understanding of what the world is really like). Again a child or a rhesus monkey cannot develop that principle if raised in virtual social and even sensory deprivation in a closet or a darkened cage. Thus, in developing the reality principle with an emerging self or ego, the child may learn to postpone immediate gratification of its drives (e.g., for food or for sex) but doesn't abandon them. It thus overcomes domination by the pleasure principle.

If no serious disturbance occurs, the person develops an accurate conception of what physical and social reality are like, of the world out there and the people in it—in psychodynamic parlance, object relations. Freud stressed the first three years of education, arguing that experience with the primary love object, usually the mother, is crucial to the child's development of that accurate version of reality and a healthy ego. Loss or mistreatment could be fatal for ultimate normal development. As discussed previously, Bowlby elaborated on that effect in his attachment theory. And Edward Gein, the killer from Plainfield, Wisconsin, was a notable example of its effects gone awry.

THE SUPEREGO

If the development of the child proceeds without undue conflict through the crucial stages of development of the ego, the child can then develop a **superego**, which produces consciousness of morality, or the capacity to differentiate right from wrong; feelings of remorse for doing bad things; and feelings of guilt that inhibit future transgressions (recall the conditioning effects previously discussed that require arousal of emotion, especially anxiety and fear). In the next chapter, we shall discuss the development of morality in greater detail.

The superego emerges through personal (individual) and cultural (norms of the membership group) conditioning, leading to the existence of **conscience** wherein reside guilt feelings for wrongdoing and the **ego ideal**. The ego ideal is the ultimate manifestation of that which the ego should strive to become (mentor, caregiver, provider), hence the important role of fatherhood or an appropriate surrogate role model, at least for boys, in addition to the mother's primacy in setting examples for the child.

BASIC FREUDIAN PSYCHOLOGICAL MECHANISM: JOHNNY AS COOKIE MONSTER

Child sees a cookie on the table. Id demands gratification: "Cookie, cookie, I love cookie!" If governed merely by the pleasure principle, the child, let's call him Johnny, grabs the cookie. Mum slaps his hand and takes the cookie away. "No Johnny, eat your muck first!" He is in pain, feeling frustration and shock, and before he has developed a well-formed ego, he merely screams.

With the emergence of the ego (a grasp of reality), he waits for mum to leave and then swipes the cookie (regression to the pleasure principle but with the emerging reality principle governing the timing). Or as he becomes more sophisticated (the reality principle and with it attendant skills are continuing to evolve), he asks for a cookie, bats his eyelashes and purrs, and if she still says no, he then coaxes, whines, and finally hollers if she doesn't come around. Here we see a conflict between the reality principle (mum says no) and the pleasure principle (Johnny wants cookie) that is crucial to his learning, and what he learns will be based on how mum reacts. Reality has emerged, and he gets it—the concept that merely because a cookie exists (or prior to that mum's breast) and his hunger drive is engaged, doesn't mean he can have it instantly upon signaling his need.

EVIDENCE OF THE SUPEREGO

With the full development of a superego, Johnny will not take the cookie when it is defined as wrong for him to do so, even if the opportunity presents itself. Or if he does take it without being observed, he feels guilt, and so may suffer tummy aches or anxiety or other ill effects. As mentioned, classical conditioning comes into play, as demonstrated in research by Miller (1941) with rats. He found hungry rats punished (by shocks) as they approached desirable food showed great hesitation and waffling, a phenomenon called approach-avoidance conflict. In a nasty but important experiment, Scott and Fuller (1965) found that hungry puppies who were shocked as they approached the meat in the cage before they tasted it would not approach the meat in the future or at least delayed much longer, whereas those who were shocked after tasting it, would not resist temptation but would concomitantly experience stress and anxiety even while they ate it.

In the same manner, punishment by parents for sexual play (fondling the genitals) during the phallic stage can lead to serious sexual conflict later, so that only sexual aggression (rape) or worse (torture, rape, and murder) or the victimization of women who are not pure or above "dirty" sex (e.g., prostitutes, other races, or some other group) becomes the only way the man or adolescent boy can overcome the conflict created and then engage in sex. Recall that Ed Gein's mother punished him for sexual interest and masturbation when he was a child but that, as he entered manhood and was obsessed with the pictures of women in the medical book *Gray's Anatomy*, she relented saying this obsession was better than consorting with the loose women of the town. Thus the icon of his life, his mother, sanctioned that extremely limited, anatomically oriented fascination.

Depending on how consistent the caregiver is in dealing with crucial events in the child's first three years of "education," the child may develop

- Virtually no superego (especially if there are major issues with ego development), which then leads to delinquency and crime;
- A faulty superego with isolated lacunae (gaps regarding certain issues, e.g., honesty, sex, aggression), which lead to weaknesses in certain areas (as mentioned previously);
- A fully functioning superego that serves him or her well in adjusting to society; or even
- An overdeveloped superego that makes the enjoyment of normally pleasurable activities (e.g., sex, affection, play) fraught with anxiety and even produces phobic reactions, a situation that can lead to crime based on guilt (Freud's original theory of crime, now discounted by psychoanalysts as the major cause) or to severe neurosis.

IN SUMMARY: THE CAUSES OF CRIME ACCORDING TO FREUD

Psychoanalysts who subscribe to Freudian psychodynamics attribute delinquency to the following causes:

1) Inability to control criminal drives originating in the id because of deficiencies in ego or superego development. Thus the delinquent is believed to possess little capacity for a) **repressing** or

b) **sublimating** instinctual (criminal) impulses of the id. (In this view, sublimation means converting libidinous or aggressive energy into activities acceptable to society, such as sports, business enterprise, or art.) The sociologist Travis Hirschi claims that the main difference between good citizens and criminals is self-control, even though they may desire the same things. Sublimation is the conceptual basis of art therapy programs, team sports programs for troubled youths, and most work rehabilitation programs. The most compelling example I can think of was described to me by a Native American friend who worked for the federal fisheries department. He introduced a fish hatchery into a prison facility for extremely troubled youths and found not only that they took an avid interest in working on the project but that some would even sneak back into the facility after they were released from prison to see how their "babies" were doing. Of course the most direct way to rechannel that energy is through engaging in sanctioned violence, as did Sidney Reilly and Billy Bishop.

2) Antisocial personality disorder (ASPD) resulting from disturbed or distorted ego development. This path of development results in the Ed Gein type of individual. Crucial stages of development in the first three years of childhood underlying ASPD include the following:

- *Birth trauma*. As discussed in the first chapter, birth is painful and can be dangerous to both mum and infant. Adrian Raine has found that difficult births when accompanied by maternal rejection are associated with later delinquency in adolescence (Raine, Brennan, & Mednick, 1994).
- *Weaning from breastfeeding*. Too early or abrupt **weaning** is associated with oral fixation—either aggressive or passive. According to Freudians, trauma here can lead to oral aggression in language as well as literally in biting, or it can result in a constant need to ingest food or drink or to chew gum or smoke, for example. Or, for males, it can lead to an inordinate fixation on large female breasts, for which *Playboy Magazine* and other purveyors of female sexuality can be thankful. On the other hand, breastfeeding to the advanced age of

24 months can lead to males who are attracted more to other erogenous regions such as faces, hips and legs, their oral stage having been sated. Freud does not dwell on the consequences for women.

- *Toilet training.* Too early or especially punitive cleanliness or **toilet training** can lead to anal expulsive or retentive personality, resulting in neurosis or delinquency. Freudians suggest messiness in humans, especially in certain types of artists, is the result of toilet-training aberrations. On the other hand, anal retentiveness is manifested in the inability to relax or in an inordinate need for cleanliness and orderliness, and may be the basis for an obsession with accountancy (just joking).
- *Punishment for sexual curiosity during the phallic stage.* If the mother panics as the child discovers his or her erogenous zones, penis, or vagina, and fondles him- or herself, for which she punishes or is seductive, neurosis or aggressive sexual deviance may result. For males, the child and the man, as discussed previously, may feel guilty for sexual interest if the parent stresses that sexual arousal is "dirty or bad" and may have to overcome the presumed reluctance of the target of his lust through coercion or rape. Or he may be overcome by an unresolved **oedipal complex**—lust for the mother—experiencing symptoms that may include attraction to inappropriate potential partners, including lust for the mother herself or for surrogates, and hatred of the father as the main rival. That can generalize to hatred of other authority figures, including teachers, police, coaches, and bosses. Or it can lead to impotence in men and, for women, an inability to enjoy sex or even **vaginismus**, the involuntary constriction of the vaginal muscles leading to painful sex or the impossibility of sex. This condition is also a consequence of being sexually abused (note the witch of Grosvenor Hotel, to be discussed).

These descriptions of the effects of disrupting development show how important it is that the child, with proper and consistent parenting, navigate through the oral, anal, phallic, latent (a relatively calm period from about 6 to 10 years of age), and genital (adolescent, pubescent years with major hormonal changes) psychosexual stages without conflict or distortion. Otherwise, primal erotic or "thanatic" energy gets fixated at a premature stage and emerges later as a psychological problem or delinquency. Thus crime, according to Freudian psychodynamic theory, is a symptom of underlying psychological conflict. To understand criminality, we must identify the specific psychic conflict, and only when it is identified and recognized by the criminal or the criminally inclined psychiatric client (the purpose of insight therapy) will rehabilitation be possible.

THEORETICAL ANALYSIS OF EMERGING DELINQUENCY

August Aichhorn (1925/1951), a follower of Freudian psychodynamics, devoted himself to studying and helping "wayward youth." He derived the concept of latent delinquency: offending that is released by life experiences (not necessarily traumatic) but only if the disposition exists within the child. Those individuals are cases of arrested personality development and can be rehabilitated only when the underlying disposition is revealed. Ophuijsen's study of youth found conduct disorder starts very early (Frankenstein, 1970). The Cambridge Study in Delinquent Development (Farrington, 2006), perhaps the most important longitudinal study of criminality ever undertaken, tracked more than 400 persons over 40 years. Farrington confirmed that early psychological and behavioral symptoms, including ego disturbance, stealing, and lying, and many physical issues were early harbingers of criminal careers.

EGO DISTURBANCE

Kate Friedlander (1947/1967) has stressed that the first three years of "education" by the mother are crucial. If the mother is absent or disinterested or deviant (e.g., through inconsistent feeding, weaning, training for cleanliness), the consequence is a disturbance in ego development (**ego disturbance**). The next two case studies underline her points.

ED GEIN AND ROBERT PICKTON: EGO DISTORTION AND FAULTY SUPEREGO

As a short documentary makes clear, Ed Gein was the inspiration behind the depiction of many fictional murderers (Screamgates, 2007). And there are parallels between Gein and serial killer Robert Pickton. Both men were raised on farms by dominant, deviant mothers; had fathers who were not involved; and experienced major traumas that culminated in their slaughtering of animals and humans.

Ed Gein, whom I described briefly in chapter 3, was a patient at the state mental hospital in Wisconsin when I was a graduate student in social and clinical psychology at the University of Wisconsin–Madison. A Freudian analysis of his bizarre behavior would focus on his devotion to his mother, who disdained and abused the feckless father, an alcoholic and later a disabled individual who was, for all intents and purposes, absent as a role model. Not only did they live on an isolated farm outside the town of Plainfield, but Gein's mother described women as immoral prostitutes in general and sex as a dirty business acceptable only for reproduction. His devotion to his mother intensified when his father died, and then his older, more rebellious brother died as well, mysteriously, during a brush fire—but not burned, rather felled by a blow to the head. Theirs being a peculiar family on the margins of society, no further inquiry was made by the authorities. Did Gein, outraged by his brother's criticism of his worshipped mother, do him in in an uncontrollable rage? Or did the mother instigate it?

Gein, though regarded as odd by his neighbors, was thought to be harmless. But when his idol, his mother, died, now isolated and with no support for a vestige of normal reality and none of the constraint created by his mother's disapproval of too much (actually normal) interest in sex, he began a campaign of grave robbing that led to his collection of body parts—vaginas, breasts, skulls stored in containers, skin made into belts, and organs found cooking on the stove. Making this collection suggests massive ego distortion at crucial stages of sexual development wherein he was erotically wired to the literal representations of sex as found in the anatomy book rather than to women as complete living entities. Thanks to his mother, he had had no experience with living women other than his mother, who was revered by him as a female icon. This reverence culminated in his dressing himself in human skin to mimic a woman, or to become her. The only actual woman he is known to have murdered was the proprietor of the local general store; her son, the sheriff, horrifyingly found her in Gein's barn, strung up and eviscerated like a deer. However, other women had gone missing in the vicinity over the years.

Clearly, Gein's bizarre sexuality stemmed from reality distortions at crucial stages of his psychosexual development and was enhanced by the absence of appropriate male or female role models. Manfred Guttmacher (1960) would have diagnosed him as suffering from **pseudopsychopathic schizophrenia**, a waxing and waning condition during which he would be more dangerous to others when, ironically, he was neither delusional nor out of touch with reality. During those times when his delusions overwhelmed him, he apparently danced under the moon clad in full regalia—human female skin.

When Robert Pickton was arrested in 2002, his lawyers were dumbfounded that such a gentle, polite, simple soul could be accused of the assault, murder, and butchering of so many women—all drug addicted—from the Downtown Eastside of Vancouver. So they took me to lunch to pick my brain. When I heard that he had been raised in an extremely primitive, semi-isolated existence on a farm dominated by a brutal mother, that there were suggestions of inappropriate sleeping and other arrangements lasting to a relatively late age, and that the father was not much in evidence, I brought up the case of Ed Gein. Although not identical, some of the elements are compelling in their similarity. For starters, there was a mother who was dominant and a father not involved as a role model.

Pickton was of borderline normal intelligence, but because of his extremely poor personal hygiene and the social gulf between his primitively functioning family (whose children often came to school in clothes and shoes soiled by the chores of cleaning out animal stalls) and the professional families occupying the growing neighborhood nearby, he was rejected by his peer group and spent his time by himself and with farm animals (Cameron, 2011). He was devoted to a pet calf that he was traumatized to discover one day had been slaughtered without his knowledge, strung up in the shed, and he was soon pressed into service slaughtering other animals, especially pigs, which apparently bear a striking resemblance during that process to human bodies. The defining moment disinhibiting him morally might have occurred when his mother pushed a badly injured boy into a ditch whom his brother had struck with his car, leading to the victim's death by drowning. Though the authorities learned of the accident through an auto body shop, no prosecution ensued.

Thus he was the product of a deadly convergence of genetic disposition (e.g., borderline intelligence and brain damage during childbirth) and lack of proper socialization by the mother. As well, he experienced the growing recognition regarding self-image that he was not part of larger, "normal" society. Accelerating the process of deviance were major ego distortion traumas through mistreatment by parents and siblings and the killing of his pet and his deep involvement in animal slaughter. Any hope for normal superego development was irreparably damaged by his mother's horrifying response to a potential crime—a response that involved covering up for the perpetrator, his brother, and callously ensuring the death of the victim.

All that was required—after all those factors accumulated in their contribution to his sociopathological and so, perhaps, consequent sociopathic condition (the latter also referred to as secondary psychopathy)—was the opportunity that he found in the Downtown Eastside while taking animal parts to a rendering plant. There he met addicted prostitutes and enticed them back to his farm with promises of drugs and money. That farm, which had functioned as a roadhouse destination, Piggy's Palace, run by his brother, had seen many addicts acting out. There on his own turf, the shy, retiring Pickton treated these women with impunity as lower forms of life for his pleasure; and, as he did with his farm animals, he disposed of them by feeding them to his pigs. Pickton allegedly claimed to an implanted cellmate, "I got 49, and I wanted 50."

SAMENOW AND YOCHELSON: THE CRIMINAL PERSONALITY

Another approach to such obviously deviant individuals was undertaken by a forensic psychiatrist, Samuel Yochelson, and his younger psychologist colleague, Stanton Samenow. They undertook a massive five-year clinical study of 240 psychiatric patients at St. Elizabeth's Hospital for the criminally insane that resulted in 20,000 pages of observations and led to the massive three-volume publication *The Criminal Personality* (Yochelson & Samenow, 1976–1986). Samenow has continued the work with updates of the original in various forms (Samenow, 1984, 2007).

First, they found that the majority of their subjects were actually sane, merely dissimulating mental illness in hope of serving easier time. Yochelson and Samenow established a group-therapeutic community that made their patients interdependent, meeting frequently in talk therapy and social support sessions to discuss issues and provide backing for one another's rehabilitation. After five years, all subjects appeared to have made excellent progress in their attitudes, values, and personal behavior, and the program was declared a success. At the study's conclusion, however, the authors arrived at the hospital to find a huge, celebratory party in full swing complete with contraband food, liquor, and illicit drugs.

The authors were, perhaps a little ingenuously, dismayed. That led to a reevaluation of the program and an attempt to discover the common problems among such offenders. After many interviews and analysis, they produced a list of 52 points of wrong thinking. Such individuals, Samenow and Yochelson reported, lie, cheat, steal, and seduce people into believing them but still consider themselves to be trustworthy. They are filled with hatred and anger at an unjust world—ready to explode and very sensitive to others' reactions to them, so, very quick to take offense. That description brings to mind the words of Charles Ng, who with his partner Leonard Lake undertook a monstrous campaign of capturing, torturing, sexually assaulting, and killing campers in the mountains of California. When an anguished victim inquired why he was assaulting her, Ng responded, "I am torturing and raping you because I hate you"(Owens, 2001).

Samenow and Yochelson reported that their patients enjoyed all aspects of crime: planning, executing, avoiding police, and manipulating the criminal justice system, even after they are returned to prison. The rush associated with activities that would make ordinary citizens fraught with anxiety is viewed as exciting and invigorating, and the perpetrators appear to experience very little fear. They are, however, claustrophobic and dread being imprisoned in small spaces for long periods of time. In fact, if confined without the opportunity to "work" the system, they can slump into a sort of pseudodepression to which the authors refer as the **zero point**. Apparently it provides the only chance for intervention. It is not true depression but a form of psychic collapse from the accumulated stress of all their deceptions so that the prisoners feel worthless, even suicidal. To Samenow, it represents the only opportunity for change, and for those who do not experience the zero point, the only option is to "throw away the key"—keep them imprisoned and away from the society they would inevitably exploit and victimize. Hare (1999), who does not subscribe to the existence of even a narrow window of opportunity for change, agrees with throwing away the key, at least for psychopaths. Samenow and Yochelson, however, do not identify their subjects as psychopaths, merely as career criminals (note Terrie Moffitt's groundbreaking work discussed elsewhere).

Their description of potential rehabilitation is similar to the **identity change process** I identified (Boyanowsky, 1977, 1984). That theory derived from distilling the crucial common elements of successful dramatic change in individuals, elements that are common to extreme interrogation, initiation rites, indoctrination, exorcism, and some Native American ceremonies such as the sweat lodge or spirit quest. All of these transformative processes require the apprehension of the individual, a person's isolation from society, and a massive increase in psychophysiological arousal through beating, starvation, sensory deprivation, increase in core temperature from a hot environment in the sweat lodge, and, often concomitantly, the taking of certain ceremonial drugs. These factors result in the triggering of the **general adaptation syndrome (GAS)** as described by Hans Selye in his classic volume *The Stress of Life* (1956).

The three-stage reactions of the GAS are 1) *alarm* that may trigger **fight or flight**, 2) *resistance* (or *adaptation*) that characterizes the body's reaction (central nervous system and endocrine system hyperarousal), and 3) *exhaustion* (wherein the organism, having used up its resources, gives in). Apparently, in order to save the organism, the mind will produce cognitions, including voices, telling the individual to embrace his or her captors, as occurred in Stockholm, Sweden, where four hostages held by a criminal gang began identifying with their captors, experiencing what is now called the "Stockholm syndrome."

Irish Republican Army (IRA) detainees (who waged a war of terrorism against Irish Protestants and the occupying English army), being Catholics, after 24 hours of confinement in the sensory deprivation of boiler suits and forced to stand in the troika position (feet apart, hands above the head leaning on a wall), reported visits from angels telling them to reveal what they knew to interrogators and to accept their enemy's program, that is, version of reality (Boyanowsky, 1976). At that point, the victim can be reprogrammed (brainwashed or converted) or can achieve a new identity, as in Native North American ceremonies under the extreme heat stress brought on in a sweat lodge. Thereupon, the person is reintroduced to the supporting community with a new identity and can receive massive social support. In the case of the IRA prisoners, as soon as they confessed, they were abandoned by their British interrogators; stranded between identities, they slumped into deep mental illness.

THEODORE SARBIN'S CRITICISMS OF CRIMINAL PERSONALITY THEORIES

Sarbin was a role theorist, a former director of the School of Criminology at Berkeley (University of California), and my academic grandfather (namely, my doctoral supervisor's supervisor)—that is, he *was* my academic grandfather until the school was shut down by Governor Ronald Reagan in 1976, purportedly for its radical leanings. Sarbin (1969) questioned the premise of pathology in the germplasm or personality. Namely, he questioned the idea that there is a defect in the constitution or makeup of the criminal. He pointed out that even sociological theories make that assumption by attributing crime to poverty although, in reality, most poor people do not commit serious crimes whereas many quite wealthy people do and get away with them, especially so-called "white-collar crimes." Also, when white-collar criminals are caught, at least until recently, almost no jail sentences are meted out, and even now jail time is given only for those with the highest public profile.

Thus, in states like California and Illinois, where there is a three-strikes law ("three strikes and you're out"), relatively minor crimes can be awarded huge sentences, even life, after three convictions, while millionaires stealing hundreds of millions of dollars are not regarded as true criminals and often get off with fines or single-digit sentences, such as that received by disgraced Canadian publisher Conrad Black (CTV News Staff, 2007). This less severe response to white-collar crimes seems odd given that, relatively speaking, such crimes cause much graver suffering and damage to society. Black, originally a great advocate of American capitalistic society and government, has since become very bitter about its "entrepreneurial" justice system wherein prosecutors (recall from chapter 1 that they are elected) seek a disproportionate sentence to achieve public notoriety and hence victimize citizens, especially those less able to defend themselves. Of course, the 150 years of prison received by fraudster Bernie Madoff, who was convicted of running a Ponzi scheme (taking money from new investors to give to those longer in the system and keeping the difference), did a great deal to reset the scales of justice. Some say he should have got life.

BIASES OF THE CRIMINAL JUSTICE AND PSYCHIATRIC SYSTEMS

Sarbin argues that the police look for criminals in the poorest and most notorious sections of a city or town and that this heightened vigilance in certain neighborhoods inevitably leads to the arrest of those most obviously deviant or mentally ill, whereas those who do not fit the stereotype are overlooked. Police stereotype people, so those who look middle class pass whereas those who look poor or mentally ill or who dress according to certain expectations will get extra attention, so evidence of their lawbreaking is more likely to be discovered. For example, according to some depictions, black gangsters and pimps wear flashy athletic clothing and drive Toyota Land Cruisers, so the police might be more inclined to stop and question an ostentatiously dressed black man driving around in that type of car rather than his white counterpart, a biasing process known as racial profiling.

So, too, does the psychiatric system show bias, identifying certain categories of people as mentally ill because they lack power or wealth or do not conform to expectations. This situation is perhaps best illustrated by what happens to Angelina Jolie's character in the film *The Changeling* (based on an actual case). She refuses to accept the boy presented to her by the LA police as her missing son and ends up being committed, through police influence, to a mental institution.

Sarbin's critique of the criminal justice system reminds me of the time I had just arrived in the UK from North America to teach at the London School of Economics and having secured accommodation near Victoria Station had wandered into the Grosvenor Hotel to engage in the English custom of taking tea. Unfortunately, the hotel dining room was packed, and I was about to be turned away when I noticed a young woman waving me to her table. Although I did not know her, I told the waiter I was joining a friend and walked over and introduced myself. She was a not unpleasant looking blonde woman, in her late twenties, who told me she was named Henny and was from Amsterdam. The only unusual aspect to her was that she suffered from strabismus: her one eye wandered like that of the "walleyed" British comedian Marty Feldman, who used the aberration to good effect in his character movie roles (e.g., in the movie *Young Frankenstein*). It is a condition that can signal either a muscle problem or an actual neural problem; most people too often conclude the individual suffers from the latter. Once I sat down, I was unable to get the attention of the haughty waiters in the busy dining room, so Henny reached into a black bag, pulled out a wand, and pointed it at the waiter nearest us, who suddenly seemed propelled, as if on a hook, to our table. I was impressed.

In fact, as we drank our tea, ate our scones, and got to know each other, Henny told me that she had been orphaned as a child and then sexually abused by foster parents. When, as an adolescent, she complained, it was assumed she was suffering from a mental disorder, so she was placed in a psychiatric hospital from which she soon escaped to live on the street. Life there was rough, and she did whatever she had to do to survive. Then one day, she met an older man who grew very fond of her and eventually took her home to live with him without putting any kind of demand on her, for which she was extremely grateful, as sexual activity was painful for her, she revealed. They were quite happy for some time until one day he apparently died mysteriously in his sleep. Since she had disclosed to a counselor who came to visit that she occasionally heard voices, the authorities decided she was mentally unfit and planned to return her to an institution, but in the nick of time, it was discovered the man had left her his entire estate. Now, as a wealthy young woman, she was able to remain independent and came to be regarded as merely eccentric rather than mentally ill. But she was lonely. Then one day on a visit to England, in a Coventry cemetery, she came across some people who were drawn to her. As she told them her story, they told her that they could tell she was not mentally ill. Rather, she was like them. She was a witch.

She was overjoyed to find her true "reference group" (people with whom one identifies) and began attending their covens, and was happier than she had ever been … but then.

"You have a problem before you can achieve full status, don't you?" I interjected.

"Yes," she said, dejectedly, "I have to have sex with the male head of the coven, and I can't."

I told her that she was in luck, that I was a psychologist and happened to know that her sexual dysfunction—vaginismus (involuntary contraction of the vaginal sphincter muscle)—was the easiest to cure and probably occurred in reaction to her having been sexually abused as a child. I gave her the name of a clinic on Harley Street that could treat her, though it was expensive.

Completely astounded, she looked at me and started to cry and to thank me, but I pointed out it was her kindness that had led to my arriving at her table. We exchanged numbers and parted. Three months later, she called and was elated to report that the therapy had worked; she had been able to pass her "entry" ceremony and was the happiest she had ever been.

That story demonstrates how poverty mixed with some purported visual symptoms of mental illness can lead to victimization, institutionalization, and stigmatization by authorities. On the other hand, having financial resources to protect you from the state and finding the correct reference group, one that gives significant respectable status to the very aspects of yourself that would have had you institutionalized, can lead to a normal self-image, desirable lifestyle, a community to relate to, and happiness. And, of course, a significant amount of money can solve many problems, including those of medical or psychological origin.

Sarbin argues that once you have a person identified as criminal and start looking for causes in that person's past (retrospective error), it is almost certain that some characteristic or event will be identified as "criminogenic." These could include, for example, parental cruelty or absence, mental disorder, and brain damage or deficit, such as lower IQ. What we don't know is how many similar individuals never commit serious offenses nor come to the attention of the criminal justice system. His criticism underlines the importance of longitudinal studies like Farrington's Cambridge Study in Delinquent Development that can determine the "vectors" (criminal versus noncriminal) of different subgroups of subjects (see Farrington, 2006; Farrington & West, 1981; Theobald, Farrington, & Piquero, 2013).

Finally, there is the need to study the individual processes involved in criminal development—for example, moral development, conformity, and environmental stress—and to study normal crime, especially white-collar crime, and its effects on the economy and on society.

Sarbin argues that rather than merely pinning down any morbid condition within any offender, we should concentrate our efforts on studying and better understanding the various major factors—often situational—that appear to be related to the commission of crimes and to burgeoning crime rates. Only through truly understanding powerful phenomena and processes such as cognitive and moral development, conformity and social support, social role enactment and reference groups, social learning, and the physiological and psychological causes of aggression—matters that govern human existence—can we hope to intervene in the human condition and reduce the commission of crimes in society. Since people all vary in their degree of socialization, conformity, cognitive development, and other factors, an algorithm that includes the degree achieved in those areas by each individual may predict a person's risk for offending. That is the reason I emphasize those processes throughout the chapters in this book.

CRITICAL CRIMINOLOGY

Sarbin's early criticism of the biases both in the criminal justice system and in the research into the causes of crime has, in the intervening years, been formalized into a theory using Marxian principles. Forms of it have also been titled conflict theory. The Marxian notion is that there is a conflict between the ruling class, which owns the means of production, and the working class, which must toil at mindless jobs to produce goods that the ruling class has promoted as desirable to the mass of people. In order to motivate those working, there must be a portion of the working class impoverished, so those actually employed will toil away in order not to lose their jobs to those desperately waiting in line. Most workers cannot afford much of what they produce. Consequently, argue theorists like Chambliss (1975), a conflict inevitably arises between the ruling class and the subservient class—with crime the product of the struggle of the subservient class to express its alienation from the established social order.

Chambliss also argues that both classes commit crimes at comparable rates, though each commits a somewhat different type of crime, with the upper classes committing more financial crime and the lower classes more violent crime. As Sarbin argued, upper classes and especially corporations commit many forms of crime—for example, patent infringement, antitrust violations, insider trading, and environmental crimes— without recriminations against them by the law enforcement authorities, whereas the lower classes commit violent and property crimes of lesser consequence and, as I noted earlier, have the book thrown at them.

Critical theory is useful for giving all of us perspective on what is happening in society, and perhaps for promoting a correction. Certainly some corrections have occurred, as the fraudulent schemes of more recent times have been met with hefty sentences comparable to those meted out for violent crimes, such as the sentence given to Bernie Madoff mentioned earlier. However, as I stated at the beginning of the book, nothing is explained until we identify who might commit a crime at a certain time in a certain place, and since most poor people, middle-class people, and "ruling-class" people do not engage in a lot of serious crime, until we identify who does, we have explained nothing.

IN SUMMARY

Many theoretical schemes, including some religious social engineering schemes, presume the child is a blank slate at birth. Not so Christianity.

Freud provides a general framework for the stage theory of human development, starting with two types of energy that articulate into the ego and superego.

Ego disturbance accounts for some of the most gruesome criminal offenders, such as Ed Gein and Robert Pickton.

Samenow and Yochelson developed a theory of criminal types based on each criminal's involvement in every element of breaking the law and avoiding capture and then prosecution.

Theodore Sarbin argues that biases in the criminal justice system lead to the conclusion that there are criminal types. He emphasizes that the study of crime should focus on the social and psychological processes involved. Critical theory outlines the study of crime as a conflict between the ruling and subservient classes.

CHAPTER SIX

THE COGNITIVE AND NEUROLOGICAL BASES OF CRIMINALITY

This chapter in *part one* traces the stages of cognitive development in the child, integrating the theories of Pavlov, Skinner, Piaget, Freud, and Kohlberg. Research that tests whether achieving a certain cognitive stage of moral development influences behavior is discussed.

In *part two*, case studies of extremely violent individuals are explained by neurological research that shows that stimulation of the amygdala, anterior hypothalamus, and **caudate nucleus** directly triggers aggression or produces calm and even affection.

PART ONE: THE COGNITIVE BASIS OF DIFFERENTIATING RIGHT FROM WRONG

Stanton Samenow may be on to something important in identifying criminals, represented by the group he studied in St. Elizabeth's Hospital for the criminally insane, as different from the rest of society (those not imprisoned) in their degree of egocentricity, lack of empathy, and personal sense of entitlement. Anyone who is psychologically relieved of the responsibility of looking after the welfare of others is much more capable of doing unto others anything that allows him or her to achieve a goal, including lying, stealing, defrauding, threatening, physically coercing, injuring, or even killing. And all of that is possible even before we contemplate whether that person is genetically prone to violence or aggression, brain damaged, or suffering from a major or minor mental or personality disorder, or, as Sarbin would say, has "pathology in the germplasm." It is fascinating that Samenow believes even some hardened criminals can be rehabilitated if you can change their thinking.

But how does thinking develop? One major theorist who was a young man when Freud was expounding his ideas spent most of his career studying his own three children. He was the Swiss psychologist Jean Piaget (Dasen, 1994). And he, too, propounded a stage theory of development that, in some important elements, mirrors Freud's. Piaget argues that children begin as undifferentiated sucking machines in the oral stage, turning everything into a nipple: finger, fist, sheet, everything. They adapt to the world through **assimilation** and **accommodation**. Assimilation is the process by which children take material into their minds from the environment, which may require altering their sense of reality. Accommodation is the effect that assimilation has on mental concepts as they develop based on what is assimilated. So a child sucks mother's nipple and, as it makes eye contact with the mum, incorporates that vision with the sensation of drinking milk to include the mum's eyes and face.

Using those mechanisms, the child progresses to the classification or grouping of objects together based on common experience. Hence perhaps the father's face as well as the mother's will be grouped together, and the child will realize there is more than one human face so that eventually humans become a class beyond just mum and dad as more people are viewed. Then, with the emergence of **conservation**, the child identifies, for example, the mum, even when she is not just a breast and two eyes but is seen from a different perspective. The child then progresses to **decentration**, the process of moving from one system of classification to another, for example, from people to dogs. I believe decentration is the basis of "making strange," as perhaps children suddenly react fearfully to faces other than those of parents or family because they are suddenly differentiating between family and others.

I remember a failed attempt to incorporate me into her family by my daughter Jennifer, who had been telling her own 22-month-old daughter, Georgia, that I, "Bhop" (a typo a niece noticed on a credit card solicitation to me that everyone adopted to differentiate me from all the other uncles and grandparents), was coming to London and would take her and their dog Kasha for a walk to the dog park. This information was imparted along with instructions on how to pick up dog droppings, a task that was new to me at the time. All went well on the walk, with Georgia chatting incessantly about the sights and my listening with pleasure, until trundling along on her push trike, she spotted a newly deposited pile of "doggie do" and warned me, "Don't eat it, Bhop!" which inspired me to laugh out loud. A very bad idea on my part.

Suddenly, it came to Georgia, who was used to being taken seriously by significant adults (her mum and dad), that, given my reaction, I was actually a stranger. She did an instant 180-degree wheelie and headed back to Jen's flat, howling like a banshee. If I tried to come closer or reassure her, she only sped faster and screamed louder, to the point where Kasha, who though very protective knew me and had incorporated me into her own family pack schema, began to worry that something was not right. Fortunately, we made it back home unscathed without anyone calling the police on the tall strange man running after the tiny screaming child riding the push trike. It took some concerted effort and time spent with Georgia to overcome that exclusion in her schema. With some relief, I can report that, twenty some years later, I have made the cut and she loves to visit.

Egocentrism, not a defect but an early stage of development, prompts the child to presume it is the center of the universe and so it cannot see the world from another perspective as someone else does. Soon the child can figure things out in the sensorimotor stage, through feeling and seeing. For example, a child might chew on a ball to tell it is soft. In the preoperational stage, the child learns to deal with physical things; it can stack blocks or count on fingers. But in the operational stage, it can, like older persons, work things out in its mind. In that way, the child develops a repository of schemas derived from perceptions, ideas, and actions that are grouped together, which it now can do in different ways. Hence, Georgia's family schema described above could change to include or exclude. Another example is playing patty cake when mum sings and claps her hands and counts rhythm. The whole sequence is a schema.

All of those progressions are stage dependent, and the child must go through each in a fixed sequence and, as with Freud's stages, cannot skip any.

THE STAGES OF COGNITIVE DEVELOPMENT

First there is the **sensorimotor stage** from birth to two years: in that stage the child discovers it can be the agent of change or action, for example, by crying or smiling or banging on a mobile hanging over the crib. And it realizes that things exist when out of sight—the basis of great delight in playing peekaboo with dad. In this recognition that objects have permanence, the child is similar to the cookie monster of Freudian psychodynamics who realizes that "cookie" exists even when mum removes it. Thus Georgia realized she had to hightail it home when the stranger (me) loomed large in her world. On the other hand, my son Alexei, at a slightly younger age, although he knew about television and watched certain programs, when he saw me appearing on the evening news, ran to the back of the TV set to see whether I was there. TV and dad were separate entities.

Then comes the **preoperational stage** from two to seven years. The child learns language and to refer to objects by images and words (e.g., truck or dolly or doggie). The child remains egocentric, so taking the role of the other, empathizing, or appreciating someone else's pain, for example, is very difficult. At this stage, the child will group things together on only one dimension (e.g., all dolls are just dolls regardless of size or dress or color).

The **concrete operational stage** emerges next at seven and lasts until 11 years of age. The child thinks logically about objects and events and can conserve numbers at age six, conserve weight at age seven, and classify objects on several parameters or arrange them on one dimension such as size, shape, or color. Dasen (1994) has demonstrated that culture can have an influence on when certain cognitive skills emerge. His study of Australian Aborigines found conservation of liquids emerged much later than in European children but that spatial awareness, more crucial to nomads, emerged earlier.

At 11 years, the child can think logically about abstract ideas and test those ideas, including "What will mum and dad let me get away

Table 6.1. Kohlberg's Model of Moral Development Compared to Other Theorists'
Developmental Models

Other Theorists		Kohlberg's Model		
		Levels	Stage	Characteristic of Stage/Level
Id (Freud)	Classical Conditioning (Pavlov) Operant Conditioning (Skinner)	A. Preconventional	Stage 1	Punishment-Obedience Orientation
			Stage 2	Instrumental-Relativist Orientation
Ego (Freud)	Social Learning (Bandura)	B. Conventional	Stage 3	Interpersonal-Concordance Orientation
			Stage 4	Authority and Social-Order-Maintaining Orientation
Superego (Freud)	Social and Cognitive Criteria	C. Postconventional, Autonomous, or Principled	Stage 5	Social-Contract and Legalistic Orientation
			Stage 6	Universal Ethical Principle Orientation

Source: L. Kohlberg (1963). The development of children's orientations toward a moral order: I. Sequence in the development of moral thought. *Vita Humana*, *6*, 11–33.

with?" So the child can consider purely hypothetical ideas (becoming a rock star), the future (being grown up and a success at business, planning to get married), and ideological problems (from justice to sharing, hurting oneself and others in the course of doing things, and fairness in dealing with others). (This stage of development is frequently called the **formal operational stage**.) Many parents recall their children protesting "It isn't fair!" when they felt they didn't get their share of candy or their turn on a ride or were told they had to go to their rooms for pushing a sibling.

Having studied Piaget's theory of child development, the American psychologist Lawrence Kohlberg (1963) distilled from his notions of evolving morality an even more articulated scheme. Although it is usually not illustrated in this fashion, I have integrated his model with the theoretical notions of Freud, Pavlov, B. F. Skinner, and Albert Bandura to illustrate the similarity if not identicality of their theoretical positions (see table 6.1).

Kohlberg developed a series of fictional stories—moral dilemmas—
to determine the level of justice that underlay a person's reasoning for
making a decision rather than judging him or her on the decision made.
For example, Kohlberg attempted to discover why a hypothetical person, Heinz, should or should not steal a wonder drug to save his wife's
life, a drug that the inventor refused to sell him for just a decent profit
(that represented only half the asking price but all Heinz could offer).
Research showed that the stages did follow a certain inviolable order
and that progress demanded an actual **cognitive restructuring**, that is,
a change in the brain, so that regression (falling back to a more primitive level) would not occur.

The **preconventional level of morality** comprised two stages. In
stage 1, the subject's rationale is based on fear of punishment as it might
be in classical conditioning where the rat or child or adult will not do
something because it might get hurt. The mediating emotion is fear or
anxiety of getting hurt or caught for wrongdoing. Thus, the amount of
arousal the child naturally experiences as fear or anxiety determines
how easily it can be conditioned, as Pavlov (1927) described, through
associating certain behaviors with punishment and thereby internal-
izing prohibitions, such as family rules put forth by parents and other
caregivers. Of course, if the child suffers from a deficit of arousal and
anxiety, that conditioning process will occur only imperfectly if at all,
as the study of psychopathy has revealed.

I recall being called up to the front of the classroom in grade 5 for
talking and having to hold out my hand to the teacher for three painful whacks of the strap. I still remember that burning sensation with a
slight shudder. Being called, walking up, and holding out my hand in
anticipation all produced extreme anxiety. My partner in crime, however, smirked through the whole process. How I admired his phlegmatic
disregard for the whole ordeal. Now I am grateful for the anxiety and
pain I felt. He spent his teenage years in youth detention whereas I
went on to play sports and become a criminal psychologist.

Also significant is whether the child experiences a lack of parental
guidance, sometimes due to the loss of even one parent, and realizes he
or she can get away with not obeying rules. Perhaps ironically, a child
that is institutionalized at this crucial stage and raised where discipline
is meted out inflexibly but not brutally could be better off regarding

moral if not emotional development. My friend had only his mother. I hope the stint in what we called "reform school" worked for him. I never found out.

But, as in most cases, if there is sufficient arousal to produce fear of punishment, then, given a sufficient amount of intelligence, the child can potentially move on to stage 2. As we have seen, even rats or puppies can achieve that conditioned response. In stage 2, the guiding principle, as devised by Skinner (1938), is instrumental or operant—what do I get out of it? Much like Skinner's rat, who figured out that pressing the lever delivers food, the child, even the psychopathically inclined child, learns to operate in this reward- and punishment-determined world of outcomes. There is no higher sense of right and wrong (but a child, if fearless enough, may defy punishment). As you can see, this stage is comparable to Freud's notion of the id, which contains the instincts for aggression and the sexual or life force and is governed by the hedonistic or pleasure principle.

The **conventional level of morality** comprises stage 3, which stresses getting along and the give and take of reciprocity or exchange, much as might occur between cooperating thieves or gangsters or being a good guy or good girl in a classroom or a peer group. Learning by imitating role models in society and the media becomes prevalent. As has been widely observed, teenagers, especially, become social blotters, soaking up fads in language, dress, attitude, music, and other media, including social media like Facebook. Recent neurological research has indicated that teenaged brains are still developing and are peculiarly open to and affected by influences they observe (National Institutes of Health, 2011). Perhaps this openness facilitates movement away from total dependence on mum and dad.

That recent research might have helped in the case of Ronny Zamora of Miami, Florida. For no apparent reason, he killed an elderly lady who lived next door when he was 15. Zamora's single mum was a Costa Rican immigrant who worked several jobs so that, for many years, Zamora was left alone for up to 18 hours each day with only a TV set for company. He was obsessed with some violent police shows, so his lawyer argued he suffered from TV intoxication. The judge didn't buy the argument, and Zamora ended up spending 25 years in prison after which he was deported to Costa Rica (Hancock, 2004). Ironically, this is not too different a career path from that taken by Raskolnikov, the university student in Dostoyevsky's *Crime and Punishment* who killed two old ladies but with more philosophical contemplation preceding the crime.

Sociologists such as Sutherland (1947) have stressed peer group influence, neighborhood role models, and the toxic effect of poverty-stricken neighborhoods to account for criminality when the adolescent is moving through this stage. Of course, Terrie Moffitt (1993) won the Stockholm prize for differentiating between those whose offending is limited to this vulnerable stage and those who persist in delinquency and criminality into adulthood. The first group, whose offending is largely situationally determined, is inordinately influenced by peers and social factors such as a poor neighborhood. The second group appears affected by genetic and neurological factors that promote persistence in criminality. It comprises those individuals we have discussed in chapter 3 and shall further consider in chapter 7.

Stage 4 emphasizes conforming to the laws of society to avoid the chaos that would ensue if people did what they wanted to do individually and idiosyncratically. Being patriotic or loyal to the government, one's country, or king and strict adherence to religious doctrine are most important. Most people function morally at one or the other of those two levels (3 or 4) according to the empirical research. And as we shall see in a later chapter, Bandura, Ross, and Ross (1961, 1963) have laid out a social learning scheme that encompasses the majority of behaviors, including aggression. I believe these behaviors fall within that level of development.

Of course, Freud would regard those behaviors at that stage to be governed by the reality principle of the ego.

As a child of eight, I was thrilled to be invited by my dad to go grouse hunting, though he had admonished me for shooting a robin with my BB gun. Knowing he was a hunter, I had expected praise when I showed him my trophy. Instead, he expressed only sorrow: "We have so few birds here and you have to shoot even those? She used to follow me around when I dug in the garden." It was like he had thrown ice water on me. I would have preferred he struck me, but he never did. He only explained that true hunters shoot only what they need and plan to eat. It was a lesson too few of my friends had been given, but I never forgot.

So he offered me a second chance that Sunday when we set off in Freddy Alder's car. Freddy was a handsome man in his late thirties who had emigrated from Germany, and my father had taken him under his wing in the mine machine shop. But to my horror, as we drove out of town, Alder described being in the Hitler Youth and then serving as a sailor aboard a submarine that torpedoed Canadian navy ships in the North Atlantic during World War II. I was so shaken that when a covey of grouse appeared and my dad offered me his .22 rifle as we walked a logging road, I couldn't hit a thing. Later, as dad cleaned the birds in the sink, I sputtered out my confusion: "Dad, Freddy was a Nazi, you hate Nazis! They killed your family. Why did we go hunting with him?"

He continued to clean the birds and said softly but firmly, "There are many evil systems, but few really evil people. Freddy was a very young man and a patriot in a country with a bad system. We must make certain Canada never has a bad system and that immigrants escaping bad systems can benefit from ours."

So Freddy was merely expressing behavior as a consequence of being at stage 4.

The **postconventional level of morality** comprises stage 5. It emphasizes the social-contract nature of laws, so they should be obeyed if they provide the greatest good for the greatest number or, alternatively, disobeyed or altered democratically if they do not. In other words, there is recognition at this stage that higher principles form the basis of democracy or any system that allows for the greater good for the greater number. On the other hand, **stage 6** moral reasoning is based on universal principles of justice, which may go beyond democratically legislated laws of the land to principles that guide prophets, visionaries, and martyrs to change the world—even at the expense of their personal freedom or lives.

Freud would regard such decisions to be governed by the ego ideal principles of the superego. In other words, people at this stage follow the credo "What I do or do not do should be based on what is intrinsically right or wrong." Examples of such individuals include Nelson Mandela, Mahatma Gandhi, Martin Luther King Jr., and perhaps even the folksinger Joan Baez, who braved the prospect of jail rather than pay taxes "toward the war effort" (as she stated) during what she regarded as the unjust Vietnam War.

One example that comes to my mind is Dr. John Reeves II, a friend and former academic colleague who came from a well-known military and athletic family in Texas. I remember meeting John for the first time when he contacted me regarding a student who had severe test anxiety problems. I was touched that a clinician would go the extra mile to help a student rather than just writing a note that the student could pass on to me. We agreed to meet at the faculty club, and I was struck by the quiet confidence that exuded from the tall, dark, handsome man with the soft-spoken southern accent who had waved to me from a wing-back chair as I entered the bar. We spoke about the student but then, as sometimes happens, we connected very quickly and talked about mutual interests, including wilderness, the sea, and basketball.

What I never learned from him, even after we had published together, was that he had declared himself a conscientious objector after beginning service in the US Army during the Vietnam War. I learned that account from a colleague, not from Dr. Reeves, who was a very modest though courageous man and who loathed to tell anyone his story. He was informed by the military that he could not become a conscientious objector after enlisting, his experiencing an epiphany notwithstanding, and was court-martialed. His case went all the way to the US Supreme Court where the justices ruled in his favor, and he became the first conscientious objector in history to receive an honorable discharge after serving in the US Army. After a stint in Canada in a clinic at Dalhousie University in Halifax, Nova Scotia, he went on to become a highly respected clinical researcher and practitioner in the area of pain control at UCLA.

EFFECTS OF MORAL DEVELOPMENT ON OFFENDING AND RECIDIVISM

Keep in mind that within the Kolhbergian scheme, a person's level of moral development attained is not based on that person's behavior but on how she or he justifies or rationalizes that behavior orally or verbally. So the question remains: How important is this theory for determining criminal behavior? Can the level achieved predict or reflect the likelihood of offending? That relationship can be measured in at least three ways: 1) by promoting moral development in a person through training and seeing whether it has an effect on delinquency; 2) by correlating the severity of delinquency or criminality with the level of morality achieved; or 3) by measuring the relationship between level of moral development and the probability of recidivism (i.e., further offending after initial conviction).

In an initial study of juvenile delinquents who were coached to achieve a higher degree of moral development, Arbuthnot and Gordon (1986) found during a one-year follow-up evaluation that these young offenders were less likely to receive behavioral referrals, had reduced rates of tardiness at school, showed improved academic performance, and had fewer police or court contacts. Stams et al. (2006) found a very strong correlation between a lower stage of moral judgment and juvenile delinquency, even when controlling for socioeconomic standing, cultural background, age, intelligence, gender, and type of offense.

Finally, in a huge (meta-analysis) comparison of many studies comprising 15,992 offenders, Van Vugt et al. (2011) found a significant inverse relation between more "mature" moral development and recidivism, with a larger effect for moral **cognition** (sense of justice factors) than for emotional cognition (feeling empathy factors). Of course, as I have discussed, empathy is part of a person's ability to experience emotion, whereas a sense of social justice is more dependent on the intellectual development of the individual. There was also a stronger relationship for production measures (the subjects' ability to describe their rationale orally) than for recognition measures (the subjects' ability to point to the printed reasoning provided). Again, active involvement requires engagement of both emotional and cognitive faculties. Correlations were not significantly different for juvenile versus adult offenders.

Those studies clearly demonstrate that moral development is relevant and may be crucial to stemming delinquency and adult criminality. How a person thinks at significant moments in the decision process is reflected in the likelihood that he or she will behave antisocially. You may recall the famous Subway TV commercial during which a doomed gangster wannabe is forced to dig his own grave while heavily armed thugs watch over him. Turning to the camera he says, "I made some bad decisions."

And so, it is important to see that imbedded within the general Kohlbergian theoretical scheme are the processes identified earlier by the major historical figures in psychology. In fact, Freud, Skinner, and Bandura are the all-time most highly cited psychologists. In other words, their work is referred to most frequently by others in the field in their own publications. Pavlov is a comparable giant in physiology. Kohlberg and Piaget are in the top 50, but clearly the former's theoretical scheme is a brilliant, eclectic creation incorporating the theories of his iconic predecessors. One can see that, as Eysenck and Eysenck (1977) argued, if central nervous system (CNS) arousal is low, it is very difficult for the individual to progress past stage 1 where further cognitive restructuring is premised on well-established primary classical conditioning mediated by fear and anxiety. Let us now turn to an examination of the mechanisms and processes in that CNS.

PART TWO: THE NEUROPHYSIOLOGICAL BASIS OF AGGRESSIVE BEHAVIOR AND VIOLENT CRIME

We all have angry thoughts. In fact, sometimes we may feel like strangling or shooting someone who annoys us, but we don't. Instead, we may fume and curse and go for a run or do something we really enjoy to distract ourselves, and those dark thoughts dissipate. Charles Whitman (Lavergne, 1997), a pleasant young man and former Eagle Scout who attended the University of Texas in Austin, loved his mother very much, his beautiful wife even more, his dad not so much. He never seemed to be able to live up to his dad's expectations, and his dad could be very physically rough on him and on his brothers and even on his mum. But his dad was far away in Florida now.

Charlie, however, was troubled by increasingly angry and even homicidal thoughts; he was so troubled he went to see a counselor at the university. It didn't seem to help as he tried to communicate how those thoughts were becoming increasingly compelling, almost having a life of their own and taking him over. Then one day he had to act. He began by murdering the two women he loved most, his mother and his wife. He left notes saying he didn't know why he had killed them and hoped what was left over from his life insurance policy could be donated to research into mental health that might help prevent a recurrence of his murderous acts. He requested an autopsy be conducted that might explain his increasingly painful headaches and account for why he felt compelled to kill.

Then, hauling a virtual armament of rifles and ammunition, he made his way up to the top of the University of Texas clock tower, the highest point on campus. He barricaded the door and, being a deadshot marksman, began to pick off passersby in the square far below him. Friends of mine from graduate school who had been there that day said it was a terrifying surreal experience as, with no apparent cause, people started dropping like flies around them. Whitman killed 16, wounding 32 others, before he was shot by two police officers. Sure enough, Whitman had a **glioblastoma**, a brain tumor, the size of a golf ball.

Thus there were two diverse aspects to Whitman. On one hand, we have the thoughtful and concerned university student who was aware cognitively that something was wrong and even wished to contribute to its analysis. On the other hand, he became the deranged killer who, in thrall to primitive centers of aggression, began firing rapidly and incessantly into a crowd and was driven to kill not only as many strangers as he could but those dearest to him. Here is a modern case of Robert Louis Stevenson's **Dr. Jekyll and Mr. Hyde** or perhaps Rodion Romanovich Raskolnikov, although Dostoyevsky did not contemplate a neurological problem in his main character. But Raskolnikov's ambivalence could have been tipped by a neurological imbalance.

Since Whitman's rampage, a controversy has raged regarding its cause as commentators blamed domestic abuse, guns, military service in the Marines, and an extraverted, occasionally cruel, sometimes violent personality. But could the brain tumor have triggered a deadly sequence of events as complex, premeditated, and skillfully executed as that which Whitman undertook? Let us examine what sixty years of neurological-behavioral research has uncovered.

AGGRESSION CENTERS IN THE BRAIN

With the advent of functional magnetic resonance imaging (fMRI), we can now actually observe which structures in the brain are activated when a visual or auditory stimulus is presented to a person. But what

Figure 6.1. The structure of the brain

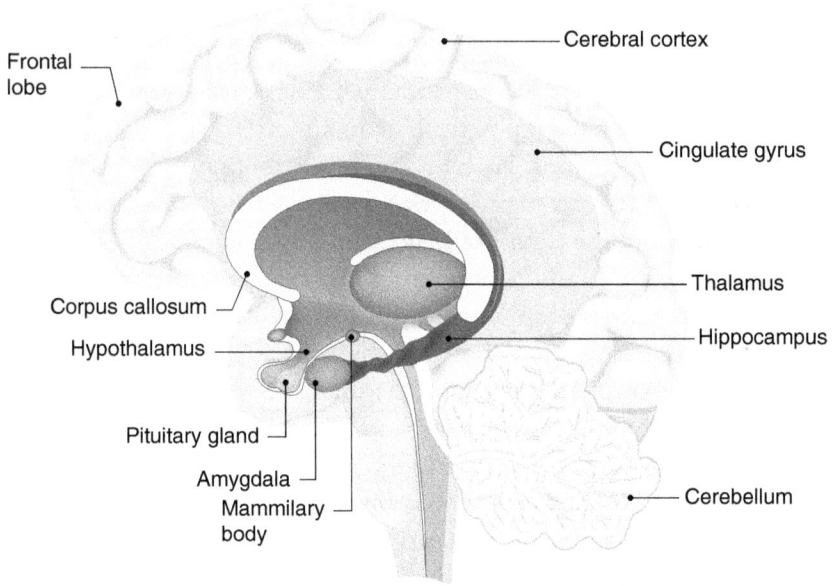

Credit: ttsz/iStock

happens when a specific part of the brain is electrically stimulated? Since the 1940s, researchers have implanted electrodes deep in the brains of humans and animals, and, using wires at first and then radio signals, they have been able to stimulate various behaviors as the animals or human patients walked about in the laboratory or in their cages or colonies or were strapped into special chairs and testing devices.

The limbic system is the area just below the cerebrum that contains several structures whose functions are involved in emotional arousal in humans and animals. One important structure is the **hypothalamus**, which is located just below the thalamus (see figure 6.1) on either side of the third ventricle (ventricles are areas of the cerebrum containing cerebrospinal fluid). Though diminutive in size, the hypothalamus is one of the most active parts of the brain and is concerned with maintaining homeostasis, that is, restoring an optimal state (set point) in the brain. The tiny but important hypothalamus controls the experience of hunger and thirst; regulates response to pain, levels of pleasure, sexual satisfaction, anger, and aggressive behavior; and is central to thermo-regulation, among other automatic functions.

Over the years, we have learned a great deal about the role of the hypothalamus in aggression. John Flynn and his colleagues at Yale raised some cats and rats together in harmony. Yet when he stimulated the cat's lateral hypothalamus, the cat ignored him and attacked its former buddy, the rat, in a very precise way, killing it with a bite to the cervical region. If the medial hypothalamus was stimulated, the cat ignored the rat and attacked the experimenter. None of those attacks was rage-filled violence, as we defined it in chapter 1, but rather very highly organized aggression, much like Whitman's (Moyer, 1976).

Moyer also describes research done in his laboratory with a rhesus monkey that had electrodes implanted in the anterior hypothalamus. The monkey, when stimulated, did not become aggressive toward inanimate objects such as dolls nor toward the experimenter. But when placed back into the monkey colony, it immediately and violently attacked the dominant monkey, and even though initially beaten back, it persisted until even the "boss" monkey's consort (girlfriend) started to change sides. When a dominant male monkey was not around, the experimental animal showed no sign of hostility, demonstrating that the stimulation triggered a specific type of behavior that was evoked only by certain stimuli in the environment, in this case, a powerful male.

Our own research on environmental effects on core temperature in humans (Boyanowsky, Calvert-Boyanowsky, Young, & Brideau, 1981; Boyanowsky, 1999) showed that, as the temperature at the anterior hypothalamus rose as a function of ambient temperature, subjects' anger and aggression, measured as intensity and duration of shocks given to an antagonist, rose accordingly, unless the subjects were made aware of the environmental source of their distress by a large thermometer set in front of them, in which case hostility and aggression dropped in spite of the increasing ambient temperature. Viewing the thermometer prompted an "Ah ha, that is why I am feeling so irritable" conclusion, which acted to control aggression. Thus, activation of the hypothalamus interacts with cognitive processes (e.g., attention to the aversive stimulation and attribution of it to an antagonist punishing you in the situation), producing increasingly intense aggressive behavior. This behavior, in itself, is counterproductive as it contributes to the psychophysiological distress of hyperthermia, which contributes to the disequilibrium experienced, and so on, in a viciously rising function—until mayhem ensues.

An early study by King (Moyer, 1976) was particularly fascinating. One patient, a very mild-mannered woman, kind, friendly, and submissive, had her amygdala stimulated. At 4 milliamperes nothing happened. At 5 milliamperes she jumped up and attacked her doctor, shouting, "If you are going to hold me better get five more men!" When King turned down the current, the attack stopped and she expressed mortification at her behavior, citing how she had felt concern about the fact that she was overcome with anger but couldn't help herself, even though expressing anger was very uncharacteristic of her normal personality.

Also Vernon Mark, Frank Ervin, and William Sweet (1972) placed electrodes in the amygdala of an epileptic girl who had, inexplicably, repeatedly stabbed a strange girl in the bathroom of a movie theater. One filmed sequence shows her calmly playing a guitar; then when stimulated, she jumps up and smashes the guitar to smithereens against the wall. When the stimulation stops, she calms down immediately.

Those experiments bear a chilling resemblance to the descriptions of the inexplicable urges to kill that Charles Whitman recorded while murdering his mother and wife just before the mayhem he wrought from the clock tower. As mentioned, Whitman had a huge tumor near the amygdala. Modern ethical criteria do not allow those early experiments to be repeated, although doing so could pin down the causal nature of such pathological conditions.

Early remedies for inexplicable aggression that could not be quelled have included drastic surgery. Narabayashi et al. (1963) in Japan reported that bilateral amygdalectomy (severing connections on both sides of that organ) produced an 85 percent reduction in violent behavior. Heimburger, Whitlock, and Kalsbeck (1966) reported a 92 percent increase in the docility of acting-out patients after they had received this surgery. One problem was that some patients in some constituencies became increasingly docile after an amygdalectomy and then began to vegetate, prompting lawsuits and a cessation of the widespread use of surgical intervention. Another reason that surgery is less used is that, as mentioned earlier, emerging ethical standards militate against such operations.

REDUCING AGGRESSION THROUGH BRAIN STIMULATION: THE WOODY ALLEN MONKEY EXPERIMENT

Jose Delgado (1963) was perhaps most famous for demonstrating on film how he was able to stop a charging bull in its tracks by stimulating its caudate nucleus remotely with his invention the "stimoceiver," which used radio waves to transmit signals.

His most elaborate experiment, however, involved a whole monkey colony. Monkey colonies are run by a boss monkey who dominates others through aggression in order to have first dibs on food and sex. Obviously, these dominant monkeys have to act out periodically to remind everyone who is the boss, so when Delgado implanted an electrode in a boss monkey's brain in the area known as the caudate nucleus and stimulated it, the young bloods in the colony noticed that he was being uncharacteristically mild and calm. Soon, one or two of the bolder members approached him, and even his girlfriend, and prodded him and then started romping about. When Delgado stopped stimulating the caudate nucleus, the boss monkey instantly snapped out of it and started cracking heads and knocking everyone back into shape, and the young bloods were appropriately cowed.

Then Delgado took the experiment one step farther by placing the stimoceiver within the colony cage. At first, monkeys looked at it curiously, but left it alone—except for one thoughtful, quiet little guy, whom I call the "Woody Allen" monkey. He wanted the food and the girl but was too small and timid to compete. Then he learned that he could control things. He would stand by the stimoceiver's controls, and whenever the boss monkey started to rage, he would simply press the button and calm him down. Woody's stock in the colony rose quite dramatically. Delgado regarded the caudate nucleus as an inhibitor, suppressor, or shutdown device. Now, fMRI research by Aron et al. (2005) has shown that caudate nucleus activity is associated with strong feelings of affection and love, so what Delgado may have done was turn a raging bull into an affectionate Ferdinand of movie fame—the boss monkey into a lover not a fighter.

Delgado (1969) became an increasingly controversial figure for arguing in his book *Physical Control of the Mind: Toward a Psychocivilized Society* for widespread brain stimulation as a way of reducing violence in modern society. It won him few friends in North America, and he returned to Spain to open a university research center. Besides the ethical problems, like individual psychotherapy, psychosurgical implants are a very expensive and inefficient way to change the world for the better, or the worse, especially when we know that implementing several social factors simultaneously can effect change in many people for the better.

IN SUMMARY

Stages of cognitive development were pioneered by Jean Piaget using his own children as subjects. The stages of moral development postulated by Kohlberg comprise the ideas of Pavlov, Skinner, Bandura, and Freud. At Kohlberg's preconventional level, which is comparable to Freud's id stage of development, are first the classical conditioning paradigm of Pavlov and then the operant conditioning of Skinner. Kohlberg's conventional level comprises the social learning paradigm of Bandura and is comparable to the ego stage of Freudian theory. The superego functions beyond physiological or social processes on a plane by itself.

Aggression centers within the brain can be triggered by social stimuli or by pathological factors such as tumors. Modern MRI and CT-scan technology has allowed us to watch the function of those centers "in vitro" without intrusive instruments. The next step …?

CHAPTER SEVEN

SOCIAL CRIMINOGENIC FACTORS

This chapter provides an in-depth exploration of the origins of delinquency. It considers 1) social learning and situational factors, integrating the theories of Bandura and of Akers with other sociological approaches; 2) familial factors; 3) the effects of the media; and 4) peer group and gang influences.

SOCIAL LEARNING AND SITUATIONAL FACTORS IN CRIMINALITY

Whenever I had to drop into my son's elementary school in late September years ago, I often spotted his friend Christian, a blue-eyed, blond, angelic little guy, age seven, sitting in the hallway outside the principal's office.

"What? Busted again, what was it this time?" I asked.

"Nothing. Just making kids laugh. I guess she doesn't like me," he answered glumly.

"Christian," I implored, "teachers look for trouble makers at the beginning of the school year. Just try being good for the first two weeks so you don't get targeted."

He looked up at me bemused and wide-eyed saying, "I can't help myself."

Happily, Christian is now a young man doing well in the family business rather than putting in hard time in the slammer, but according to theorists Travis Hirschi, a sociologist, and Albert Bandura, a psychologist, the most basic and significant difference between normal people and chronic criminals is lack of self-control or **self-regulation.**

Did Christian escape the downward spiral into serious delinquency because his parents "cemented" his social bond, as Hirschi would hypothesize, by discipline, constancy, and example? Or did his true personality develop control as he matured? Or did his reference group—those people with whom he identified—change as he approached the critical age of adolescence, when crime appears to take over so many young people? Gottfredson and Hirschi (1990), as sociologists, are vaguer than Bandura in defining the critical factors that lead to delinquency. Bandura (1976), as a psychologist, constructs the factors more precisely to identify those that are necessary and those that are sufficient to produce certain outcomes. Central to this process is the concept of **reciprocal determinism**, namely, that cognitive processes and social environment both affect the individual and each other.

So both the characteristics of the individual and powerful factors in the environment make a difference. To see how the theory evolved, let us look at the first conception of aggression in the social learning paradigm, flowing from Freud, whose most parsimonious paradigm (i.e., the one in which the most data are explained with the least number of concepts) proposed that aggression was simply an instinct. But when does aggression show itself? Certainly not constantly. So instinct is not a sufficient cause. To elaborate on that concept, Miller (1941) argued that frustration experienced by an individual—by having a goal blocked—increased the probability of that person's committing an aggressive act. Frustration-aggression theory held sway until it became clear that not only frustration but other irritations as well led to aggression. But in some circumstances, aggression wasn't necessarily always the outcome of that process.

Bandura (1976) proposed that the precursor of aggression can be not only frustration but 1) any aversive experience, meaning one that arouses negative emotions (e.g., an insult, pain, a noxious noise), or 2) merely an incentive inducement, that is being offered a reward. Those motivating experiences lead to either emotional arousal or to the anticipation of certain consequences (e.g., being paid, having sex, gaining the admiration of your peers) or any combination of those. Once these motivating experiences are in play, not only aggression follows. The same motivation can lead to achievement (I'll show them!), withdrawal and resignation (Let me out of here!), or psychosomatization (i.e., getting a physical symptom such as blushing, shortness of breath, asthmatic attacks, or pains in the gut). In addition, as Bandura pointed out, the individual can self-anesthetize by taking drugs or alcohol or can, most rationally, engage in constructive problem solving. Suddenly, a very simple, parsimonious idea had become very complicated and was no longer restricted to the explanation of aggression. Rather, what these motivating experiences caused reflected the response repertoires of children, adolescents, and, eventually, adults. Outcome is based on the richness of the repertoire of responses they have available.

Thus, unlike within the reactions of many animals, the causal link does not necessarily produce what animal behaviorists call a **fixed action pattern**. For example, when a wolf—powerful, skilled, and deadly—becomes hungry, she goes hunting. When she spots a deer, she attacks in the most effective way, a fixed action pattern. On the other hand, let's examine the case of a youth in the ghetto of an American city being embarrassed by a peer in front of his friends. Depending on his repertoire of skills, he may lash out with a fist, knife, or firearm. Or he may, if he has the verbal agility, lash out with a barrage of insults directed at his antagonist, denigrating his antagonist's physical sexual endowments (or lack thereof), his clothes, or his sister or mother or girlfriend, and thereby embarrassing his rival. In the process, he makes everyone laugh and admire his own verbal dexterity and, in turn, has his social status reinforced, even elevated, without lifting a finger. Should his rival retaliate orally, the verbal battle is on. Should his rival resort to physical aggression, the attacker loses face and our youth has won, unless the retaliation is fatal, then both lose.

This sort of verbal fight is, in fact, the basis of "rapping" in the black ghetto, as reported in a 1969 article by Thomas Kochman. Now, of course, rap and hip-hop are widely recognized only as genres of commercial music and not for their utilitarian origins in deflecting or diminishing physical aggression. Oh if only they had remained so! My son and I still alternate selections on the radio during road trips.

Perhaps, not surprisingly, my choice is never hip-hop. His is never country and western nor medieval music, blues nor jazz. But I am hoping that repeated exposure will pave the way to broadened taste.

The sociologist Ronald Akers (1985) further developed the theory of **differential association**, propounded by Edwin Sutherland (1947) decades before him, that crime is learned in small interaction groups. Akers's version of this idea, dubbed "social learning theory," stressed that reinforcement of criminal behavior is the key factor. So far, most of the support for Akers's theory is in the area of drug-taking behavior. Bandura's argument is that the child and the adolescent learn too much too quickly for direct reinforcement to be the basis of much learning and demonstrated so in what is now one of the classic experiments in social psychology.

Bandura et al. (1963) showed small children a film of an adult doing various unusual, aggressive things to a "Bobo Doll," an inflated clown doll weighted at the base to stay upright. Later they filmed the children doing identical things to the doll without having received instruction or reward. That experiment, deceptively simple in its elegance, demonstrated that children learn even complicated acts constantly and do not need to be rewarded either to learn or to perform those acts. The idea seems self-evident now, but in those days, the learning paradigm in vogue (comprising stimulus-response-reinforcement) could not explain the results. That is what is known as a paradigm changing experiment. Of course there was an element of reward in the children's seeing the reaction of the Bobo Doll (e.g., bobbing backward violently upon being struck), hence the efficacy of the particular blows.

Thus, learning through observation of the behavior of others, of "models," known also as **vicarious learning**, is the most powerful ubiquitous form of learning. Bandura argued there are different types of models. The first type of model is the live model, an actual individual demonstrating or acting out a behavior. That is obviously the basis of the tremendous influence wielded by parents, caregivers, siblings and peers, fellow gang members, peer group mates, and, finally, authority figures such as army and police officers performing their duties.

Gerald Patterson (1993) has embraced the notion of the importance to learning of live models to develop his **coercion theory** of child development wherein the parents use an authoritarian approach to discipline based on their personal desires rather than providing rewards contingent on the good behavior of the child and punishment for the bad. Thus the rule is "Do this because I say so!" rather than behave so as to produce a socially desirable outcome. The child develops a negative reaction to the parents' demands, which escalates if the parent then withdraws demands. Also, argues Patterson, the child will, having experienced the efficacy of force in word or action, go on to use coercive techniques in its interactions with children and other adults. As that pattern continues, the child becomes progressively more antisocial.

Second, there are instructional or verbal models that lay out descriptions and explanations of behavior. We get verbal instructional models from a teacher, imam, preacher, or coach urging us to do or not to do specific things. Patriotic and fight songs, whether in military marching or football rallies, exhort the singer and listeners to higher degrees of aggressive behavior. Similarly, as Sutherland and especially Akers argued when expounding differential association theory, those who observe or experience aggressive and deviant behavior in close interpersonal interaction within delinquent groups are much more likely to become criminal. Many things are learned by the child but only those that are constantly reinforced will not fade; those behaviors will go on to form the basis of a child's regular repertoire of behavior and will be performed repeatedly. In that sense, Akers's and Sutherland's points are well taken.

Third, there is the **symbolic model** that involves a character, real or fictional, performing certain behaviors in films, on television, or online. So pervasive is the power of such models that commercials now display a disclaimer telling people watching at home not to imitate the amazing feats of closed-track stunt drivers or of skydivers and the ill-fated antics portrayed in the wildly popular *Jackass* films. The Canadian film director Ted Kotcheff once described to me how the London police pleaded with him not to show a suicide on the subway in one of his productions for BBC television, but he pooh-poohed the plea and went ahead. The morning after the show aired, the police called to tell him several people had already killed themselves in exactly the same way. In a series of clever field studies, David Phillips (1986) of the University of California Santa Cruz found that homicides increased when a major boxing match was aired—especially if the victim resembled or was similar in some way to the one defeated—and decreased when execution (i.e., capital punishment) got a lot of exposure in the media. That deterrent effect was of short duration, however. Perhaps all are.

So, Bandura argues that because a child does not imitate a behavior does not mean it has not learned that behavior. However, reinforcement or reward, as delineated by Dollard, Doob, Miller, Mowrer, and Sears (1939), Miller (1941), and Akers (1985), can influence a behavior's performance. But not everything seen is learned. Some things are not attended to significantly; other things are too complicated. Memory is limited, and physical or mental or physical capacity to learn and reproduce the behavior will ultimately determine what is internalized cognitively. For example, much as NFL fans try to emulate New England Patriots' quarterback Tom Brady in pick-up games of touch football, they fail miserably, despite wearing a jersey with their role model's number on it. In fact, not even his skilled colleagues in professional football have managed to do so.

Research has shown that not only externally administered reinforcement or reward in the learner's environment is crucial but also internal cognitive rewards such as pride, sense of accomplishment, satisfaction, sexual gratification, satiation of hunger, euphoria, and laughter. Those internal rewards are immensely reinforcing, as Hirschi might argue also. Consequently, the importance of internal states and thoughts has helped link social learning theories to cognitive development theories such as Piaget's, Kohlberg's, and Freud's. Internal states and thoughts might explain also why Patterson's coercion theory is so compelling in its analysis of the gestation of antisocial behavior. Claude Brown describes his thoughts as a New York City youth:

> Mama seemed silly to me. She was bothered because most of the parents in the neighborhood didn't allow their children to play with me. What she didn't know was that I never wanted to play with them. My friends were all daring like me, tough like me, dirty like me, ragged like me, cursed like me, and had a great love for trouble like me. We took pride in being able to hitch rides on trolleys, buses, taxicabs and in knowing how to steal and fight. We knew that we were the only kids in the neighborhood who usually had more than ten dollars in their pockets. There were

other people who knew this too, and that was often a problem for us. Somebody was always trying to shake us down or rob us. (Brown, 1965, p. 13)

THE ORIGINS OF DELINQUENCY

As mentioned previously, long ago Aichhorn (1925/1951) had argued that delinquency emerges as a function of life events, not necessarily traumatic, occurring to a subset of individuals who already contain the latent elements of antisocial behavior in their constitution, those elements that Raine identified. Farrington and Welsh (2007) describe the most important individual factors in predicting offending as low intelligence and low educational attainment, certain personality and temperament factors, lack of empathy, and a high degree of impulsiveness. The strongest family factors are large family size, poor parental supervision, parental conflict, and disrupted families. The environmental factors are growing up in a low socioeconomic status household, associating with delinquent friends (Akers's point), attending schools with high delinquency rates, and living in deprived areas, points emphasized by Sutherland. Many of those environmental factors can be seen as sources of differential association and reinforcement, the process emphasized by Akers through which various interactions endorse favorable definitions toward breaking the law.

If we analyze such factors, the personal characteristics revealed are those that other researchers have identified in individual offenders, especially those with psychopathic tendencies. Of course, large families suggest less ability (time and effort available) to focus on children who are troubled, a deficit exacerbated if a family has quarreling parents or a single parent. Finally, children are at great risk if they live among other children in similar circumstances: a cascade of causal factors.

Although differing slightly, Glueck and Glueck (1950) identified many of those factors in their study comparing 500 institutionalized boys with 500 matched controls. And to reiterate, in a study of young delinquents that has received a great deal of attention, Terrie Moffitt (1993) has identified two vectors of offending: adolescent

limited and **life-course persistent criminality**. Those whose antisocial behavior is limited to the adolescent years make up the largest
group, and those whose offending is life-course persistent the smaller. She describes a process within which biological factors and the
early family environment mutually influence one another: negative
environments worsen negative traits, and negative traits increase the
exposure to negative environments. Obviously, Bandura's concept of
reciprocal determinism has influenced her thinking. By late adolescence, those traits conducive to antisocial behavior are so entrenched
that changing a person's behavior may be nearly impossible. By contrast, adolescent-limited antisocial behavior is not driven by individual traits but rather by peer influence and other situational factors,
and it eventually comes to be abandoned. In a 2018 review, Moffitt
affirms that such bifurcation of adolescent offenders has stood the
test of time as a major principle of behavior and should form the
basis for social policy.

That theoretical algorithm harkens back to Lombroso's ideas of over
100 years ago. Moffitt argues that multiple minor physical anomalies
that reflect neurological impairments along with mistreatment by parents are two of the significant causes of future serious delinquency.
Raine, Brennan, and Mednick (1994) found that birth complications
combined with maternal rejection were strongly predictive of future
offending. Thus, there is mounting empirical evidence that individual predilections interacting with powerful environmental influences
collude to produce both adolescent-limited and life-course-persistent
offenders.

MEDIA EFFECTS ON AGGRESSIVE BEHAVIOR AND VIOLENT CRIME

With the advent of wildly popular comic books depicting violence,
aggression, and crime, a minor panic ensued in the United States. It
was fueled by the 1954 testimony, before a congressional committee,
of psychiatrist Dr. Fredric Wertham that, indeed, the sordidly violent
comic books flooding the market in the thirties and forties produced
antisocial effects:

The general lesson we have deduced from our large case material is that the bad effects of crime comic books exist potentially for all children and may be exerted along these lines:

1) The comic-book format is an invitation to illiteracy.
2) Crime comic books create an atmosphere of cruelty and deceit.
3) They create a readiness for temptation.
4) They stimulate unwholesome fantasies.
5) They suggest criminal or sexually abnormal ideas.
6) They furnish the rationalization for them, which may be ethically even more harmful than the impulse.
7) They suggest the forms a delinquent impulse may take and supply details of technique.
8) They may tip the scales toward maladjustment or delinquency.

Crime comics are an agent with harmful potentialities. They bring about a mass conditioning of children, with different effects in the individual case. A child is not a simple unit which exists outside of its living social ties. Comic books themselves may be the virus, or the lack of resistance to the social virus of a harmful environment. (Wertham, 1954, p. 118)

At first blush, Wertham's conclusions all make sense, but his methodology as a forensic psychiatrist was to ask juvenile delinquents in his care whether they read comics, and they all confirmed that they did. What was not glaringly obvious to him and the committee, for some reason, was that if nondelinquents (e.g., a control group) were asked the same question, virtually all of them would probably have affirmed that they too read comic books. Such flawed "expert" research and testimony is perhaps why Canada followed suit and listed "crime comics" among prohibited media in section 163 of the Canadian Criminal Code. To give a more recent example, a group of Canadian researchers wished to study the effects of exposure to pornography on male adolescents. But they could find no control group. That is, by age 14 years, every single male they interviewed had seen pornography, yet sexual violence against women and children has declined dramatically in the past few years.

In spite of Wertham's testimony, comics survived and moved on to much more sordid and sexually and aggressively explicit material during the 1960s through to the present. And comics have generated major movie "franchises" from *Spider-Man* to *Deadpool*. Our question is, "Did extreme violence and aggression follow suit?" Let us see.

The next significant work of psychologists regarding the effects of media on antisocial behavior was pioneered by Leonard Eron, who almost accidentally during a study of family influences on child development discovered that children who watched violent television programs at age 6 to 10 engaged in more deviant and delinquent sorts of acts. Follow-up studies of those children found that, 15 years later, those who had preferred violent programs as children were more likely to engage in aggressive behavior as adults (Huesmann, Moise-Titus, Podolski, & Eron, 2003).

That elegant and methodologically impeccable study found antisocial effects for both boys and girls who identified with aggressive characters in those TV programs watched as young children. Clearly there is a link between viewing violence and aggression for some individuals, an outcome Bandura would certainly confirm.

Two questions come to mind about the relationship. The first is one that Moffitt might ask: Do the children who much prefer violent programs at an early age differ from other children at the outset? The second question is this: How socially significant is that uncovered effect? Given that violence and mayhem and access to it have exploded not only on television and in film but on the Internet, where just about any type of unsavory, violent display is available to almost any viewer, if the relationship were powerful, widespread, and robust, wouldn't it be reflected in a commensurate rise in violent crime, especially aggravated assault and homicide? One would think so, yet, as mentioned previously, violent crime rates in 2011 in the United States fell for the fifth straight year to almost historic record lows, according to the Federal Bureau of Investigation. And since then the overall trend has continued, with a few years (2012, 2015, and 2016) showing small increases (FBI, 2019). Rates in Canada have similarly declined between 2007 and 2017 despite the explosion and increasingly appalling nature of material available to be viewed (Allen, 2018). Perhaps the fact that the demographic profile of both countries is aging may be a significant factor since young men are the most likely to engage in violent behavior—followed by young women at a significantly lower rate.

THE COUNTERPHOBIC RESPONSE

Then again, there may be another effect of viewing violent crime and aggressive behavior. In a series of studies ranging from field research in response to the brutal murder of a coed on the campus of the University of Wisconsin to experiments on university campuses warning subjects of recent attacks on women, my colleagues and I (Boyanowsky, Newtson, & Walster, 1974; Boyanowsky, 1977) found that one of the motivations for seeking out films filled with violent and aggressive content was coping with fear of assault aroused by threats to oneself, something Otto Fenichel (1946) had labeled "the **counterphobic response**." Exposing oneself to fear stimuli in a safe environment allows one to cope with the fear and can even translate it into a thrill, hence, as we discovered, the tendency for teenagers to go to horror and especially "slasher" movies on dates. In retrospect, counterphobic behavior is essential to life. Otherwise, we would develop multiple phobias and neuroses trying to avoid everything that frightens us. So too, Doob and MacDonald (1979) found that people merely living in high crime neighborhoods watch more crime shows.

DELINQUENCY AND CRIME IN GROUPS AND GANGS

How does one study the reality of an adolescent gang and measure its actual effects on residents who live nearby, headlines in the media notwithstanding? Below I delineate a research approach to deal with one such situation.

A VIOLENT YOUTH GANG: MYTH, PERCEPTION, AND REALITY

THE CRIME SCENARIO
According to strident media accounts, a neighborhood of Vancouver had been taken over by a drug-taking, glue-sniffing, violent gang of

juveniles. "Animals set man on fire," screamed one typical headline describing how adolescents had apprehended an enemy gang member, beaten him severely, and then poured lighter fluid on him and set him on fire, and as he lay writhing on the ground had ridden over him back and forth on their bicycles (Boyanowsky, 2012a). Another story described how when a husky young man, a body builder, had come upon a couple of kids vandalizing his vintage Chevrolet Corvette, he had banged their heads together whereupon they started screaming and shouting and within seconds two dozen or more adolescents descended upon him, armed with baseball bats and chains, and put him in hospital with severe injuries.

Consequently, Ocean Park (not its real name) was in the throes of a social and moral panic. The public was outraged, demanding that the authorities apprehend the group that was plaguing its streets, terrorizing its citizens. Some social services, however, questioned whether the gang even existed, pointing out it had long been known that, contrary to public perceptions, gangs were not the primary source of adolescent crime (Haney & Gold, 1973).

THE OCEAN PARK STUDY

At that time, I had research interests in the area of perceptions and the origins of crime. I had studied how young people in different contexts can be stereotyped and had found that the media, both journalistic and dramatic, can shape a person's views of his or her world. Also, I knew that these stereotypes and media portrayals both contributed to fear (Doob & Macdonald, 1979) and could be used to reduce fear (Boyanowsky, Newtson, & Walster, 1974; Boyanowsky, 1977). So I proposed to determine whether the Ocean Park gang existed—as a gang—and if so, to find out how extensive and stable it was and to compare against the media reports about the gang how it was viewed by people who came into daily contact with it versus those in the neighborhood who knew the gang only through those media reports.

ECOLOGICAL ANALYSIS

That approach I took, dubbed an **ecological** analysis, derives from the Chicago school of sociology (Shaw & McKay, 1942) and has two dimensions: physical ecology and social ecology. Physical ecology represents the setting of the gang's activities and the distance of respondents from Ocean Park, where the gang conducted its activities. Social ecology, or symbolic interaction, as created by G. H. Mead (Mead & Morris, 1934) and described in Ascani (2012), represents the relationship various sectors of the community had with the alleged gang and how from those interactions the gang's identity was formed.

PHYSICAL ANALYSIS

To begin the physical analysis, I enlisted two research assistants to interview 20 residents of Ocean Park (OP) and 20 residents of a neighborhood nearby (dubbed Mountain Park or MP). These neighborhoods were separated by some distance, both physical and socioeconomic. A large forested hill containing another major park was between them, and the second community was middle and upper-middle class comprising detached single-family homes with gardens, in contrast to the assisted-housing tenements and modest working-class bungalows of the study area. For purposes of the study, the Ocean Park area was further divided: the first section comprised those persons resident on the street that fronted directly onto the park and the second, those resident one street and two streets removed from the park.

SOCIAL ANALYSIS

Using a social set of criteria, we placed different sectors of the community to be interviewed on a social distance spectrum beginning with those closest to the adolescents to be studied and ranging to those most socially distant. Those so placed included, from the closest to the most distant, 10 parents of alleged gang members, 10 social workers, 7 merchants in the area, and 6 police assigned to surveillance of the gang's territory.

THE ECOLOGY OF THE SETTING

What we found in Ocean Park ran contrary to the research of the Chicago school (Thrasher, 1926) and the Cambridge Study in Delinquent Development (Farrington & Welsh, 2007), which provided bleak descriptions of the physical environment within which gang members and youths at risk lived in both the United States and the UK. The Ocean Park area had not only government subsidized apartment buildings and small, older detached cottages but a great deal of green space, many trees, and a great many sports and recreation facilities. There were baseball and soccer fields, a gymnasium, an ice-skating and hockey rink, and exercise facilities. It was not the setting anyone who was familiar with gang research in the United States or the UK—but not with the Vancouver area—would have expected to encounter.

GANG MORPHOLOGY: WHO BELONGS?

In contrast to American, other Canadian, and British studies of gangs, our study found that very few of the gang member families were of Native American or African origin, and, in fact, most were not recent immigrants but were at least first or second generation Canadians from the UK, Europe, and elsewhere. Most startling, however, was that all of the parents interviewed were young single mothers in their twenties and early thirties. Their general comment (like that of single mums in US city ghettos) was how difficult it was to meet appropriate males who could become partners, a situation acutely experienced by the inter- viewers who were two attractive young men. They sometimes reported some difficulty in extricating themselves gracefully from the interview- ee's apartment. The mothers reported being stuck in the apartment with multiple children and so, any child that proved disruptive would be banished to the outdoors as often as possible, even at an early age, a fact also noted in the Cambridge study.

THE MEASUREMENT INSTRUMENT

To maintain methodological consistency, we gave all respondents the same questions to answer orally on an 11-point scale designed like a **Likert scale**. That scale ranged from 1 for total disagreement to 6 for a neutral opinion to 11 for total agreement with a series of statements made by the interviewers. Since the results were statistically quite clear, for the purposes of this chapter, I will restrict myself to descrip- tive reports. For instance, the local OP respondents disagreed that the gang members were merely a group of harmless kids, in contrast to the distant MP respondents who felt that, indeed, they were "only kids." Social workers preferred to believe there was a "group" rather than a gang, though they used the term gang themselves in conversation, but the police argued most emphatically that a delinquent gang existed. As might be expected, mothers were not sure. In any case, it appears that self-reference to gang membership was widespread, as the interviewers noted graffiti on many walls, fences, and public buildings that read "Ocean Parkers Rule" throughout the gang's territory, especially where it abutted a rival gang's "turf."

MP respondents tended to believe the gang members spent only three to four hours per day together, whereas the OP residents were of the opinion that gang members were together twice as long each day, especially in the summer when they were seen to spend the whole night hanging around in the park. Police, mothers, and even social workers concurred. That discrepancy demonstrates the limitation of studies that use only one source of information to determine the reality of the situation.

SIZE AND GENDER MAKEUP OF THE GANG

The three most knowledgeable groups, mothers, social workers, and police, as well as MP respondents, felt the membership ranged in age from about 12 years to 18 years, especially among the peripheral members who numbered 50. However, the delinquent core group was considered to be slightly older, ranging from 15 to as high as 20 years old and numbered 15, with females comprising about 20 to 30 percent of the gang. According to the police, females also committed assaults, especially on non-gang members in schools in order to extort money for drug purchases. In addition, according to police and OP respondents, all members were sexually active, usually in the summertime and in the park. The same sources said that the females provided sexual favors to a succession of males. One elderly woman, among only a small group living near the park that was willing to speak extensively, described working in her garden when she suddenly realized gang members were engaged in sex just across her fence. From past experience, she was so terrified of being discovered that she crawled on her belly all the way back to her house to escape detection.

SNAPSHOT SUMMARY

The gang is indeed a group of juveniles consisting of 15 core members of whom one third are girls ranging in age from 13 to 20 years. They reportedly spend much of their waking time together. From a symbolic interactionist perspective, the gang exists and is labeled delinquent by significant others in the immediate community (OP) based on their interactions with it and by self-identification, but not by the distal community (MP), which knows about this group of juveniles only through media reports.

Only the social workers disagreed with the statement that "gang members were responsible for most of the crime in the neighbourhood" and that they used tobacco, alcohol, and drugs. Respondents were uncertain whether gang members were addicted to hard drugs (e.g., heroin, crystal methamphetamine).

It was commonly agreed, especially among OP and MP respondents, that most of the gang members got in trouble with the police, and, surprisingly, gang members' mothers concurred. Those respondents also agreed that gang members went looking for trouble. Merchants described how members would "swarm" their places of business, grabbing as much as they could before anyone could respond, and then vanish into the trees in the park. The gravest incident described how several gang members entered an empty ice cream parlor; locked the female attendant in the walk-in freezer, blocking the door; stole as much as they could; and then ran away. It was just by lucky chance that an entering customer heard the faint cries of the attendant in the freezer and was able to rescue her before she was seriously injured or even died from the cold.

FUTURE PROSPECTS

In response to the statement that "kids like this grow up to be hardened criminals," both OP and MP residents were relatively undecided, but local merchants, police, and once again, surprisingly, mothers of gang members moderately agreed. Only the social workers demurred. On several occasions they introduced the interviewers to individual gang members and pointed out how pleasant they were as individuals. "Look, they are only little children, not monsters," they insisted, and indeed, as individuals, gang members were indistinguishable from any other adolescents. Note again the powerful conformity effects my colleagues and I discovered in experimental groups, effects that work to transform reasonable individuals into an antisocial group entity, as Claude Brown (1965) described earlier in this chapter.

MEDIA EFFECTS

Although social workers contended that the image of a violent, adolescent gang had been created by overreacting media coverage, two findings tended to discount that explanation. First, the distant MP community respondents tended to view the gang less extremely than the OP respondents who lived in the park vicinity. One would expect to find the opposite if the "gang" were a purely media-created phenomenon. MP respondents also displayed much less fear of the gang. The only issue on which the MP community could be construed to be more negative was in its greater belief that gang members were addicted to hard drugs. The OP respondents disagreed, based on personal observations, noting that gang members seemed to drink beer and other alcoholic beverages, sniff glue, and smoke tobacco and marijuana and were only occasionally seen to ingest crystal meth.

Second, as mentioned, there was markedly greater fear of the gang in the OP community than in MP community. That state was most emphasized by the fact that OP residents fronting on the park would not answer their doors to the interviewers, at best peeking at them from behind curtains and waving them away. Less negatively, OP residents one street away did open their doors but with great trepidation and hustled the interviewers inside, explaining that residents who were seen to be speaking with authorities had been assaulted and had had their vehicles and houses vandalized. Residents three streets away from the park were visibly less anxious, friendlier, and more willing to discuss the gang. On the other hand, all MP residents were completely sanguine about being interviewed. One can only speculate that had we been able to interview the residents fronting on Ocean Park, our results would have been even more extreme.

Media effects, then, did not create the climate of fear but proved useful in bringing attention to the gravity of the situation. The police were reservedly grateful for the media coverage of the gang, as were the mothers who said that it was one way they could keep informed of the more grievous misdeeds of their children. On the other hand, the police decried the notoriety the gang received because of the media coverage, which police thought romanticized gang membership and crystallized the renegade identity of the gang. That coverage, they felt, might even put pressure on the gang to be more extremely antisocial than it otherwise would have been, an analysis that concurs with a symbolic interaction explanation.

EXPLANATIONS AND CAUSES

The ecological explanation of the Chicago school (e.g., Thrasher, Becker, and others) is that gangs are spawned in transitional parts of cities. Those neighborhoods are desolate in their aspect, having poor and overcrowded housing and lacking recreational facilities or good schools, and they are the neighborhoods of successive generations of immigrant families. Such families from abroad or from rural areas are often in dysfunctional states due to unemployment or underemployment, hence impoverishment, and they very often lack proper role models, especially for young males. Eventually, some families are successful and move on to be replaced by other similarly disadvantaged groups.

The irony is that, although containing the low-cost or assisted-rent housing that virtually all of the families of gang members occupied, Ocean Park is quite scenic with the tenements abutting older working-class but well-cared-for bungalows. In addition, there is the park itself that is quite extensive, beautifully treed, and containing, as mentioned at the outset, every conceivable kind of recreational and sports opportunity. However, the climate of fear extant was so severe few adults and younger children ventured into the unsupervised park of trees and grass, especially in the evening and after dark.

If the gang was not a media apparition and not a product of a deprived environment, wherein lies the explanation for its existence? Do the causal factors lie in other environmental, sociological, social-structural, familial, economic, or psychological factors? First, basic environmental causes can be set aside as no comparable gang existed in MP, the control community, which had its own beautiful, densely treed, intensely used park. Certainly no gang existed in OP until low-cost housing was created (over protests from local residents several years before, who, as a result, won the extensive recreational facilities from government planners). A sociological explanation, then, holds some water, as we discovered that, contrary to what the police attested (that the kids came from normal, intact families), every parent of a gang member interviewed turned out to be a single mother usually with more than one child.

ECONOMIC FACTORS The reality was that, although the park had extensive recreational facilities, admission to most places demanded a small user fee that for middle-class families would not be a problem but that for single mothers with several small children was a major obstacle to regular use. Even simple things were beyond reach, like using the gym, and they certainly could not afford to have their children join sports teams requiring registration fees, equipment, and other expenses. So the park itself became the constant default location of activity.

FAMILIAL ISSUES Mothers protested that they had little time for recreation themselves while taking care of their children, and in the absence of suitable males for whom competition was quite strong in the neighborhood, they would gather in small groups of women to drink alcohol and smoke tobacco and marijuana. They claimed that competition for males was so strong that sexually promiscuous behavior was the only way to attract men, which, even they admitted, did not allow for good role modeling for the children. And it also resulted in their focusing less on their children's adjustment to spend more on their own: thus they became self-absorbed, which led us to speculate that solving the mothers' social adjustment problems might allow them to focus more on the children.

Although the physical environment, unlike those in US city ghettos and UK projects, was not bleak, toxic, and fraught with danger, and so seemed not to contribute to the delinquency of the children in OP, the life circumstances of the mothers—single and lacking in appropriate male companionship—was remarkably similar to those described by some African American mothers. One circumstance relates to the scarcity of male partners and role models, in part because African American young males have high mortality and imprisonment rates (Pathak, 2018) so are in the minority in many neighborhoods. Thus, women would likely feel peer competition pressure because of this scarcity of young men, and men would be less inclined to make a commitment to any one woman. This was certainly the circumstance that the young women of Ocean Park described to us.

By comparison, the downtown eastside of Vancouver, its oldest neighborhood, for 100 years was the center of crime and drug activity. My wife and I recently lived for a year in a row house built for Eastern European immigrants in 1903 as rental housing, coincidentally (my parents are from Ukraine; she is from Transylvania). Serious drug addicts still roam the streets today. However, we couldn't afford to buy there as the area of ramshackle late-Victorian dwellings protected by heritage status was in transition. The streets are also currently thronging with young couples, hipsters who love the idea of living downtown. And the most likely violence to be feared is being knocked over by a young woman cycling down the street with a baby buggy in tow. Most households comprise intact couples either heterosexual or LGTBQ, and children of all ages play in the streets and parks. Delinquency is not a problem. My point is the importance of stable family life in the prevention of delinquency.

PSYCHOLOGICAL ISSUES We concluded that the problem of the Ocean Park gang began with the construction of social housing that attracted families on living assistance, very often headed by single mothers with more than one child. The mothers described how the relatively benign physical environment of the project alleviated any guilt they felt in sending the most difficult kids outdoors to spare themselves the anxiety and tension wrought by volatile, easily bored, and disobedient children in quite crowded apartments where two or more kids shared a bedroom. Farrington, Piquero, and Jennings (2013) report that children in England are often banished outside for hours at a time into much less salubrious environments at an age as young as three or four.

CRITICAL NUMBERS
As kids spend hours and then days in the park, they run out of activities to amuse themselves, especially as they approach adolescence, so they seek excitement, drugs, money. In the absence of more creative activities, they inevitably engage in violence—with one another, with passing residents, with other kids and merchants. This violence occurs especially when inhibitions, usually minimal among preadolescents and teens, are further reduced by the use of alcohol and drugs, which in turn require money. Hence, break-ins and shakedowns are undertaken.

Exacerbating the situation is the fact that many are barred from using the recreational facilities by such a simple obstacle as a small user fee their parents cannot pay and the adolescents refuse to pay. Or, more seriously, the young people have been flagged and barred from the facilities for causing disruptions or even damage on past occasions.

As more kids become pariahs, they convince others to hang out with them as "all of the kids are hanging not going to a lame game at the rec centre." As Boyanowsky and others showed in several studies (Boyanowsky & Allen, 1973; Boyanowsky, Allen, Bragg, & Lepinski, 1981), conformity to the group is so powerful an effect that only a constantly present, dissenting social supporter—a father, mother, or sibling, for example—can aid someone in resisting group pressure, even though the individual may privately wish to do so. And once the social supporter is absent, the individual returns to the fold. What the housing situation has done is create a critical number of children with similarly problematic behavioral dispositions who are thrust into each other's company for inordinate numbers of hours. Ron Akers, propounder of the social reinforcement theory of delinquency, would argue that the outcome was based on a system of mutual reward for deviant behaviors.

ESCALATION

Thus, in the absence of resources or more creative activities, children at risk remain together as one hour lengthens to eight hours and day becomes night—and the number of these children reaches a critical mass. Soon there is a gang engaging in activities from chatting to roughhousing with one another to smoking marijuana and engaging in sex, from deciding to swarm a store to beating up some passing kids, vandalizing a car, or snooping around yards looking for open doors and windows in order to enter and steal something of value. As studies of young offenders have shown, it is the child who is easily bored, suffering from attention deficit disorder, and so impulsive and risk taking that emerges as the leader (Quay & Werry, 1986). The group then moves from play to wandering to swarming to any exciting opportunity that arises, including engaging in fights with other groups of adolescents or vandalizing cars and property in the neighborhood and instilling anxiety and fear in the residents. And ultimately, the group comes to the attention of the authorities and the media that, in turn, enhance its status with adolescents in similar circumstances who normally would not engage in such activities but are now drawn to the group because of its newly gained notoriety.

You may have read William Golding's chilling novel *Lord of the Flies*, made into a fine film directed by Peter Brook in 1963 (Golding, 1954). The theme of *Lord of the Flies* is that people, especially children, once the veneer of society is removed, revert to a primitive and violent state fraught with fear and characterized by brutal violence. Only the constraints of society inhibit those tendencies, and for the OP gang, they were potentiated by its members having had no appropriate male role model at home. So, after these adolescents spent days together in the park in relative isolation, as happened on the island in the book, the most dangerous and risk-taking individual became the leader.

THE FOLLOW-UP STUDY

Several years later, armed with the list of addresses of the families of the original gang, a researcher was dispatched to Ocean Park to determine the state of the gang. To her surprise, the gang no longer existed. Many had moved but many of the families still there no longer had children of the age at risk (13 to 18). Other families had moved in, but perhaps at-risk children (i.e., ADHD, compulsive, risk-taking children), no longer existed in sufficient numbers to feed on one another and create an extreme culture of delinquency. Also, children in the years following the study of the gang had begun to be treated with Ritalin for ADHD, a drug that has been shown to reduce delinquency among such male children, those who in the past would have been the ringleaders. Thus those children would, at the appropriate age, not be so disruptive, and so could participate in hockey, baseball, volleyball, ringette, basketball, and soccer—organized group activities that were offered at the rec center. In fact, clerks claimed the present crop of kids was proud of the center and that there hadn't been an incident for more than five years. In addition, a very low yearly fee for rec center membership, one that all families could afford, had been instituted.

COMMUNITY EFFORTS

At the time of the original study, several residents had revealed that vigilante responses to "get our park back" were arising. Police admitted that pressure had been put upon authorities by citizens' groups to "crack down" on the gang whenever its members convened in large numbers. So the combination of increased community activity in concert with police intervention may have resulted in juveniles choosing to engage in their illicit activities (e.g., drug taking, break and enters, car theft) in much smaller and less detectable groups, as cited by Gordon and Foley (1998) in their Vancouver area gang study. Other previous members interviewed in the follow-up revealed that since becoming of legal drinking age, they sought out bars for their entertainment.

PHYSICAL ECOLOGY

Additional measures to deter gang activities had been implemented, such as thinning trees so view planes were established in the park and installing more and brighter light posts that were kept lit during the night. Those measures resulted in two outcomes: the park was no longer used for fights with other gangs and, as one former member stated, "A lot of guys just started hanging out alone or in smaller groups." As one resident, who was a baseball coach and a father, exclaimed, "We took our park back. They didn't want to be hassled all the time [by police] as members of a gang." Thus, they became more concerned about being harassed by the police than being beaten up by members of other gangs and so just avoided the parks.

THE CONCLUSION

The nub of the problem was the existence of an identifiable gang that came to represent deviance. A combination of eventual maturation, progression to adult crime, and harassment by citizens and police made gang membership less attractive. As some merchants, real estate agents, and police commented, the gang had been the problem, the cause of public fear and anxiety. One must acknowledge the power of conformity processes: people in large or even smaller groups can more easily be induced to beat someone up, trash a store, or burn police cars. (Consider, for example, the post–Stanley Cup riot of 2011 in normally peaceful downtown Vancouver wherein hundreds of young people committed millions of dollars of damage and even assaults on individuals who tried to stop them.) So too, the Ocean Parkers had occasionally acted out of conformity and had instilled fear in the community. But similar criminal acts—buying and selling drugs, breaking and entering, car vandalism, threats against residents, and even public drunkenness or displays of sexual behavior—still occurred, although these were no longer linked to a gang in the mind of the public. Consequently, public fear of the gang was assuaged.

THE VANCOUVER GANG STUDY (1998)

A study of gangs in the whole Vancouver Lower Mainland confirmed that street gangs, unlike criminal organizations, come and go in waves for some unfathomable reason. As Gordon and Foley (1998) claim, there is no satisfactory explanation for the cyclical patterns of street gang activity in Vancouver. They hypothesized that the following factors had reduced gang activity:

1) Aggressive targeting of key individuals by police when given the appropriate resources through considerable public and political pressure led to the demise of gangs at a certain period.
2) Highly publicized acts of extreme violence that exceeded even the members' notions of acceptable behavior produced revulsion that deflated the romantic and entertainment value of belonging to a street gang.
3) Maturation of gang members, who, like criminals in general, "mature" out of criminal activity in their twenties, reduced membership.
4) The death or neutralization of leaders through drug abuse or at the hands of others weakened the gang.
5) Community-based programs dried up the supply of prospective new members.

The Vancouver-wide study of 128 gang members on probation underlines the usefulness of studying one gang in depth, as that study's conclusions differ very little from our own. Certain generic factors are common to all gangs. Unlike the physical and social-ecological explanations given in the Ocean Park study, however, the Vancouver study found an overrepresentation of visible ethnic minorities among whom youths of Vietnamese origin were the most prominent. That finding is in contrast to the fact that recent immigrants who are members of visible minorities are traditionally underrepresented in crime in Canada. They conclude that gang members are drawn to the lifestyle by social or economic inequality. For instance, young new immigrants have trouble integrating into peer society because of language or other cultural difficulties and so take refuge in gangs comprising their language and cultural background or in response to the pressure created by economic hardship. It must, however, be cautioned that, ironically, many gang members also come from middle-class or better backgrounds. Also, the conclusions of Gordon and Foley must be viewed circumspectly because those researchers used a very biased sample: unlike in our Ocean Park research, Gordon and Foley studied only gang members who had been convicted.

One Chinese gang member from a middle-class family who came to speak to my class while on remand was involved in a Vietnamese gang whose members he described as terrifyingly ruthless: "They are small guys, but they don't back down, so if you get into a fight with them, one of you dies." Why was he involved? "I'm not smart like my brother who is in your class. I can't get into university, so I can wash dishes for minimum wage at the Night and Day [a restaurant] or jack sports and muscle cars at $5000 a pop. Every night. And I have tried to stop, but I eventually go back to the life." Too true, in a lame attempt at money laundering, he was nabbed for giving kids at an arcade $50 bills to get change. After the third time it occurred, the attendant called the police. A prime example of Merton's **strain theory** of delinquency. Merton (1957) argued that certain members of society, although unable to achieve commonly desired goals such as money, cars, status, and attractive mates due to racism, social deprivation, lack of intelligence, unwillingness to work hard, or a multitude of other factors, nevertheless pursue these goals through engaging in crime. Consider the example below.

THE INDO-CANADIAN BLOODBATH
In the documentary *A Warrior's Religion* by Mani Amar (available on YouTube), the filmmaker interviews gang members and members of the Sikh community in an effort to understand why more than 80 (and counting) young Sikh men have been murdered in suburban Vancouver in recent years. The speculation on the part of the Sikhs ranges from

families who work too hard and don't provide enough guidance and discipline to the fact that many Sikhs are extremely materialistic and that boys are favored to the point at which they start to experience unrealistic expectations about themselves and so delve into the life of gangsters as a way of acquiring all of the benefits—money, cars, beautiful women—without achieving very much in conventional society. Of course that motivator of crime, the desire to escape frustrated ambitions and take a shortcut to pleasure and success, has been documented widely among criminals and postulated by Merton (1957) and Agnew (1990). And Akers (2000) discusses drug taking in many cities in the United States as a way of managing the unpleasant feelings associated with frustration and the resultant dissatisfaction, resentment, and anger. Thus one could characterize this precursor of crime as a **morbid sense of entitlement**. The fine Deepa Mehta film *Beeba Boys* (2015) explores that causal chain in exquisite fashion.

But those strains first delineated by Merton (1957) occur universally. So why did they become homicidally epidemic among young Sikh men, most of whose families are respectable workers or businessmen, and most poignantly in the Vancouver area? As I pointed out in the Ocean Park study, critical numbers of individuals in the same social circumstances will often foment a gang problem whereas a few persons or small groups in a comparable social environment will not, other than committing the same types of crimes as individuals. So significant numbers of "entitled" Sikhs shared a common fate and frustration. But why in Vancouver did it burgeon into a major gang war?

SOWING THE SEEDS OF VIOLENT GANG CRIME

Several members of the Babbar Khalsa terrorist organization who fought the government of India and lost in a bid to create the Sikh nation of Khalistan were allowed to migrate to Canada even though European countries had warned of their aggressive activities and commitment to solving problems through violence. Most prominent among those immigrants were Talwinder Singh Parmar and his right-hand man Ajaib Singh Bagri, who settled in Vancouver, a city that contains the largest Sikh community outside India. Several attacks, some ending in homicide against moderate journalists and politicians, followed in the ensuing years, culminating in the 1985 plot to blow up Air India flights from Montreal and Tokyo. The Japanese bomb plot resulted in a bomb's exploding prematurely in Narita International Airport, killing two baggage handlers and injuring four other people. But the Montreal flight ended much more tragically—with the killing of 329 people. Charges were laid for 331 cases of first-degree murder in 2000 against Bagri and a third militant Sikh, Ripudaman Singh Malik. Parmar had died in India in 1992. Despite wiretap evidence, witnesses' testimony, and the bomb maker, Indirjit Singh Reyat, pleading guilty to manslaughter, the judge ruled that the evidence was not strong enough to convict Bagri and Malik, so they were set free after costing the Canadian government almost $20 million in legal fees for defense counsel for them. They had claimed destitution despite the fact that Malik, at least, was a wealthy businessman. A later inquiry established by the Canadian government concluded they were responsible, but no one went to prison other than Reyat.

Thus a toxic brew was created by a self-identified religion of violent solutions committed to killing its foes, a generation of pampered and entitled young men raised in that religion and culture, and the demonstration (massively rewarding) that even in Canadian society, lawbreaking and extreme violent crime and homicide go unpunished. Together, those elements served to create not only gangs but competition among gangs for the lucrative drug trade of which the Vancouver metropolitan area had become the nexus. Those conditions notwithstanding, most Vancouver Sikhs do not resort to crime. On the other hand, although Babbar Khalsa is on the terrorist exclusion list in North America, its cells continue to threaten death worldwide to anyone who displeases them.

It is remarkable that the spate of killings in the Sikh community in the Lower Mainland (Metropolitan Vancouver) has recently been overshadowed by an even bigger outbreak of gang warfare among competing gangs; most notoriously, the Red Scorpions, headed by the Bacon brothers of Abbotsford, are vying with the International Soldiers and the United Nations Gang, among several others. Five fatal gang-related shootings in the Lower Mainland took place as recently as the autumn of 2018 (Saltman, 2018). The United Nations (the intergovernmental organization not the gang) has identified Vancouver as the most integrated city in the world, a fact now reflected even in its most notorious criminal elements. But does that fact add to the pride of smug Vancouverites who feel they live in the "best place on earth" (the governmental slogan for British Columbia)? Probably not. Another long-term criminal gang, constantly under attack by police, also continues to function in Vancouver: the Hell's Angels. The biker gang is widespread through North America but just recently was officially identified by the Manitoba government as a criminal organization. Thus it is exempt from the protection of certain civil rights. Police in British Columbia and elsewhere in Western Canada are attempting to dismantle its operations by using the law that allows seizure of all property obtained through criminal acts.

THE SOLUTION

All these organizations are sustained by the illegal drug trade. In an essay originally published in the *Vancouver Sun* as an op-ed piece, I argue that illegal drug trade in British Columbia is so lucrative that arresting and imprisoning gang members, especially the heads of gangs, merely creates job opportunities for new recruits (Boyanowsky, 2012b). Those recruits are now largely from comfortable working-class and even upper-middle-class families, so the traditional interventions mounted with youths in the United Kingdom, the United States, and elsewhere are basically irrelevant to the present situation in Vancouver and elsewhere in British Columbia. I point out that alcohol, pharmaceutically the most dangerous drug, whose prohibition triggered the largest crime wave in North America during the 1920s, is now dealt with through regulation. Consequently, hardly anyone kills anyone about alcohol except in gang warfare in Nunavut. In that territory, alcohol is illegal due to the aboriginal government's recognition of the special sensitivity of its indigenous population to alcohol's negative effects. So in that locale there is serious alcohol-related gang violence because the region is a black market for bootleggers. Thus, decriminalization and mere regulation, similar to the approach applied to alcohol throughout most of the world, should replace the failed war on drugs and apply to every drug. Despite widespread outrage at that suggestion, the example of Portugal, which decriminalized all drugs well over a decade ago, shows that regulation does work to reduce crime, and drug use does not soar (Greenwald, 2009). Even the use of marijuana by young people has declined. Today, marijuana is legal in Canada. Thus the country becomes an ongoing experiment.

IN CONCLUSION

What I have shown is how a violent youth gang is created by critical numbers of adolescents residing in a concentrated area, its beauty notwithstanding, who spend a great deal of time together unsupervised. The psychological propensities of a few produce deviant leaders among them. But such gangs disappear when the critical numbers of adolescents at risk are reduced and dispersed. Ethnic criminal gangs recruit new immigrants who seek refuge and belonging when they are vulnerable due to language deficits, lack of familial supervision, and the need for finances in a new country. Sometimes, gangs are even spawned because a critical number of entitled young men are raised in a violent culture at a certain moment in history. Most mature criminal gangs, however, comprise individuals from one ethnic group or many because the financial rewards of the drug trade are so enticing for those with unfulfilled, perhaps unrealistic, expectations that they will risk prison or even death to reap those benefits.

The solution lies in changing the laws. A few years ago, I was invited to participate in a videoconference at the United States Consulate General in Vancouver in order to receive a briefing on dealing with the drug gangs, especially the cartels operating along the Mexican border. Once the moderator in charge of American policy, speaking from Washington, DC, finished his overview, he asked whether there were any questions. The room was full of young, impressive looking men and women, all from the FBI, CIA, RCMP, Vancouver Police Department, and Canadian Security and Intelligence Services. Then there was me, the lone gray-bearded academic. No one spoke. Finally, I said I had a question. They all turned to me, shocked and bemused, when I asked, "Has the US government considered legalizing all drugs?"

I was astounded when the moderator responded without hesitating, "Well, now that Obama is in the White House, it is at least on the agenda for consideration." Perhaps progress is possible. But then the political scene is very changeable, as we have come to note since November 2016.

IN SUMMARY

Children learn through observation as Bandura demonstrated (i.e., through vicarious learning rather than just through reinforced responses).

A combination of individual risk factors and environmental risk factors promote delinquency.

Media effects can influence aggressive reactions, but the overall trend, despite increased violence in the media, has been a reduction in violent crime—and viewing violence can also be a way of reducing fear.

Studies of gangs in the Vancouver area include those focusing on adolescent "park" gangs, ethnic gangs involved in the drug trade, and Indo-Canadian gangs. There is an inordinate number of middle-class Indo-Canadian gang members who suffer from the effects of the gap between expectations and what they can achieve without ability, education, and hard work. This situation, as an impetus to crime, is consistent with strain theory.

CHAPTER EIGHT

SOCIOPOLITICAL CRIMINOGENIC FACTORS

SOWING THE SEEDS OF SLAUGHTER

Although aggression against individuals and groups is not only common and probably limitless in its intensity and magnitude and the use of it by groups familiar to us at its most extreme is well known (e.g., the dropping of the atomic bombs on Hiroshima and Nagasaki, the firebombing of Dresden), the use of such aggression in a violent form is more palatable in the context of war. Very often, the justification of its application is ultimately the saving of lives (like so many other policy decisions, e.g., the internment of Japanese in World War II and of Ukrainians in Canada from 1914 to 1920). Another justification is revenge for past injury (the 400-year-old Serbian memory of the razing of a church and the building of a mosque on the site by Muslims).

Aggressive action can be framed as a policy decision regarding the greater good for the greater number (e.g., the Irish famine engineered by the English or the forced starvation of several million Ukrainians by Stalinist Russia in 1932, now referred to as the Holodomor, or the systematic elimination of six million Jews in the Holocaust). It can be done instantly or through indirect actions; it can be done remotely, as in aerial bombing, or in an "industrialized" form, such as deportation, internment, and systematic execution. However, when a government exports all foodstuffs and leaves its citizens to starve, sociopolitical explanations may suffice. Thus, when Western pro-Communists, such as *New York Times* Pulitzer Prize–winning correspondent Walter Duranty, witnessed the forced, mass starvation in the Ukrainian part of the USSR, he commented, "You can't make an omelette without breaking eggs" (Taylor, 1990, p. 185; Conquest, 1986).

Bandura refers to such characterizations as "**neutralization,**" that is, the smoothing over of the horrendous nature of the policy and its consequences. Agnieszka Holland's (2019) film *Mr. Jones* shows how Western journalists in Moscow folded under threats from the Kremlin in order to suppress the horror of millions dying in the Ukraine while journalist Gareth Jones desperately tried to get out the story. In his attempt to break the story, Jones confers with another young writer, George Orwell, who is so struck by Jones's chilling tale that he is inspired to write *Animal Farm*.

In those processes of sanctioned aggression and its neutralization, the individual is only a cog in the machine and has a very circumscribed role, even if it involves pressing a button to open a bomb bay door or to release poison gas, even if it means removing food from starving people under gunpoint. One doesn't usually have to engage in the individual infliction of pain, mutilation, and death over and over or repeatedly confront the horrific consequences by witnessing the deaths of hundreds, thousands, and even hundreds of thousands of human beings.

When, however, one wishes to create the circumstances for mass killings at a technologically primitive level, the repeated intimate involvement of thousands of previously innocuous people in the carnage is necessary. Consequently, there is a multistage process that must be followed and several psychological and social conditions that must be fulfilled.

First, a target group must be identified that is clearly but not massively different from those who are identified to be the perpetrators. Societies are more prone to mass killings if they officially underscore differences among groups—for example, Christian versus Jew (rather than merely German), Jew versus Arab, or European versus Beothuk (the extinct aboriginal tribe of Newfoundland). If the target group is small, targeting it is easy, but advocating drastic actions against it is more difficult, as the group presents a trivial problem. Although even relatively transitory or ephemeral characteristics can be identified and recruited to the task, this targeting will often merely promote xenophobia (which is a basic human reaction experienced from infancy and grounded in sociobiological motivation). Targeting is more likely to lead to aggressive action when a threat is identified, such as immigrants taking jobs or farmers taking land or, better yet, immigrant farmers, who became the target of cattle ranchers in Montana during the 1800s.

This dispute between cattle barons and European immigrants is the focus of the film *Heaven's Gate* directed by Michael Cimino (1980). That film documents an event now loath to be discussed by present-day citizens because survivors have been assimilated—by name change (for instance, Boyko to Boyd), occupation, and intermarriage—into the positive folklore of the American West. In the Canadian West, specifically in Alberta and Saskatchewan, the arrival of those immigrants in part triggered the formation of the Ku Klux Klan among the original white Anglo-Saxon populace. M. Sherif, Harvey, White, Hood, & C.W. Sherif (1961) and Tajfel (1982) have both illustrated how easy it is to produce the differentiation, denigration, discrimination, and hostility necessary as a first step. Boyanowsky and Allen (1973) have shown how ingroup self-identity, that is, identifying only with a specific group such as white Anglo-Saxon Protestants; the threat of censure from that reference group; and, finally, those ubiquitous ingroup conformity processes discussed previously motivate the distinction. Perceived threats (real or concocted) to one's group inspire the requisite initial hostility.

If the target group is large, more enduring characteristics that resist assimilation or subsummation within a larger, inclusive category (Canadian, Catholic, Christian, human) may be required. How then, once a group has been targeted, isolated psychologically, and characterized as posing a threat or having perpetuated an injustice, does one initiate the killing? I believe it is through a multifactor process involving elements of disinhibition, personal predilection and grievance, conformity processes, and a certain societal state, in concert with 1) official sanction and 2) official exhortation—"cheering on" the murderous masses. In 2010, President Jacob Zuma of South Africa sang "Shoot the Farmer, Kill the Boer" as horrific attacks (rape, torture, and murder) against white farmers escalated, thereby sanctioning their perpetration (Chung, 2017). Using similar terrorism tactics, nearby Zimbabwe has been just about "cleansed" of white farmers.

I have proposed a "Pyramid of Crime" that illustrates the interaction of personal predilections with societal state. In that model (figure 8.1), the political structure of all countries is arranged in a rectangle in one of five tiers, with the top tier comprising regimes that are monolithic and homogeneous ideologically, religiously, or ethnically and, most importantly, totalitarian. These countries impose the maximum social control. On the other hand, the traditional criminogenic factors of **outgroup/ ingroup loyalties and discrimination**, whether economic, religious, or ethnic, are minimized.

Aggression and violent crime are nevertheless vestigially present within countries placed at the top of the pyramid. A tiny percentage of the population commits antisocial acts triggered by psychotic delusions, psychopathy, or concomitant moral turpitude and crimes of passion. Official government response is swift and harsh with a massive general deterrent effect. Examples might include Afghanistan under the Taliban, Saudi Arabia, the former Soviet Union, and North Korea and China at their communist peak, with Singapore a little below them.

The viciousness of Saudi law enforcement was perhaps best exemplified for North Americans when William Sampson, a pharmaceutical representative of joint Canadian-UK citizenship, was arrested. Sampson, who used to hang out in Riyadh's illegal bars, was named under torture by his friend Raf Schyvens (who later lamented his claim) as involved in a car bombing. Schyvens had been arrested earlier when a crackdown on those illegal bars was instituted. Sampson was thrown into prison where he was tortured and raped until he confessed to the bombing and was sentenced to be beheaded, but after 31 months of worldwide and some Canadian government protest, he was released in 2003. He was a broken man, a former outdoorsman who could no longer walk properly more than 200 meters. He died of a heart attack in 2012 at the age of 52 (Nonato, 2012).

Even more extreme was the action of North Korea's young dictator Kim Jong Un, who declared his uncle, Jang Song Thaek, and several others to be "anti-party, counter revolutionary factional elements" and "despicable human scum" (Fisher, 2013). Those code words suggest they had questioned some of the "hermit kingdom's" policies; reputedly, they were fed to starving dogs (Dier, 2014). Whether the story was true or not, the general deterrent effect of such actions results in very few people being willing to question the authority of such regimes or to commit any action that might be construed to be illegal.

The second tier comprises countries that are socially democratic and promote equality of both a level of welfare (food, shelter, health, and education) below which citizenry need not fall and opportunity. This access to opportunity is inclusive enough to offset ingroup versus outgroup hostilities and is facilitated if multifactor homogeneity exists, such as was the case in Scandinavia and, until the late seventies, in the United Kingdom and, to a lesser extent, in Canada. That status is now threatened by the massive numbers of refugees who have been admitted to Sweden and Norway, shattering homogeneity in those countries.

One direct result was the mass murder in Oslo and on Utøya, a vacation island for union workers' children. In total, 77 innocent men, women, and, mostly, children were murdered by the self-declared fascist Anders Behring Breivik. Breivik's hatred was spawned by the influx of Islamic refugees for which he blamed the socialist worker's party and feminism (McIntyre, 2011). His punishment for that atrocity by the state was in stark contrast to the brutality of the Korean and Saudi regimes. He was given 21 years in detention and even sued the government for cruelty for placing him in solitary confinement. Such horrific incidents notwithstanding, Scandinavia retains a low crime rate.

The level of violent crime in the countries placed in this tier (2) is higher, as they have less totalitarian control, but it is still relatively low. Also, the establishment of individual constitutional rights allows individuals with primary psychopathic tendencies (lack of conscience, empathy, and lack of shame for being sanctioned by their group) to exploit the system, giving them more room to operate (as with Breivik). As group diversity expands with immigration and total integration-assimilation is not achieved, or no longer held out to be of paramount importance, problems stemming from lack of consensus of values among groups increase, as does violent crime. In fact, lack of official support for assimilation can promote the violent activities of imported violent groups such as the Mafia, Asian triads, and Russian, Indo-Canadian, Iranian, and Caribbean gangs, as well as the formation and increasing violence of homegrown gangs, for example, aboriginal gangs in Canada or black gangs in the United States. As a result, a significant minority is involved on a regular basis in violent crime, but it usually does not significantly impinge upon the larger community. Fear of violent crime is thus not a major motivating force.

Countries in the third tier are characterized by right-wing, individualistic democracy, wherein spiritual salvation and success or failure are largely attributed to the individual and protected by a strong constitution of individual rights. The result is a society of winners and losers, most of whom are basically law-abiding. If they are successful, fundamentally religious in the tradition of the society (e.g., Christian in the United States), or connected to the political process, they subscribe to the overall view of their society. But if they perceive themselves as outgroup members with personal responsibility to take care of their primary subgroup, they never achieve the attachment to a larger societal ideal of unity of purpose and existence.

Thus, not only do primary psychopaths have even more room to operate, but there are more secondary psychopaths (sociopaths), individuals who have been traumatized by their personal developmental experiences, who (like Harlow's monkeys and Romanian orphans) suffer from inadequate empathy, muted central nervous system arousal and consequent emotional arousal to stress, and, ultimately, arrested moral development. They, in turn, will recruit others to a predatory lifestyle rather than subscribing to a universal moral and behavioral code, a code that has always been perceived as partitioned (i.e., applicable only when dealing with people like themselves). Predation on the haves for a significant portion of the have-nots is the ongoing state of affairs and waxes and wanes only with factors such as the economy, age and other demographics, and the perception of external threat (e.g., war or foreign invasion), a factor that tends to reduce animosities among internal groups. In a series of famous field experiments, Sherif demonstrated that groups competing for scarce resources will engage in conflict unless a superordinate goal forces them to cooperate and overcome perceived group differences (Sherif et al., 1961).

Such factors, of course, are added to those already operating in tier-3 countries and also experienced in tier-2 countries. But with increasing inequality and disunion, a significant portion of the population, marginalized groups, and those of personal predilection toward crime, who have much more opportunity to escape detection, prey on the public both on the street and in the boardroom. The United States is the prime example, with the United Kingdom and Canada approaching it, as right-wing, individualistic philosophies begin to penetrate their political and economic fabric. Fear of crime (of the "Other," i.e., those who are impugned for not sharing one's values) is a major motive guiding many lifestyle, political, and economic decisions in tier-3 countries.

On October 30, 2018, a lengthy report in the *Montreal Gazette* revealed the extent that organized crime had penetrated Canada, much in the manner that it has beset the United States for many decades. It revealed a conversation that had been overheard on a police wiretap. The speakers were Gregory Woolley, 46, a former Haitian street-gang member who had risen to become an associate of the Hell's Angels, and two alleged Mafia leaders, Leonardo Rizzuto, 49, and Stefano Sollecito, 51. They were meeting in the Little Italy offices of lawyer Loris Cavaliere, where Rizzuto worked as a lawyer. Discussed were problematic drug dealers, tax on using territories for dealing, and other matters. However, when Rizzuto was brought to trial, he was acquitted because the judge ruled that the wiretap evidence, though legally obtained, violated lawyer-client privilege as it eavesdropped on a lawyer's office (Cherry, 2018). Thus, in a democracy, in contrast to places like Saudi Arabia and North Korea, gangsters can invoke constitutional rights that allow them to live in a universe parallel to that of normative, law-abiding society.

The fourth tier is occupied by countries in devolution (wherein superordinate, inclusive control systems have been disrupted or have disintegrated) or by those struggling to cope during postcolonial independence (wherein the force and clear prescriptions of imposed regimes have been removed, often with scant preparation, leaving a consensus vacuum). With the removal of superordinate conceptual primary identification (e.g., we are all Americans, Christians, Muslims, British Empire citizens) and the loss of the central government's ability to impose its will, the human tendency is to grasp, often nostalgically, at historic, geographic, ethnic, and ultimately genealogical (tribal) units of identification (see, for example, *Blood and Longing*, by Michael Ignatieff, 1993). People are no longer, for example, Soviet citizens, communists equal under the law, but Ukrainians, Romanians, Germans, and Georgians. Age-old distinctions, religious and tribal, and grievances, rather than similarities, are trumpeted and become the basis of identification, governance, love, and hatred. Another prime example is the former Yugoslavia that disintegrated into Bosnia, Croatia, and "remnant" Yugoslavia and then further into Kosovo with Serbs, Croats, and Muslims forming warring factions to slaughter those with whom they had previously lived in peace as neighbors. These combatants were not bush-dwelling, uneducated tribal warriors but worldly, PhD-holding, BMW-driving sophisticates of the highest order.

The Bosnian War put the lie to the belief that education would serve as a prophylactic for mass murder (of course, education had not served the Nazi leadership in that way either). On March 24, 2016, Radovan Karadzic, former head of the Bosnian Serb government, was convicted of genocide in the Srebrenica Massacre (which aimed to kill every able-bodied Bosnian Muslim male) and of war crimes and crimes against humanity. He was sentenced to 40 years in prison. Karadzic was a psychiatrist and the author of several books of poetry, yet still he committed crimes more horrendous than another fictitious psychiatrist, Hannibal Lecter, famously portrayed in *The Silence of the Lambs* and other novels and films in that series. Karadzic acted "in the service" of ethnic cleansing and ridding his country of other ethnic and religious groups—tribalism at its most brutal.

Opportunities abound for profiteers of all stripes—religious, commercial, and ethnic—to take advantage of the situation in tier-4 countries, to take control of business, land, and people's hearts. And so, in the absence of effective central control, of police, and, often, of even the army, demagogues can have maximum free rein. These demagogues include messiahs, chiefs, warlords, and gangsters—some idealistic but others narcissistic and psychopathic. Standards of behavior are made up as one goes along, and the criterion of success is recruiting followers, who, in a state of maximum ambiguity and, among the adolescent young, suggestibility, are at least tempted and sometimes even eager to belong to something clear, powerful, and protective. (Recall my own disappointment in my dad when he rejected my attempt to regard the former German sailor as a member of an outgroup.)

In these circumstances, citizens become neo-Nazi skinheads or Islamist extremists, joining groups such as **ISIL** (the Islamic State in Iraq and the Levant) and commanding resources—whether wealth

(US currency, gold, or diamonds), territory, a large following, control of the media, or military firepower (including Kalashnikovs or even rocket launchers and tanks). Unless control is established, a majority of the populace may become engaged in activities that would previously be defined as seriously criminal or violently aggressive behaviors but are now lauded and even promoted on YouTube. Consider, for example, the beheadings of US and Western European hostages by ISIL (ISIS).

The fifth tier is occupied by countries characterized by the chaos of civil strife, once hostilities have broken out, or even total war. Under those extreme conditions of ambiguity and fear, few individuals or groups can remain neutral or outside the influence of the warring parties, and so the majority become actively involved or complicit in behavior that would under peaceful circumstances be perceived as criminal, just to survive. The opportunity arises then for demagogues (leaders promoting hatred of the Other) to identify the enemy or out-group and to give the sector of the populace within their control only two options: to engage in the conflict or to be regarded as part of the enemy. Under conditions in which societal consensus no longer exists, common fate (we are all in this together) must be established within the group, so an incident must be exploited or concocted or an historic grievance brought to the fore, and a method for promoting conflict must be developed, one that exploits the personal predilections of individuals who are willing and able to carry out the aggression and, through group processes, to recruit others to the task.

As Dutton et al. (2005) described, Rwanda's colonial rulers, the Belgians, had favored the minority Tutsis in terms of education and jobs and most other benefits. In conditions similar to those delineated previously, the situation after Rwanda achieved independence in the 1960s had deteriorated into civil war by the 1990s, until all unifying influences and superordinate categories (religious or political) had been eliminated and, for the two largest groups, you were either Hutu, the majority, or Tutsi, the largest minority. The situation was characterized as a struggle for survival, one against the other, with the Hutus having previously been mistreated in favor of the Tutsis. The instigating event of the Rwandan genocide of 1994 was the killing of the Hutu leader when a rocket downed the aircraft he was traveling in. A great deal of fear had already been generated by the activities of the Tutsi rebels in the north, so the situation was presented over state radio as kill or be killed. The killing of Tutsi and politically moderate Hutu began. Although many of the Hutu militia were equipped with firearms, much of the killing involved very intimate interaction and personal involvement in killing. Machetes were used, and many killings were preceded by mutilation and even the killing of children first in front of the parents before they were killed.

Although such incidents may not have been in the majority, they probably occurred because inverted norms (i.e., violent aggression as the norm) and the exhortations by authority figures to kill as many "enemies" as possible brought to the fore individuals who operate in all countries, regardless of what tier these countries have been assigned. Perhaps some act as dictators in tier-1 countries or merely as minor deviants, sex offenders, or killers, but under the severe constraints of the state, they have very little opportunity to make a major impact (unless they work for the state, e.g., in Argentina or Iraq as torturers). In the chaos of the tier-5 country, however, they break no norm or law but, by leading the carnage, actually set the standard of success or excellence through achieving a high body count. Fed initially by their need for excitement as psychopaths, uninhibited by conscience, and perhaps buttressed by any personal fantasy or grievance they could recall or conjure up, they killed many and were rewarded with the terror, pain expressed, bloodletting, and taking of lives that their horrid efforts produced.

But given their rapid central nervous system inhibition, they would not be efficient serial mass murderers. Perhaps, after only a couple of days, it became too easy, as others pitched in—first the secondary psychopaths, deadened emotionally and morally by personal trauma, and finally the dissocial psychopaths (temporary killers, like those in the Japanese army in World War II). According to Robert Hare, those temporarily psychopathic types are psychologically normal individuals recruited, I believe, to socially pathological actions by a combination of obedience to authority and conformity processes; they are motivated by following the behavior that their peers are engaging in. That situation creates a compelling social reality even though, in actuality, outside of the social pressure situation, it is one that may be against their personal beliefs. Asch (1951) found some individuals actually changed their beliefs, but most presumed changing their beliefs was a matter of optics. Milgram (1963) demonstrated that a majority of subjects would aggress dangerously, even in a laboratory, if exhorted by a minor authority figure—the research assistant. In the mass media, Hutus heard their leaders exhorting them to extinguish all Tutsis and that social reality was couched in terms that stressed Tutsis would otherwise soon be doing the same to them and their children if they were not eliminated.

Ironically it was most likely the tertiary majority, the so-called normal killers, or dissocial psychopaths, in thrall to the mesmerizing passion of the slaughter, who eventually carried out the bulk of the killings. Although each militia unit would have "benefited" from a "leader" who pushed the boundaries, sadism, torturing, and mutilation are not very efficient activities in the exclusive pursuit of the more ambitious goal of maximum body count and genocide. That person's role would have been to serve as the expander of boundaries, whose increasingly horrific atrocities, engaged in to ward off the encroaching boredom of mere killing, disinhibited others' own killing activity and made their efforts seem more circumscribed, less self-indulgent, and, though equally homicidal, more palatable by comparison. Eventually, Tutsis, by definition and by the habituation of mass killing, came to be defined as appropriate targets for slaughter, although many variations and inconsistencies occurred. These inconsistencies are not peculiar to genocide. During the My Lai incident in Vietnam (Dutton et al., 2005), US troops methodically machine-gunned women, old men, and children, but when the soldiers stopped for lunch, they offered some of the surviving kids sticks of gum. Similar incidents probably occurred when the early French and English settlers, along with Mi'kmaq imported from Nova Scotia, were eliminating the indigenous Beothuks of Newfoundland.

It is interesting to note that Marnie Rice (1997, 1999) has also proposed psychopathy not to be a mental disorder but rather a failsafe personality type devised by nature to allow survival of the species in extreme situations (perhaps, as described in the sociobiological example, by not sounding the alarm at the approach of the enemy so as to survive at any cost). But the psychopath of any type causes havoc in most societies (tiers 1 through 4).

Figure 8.1. Pyramid of Crime: A representation of the proportion of the population in countries characterized by different types of sociopolitical
ecology who commit serious violent crime

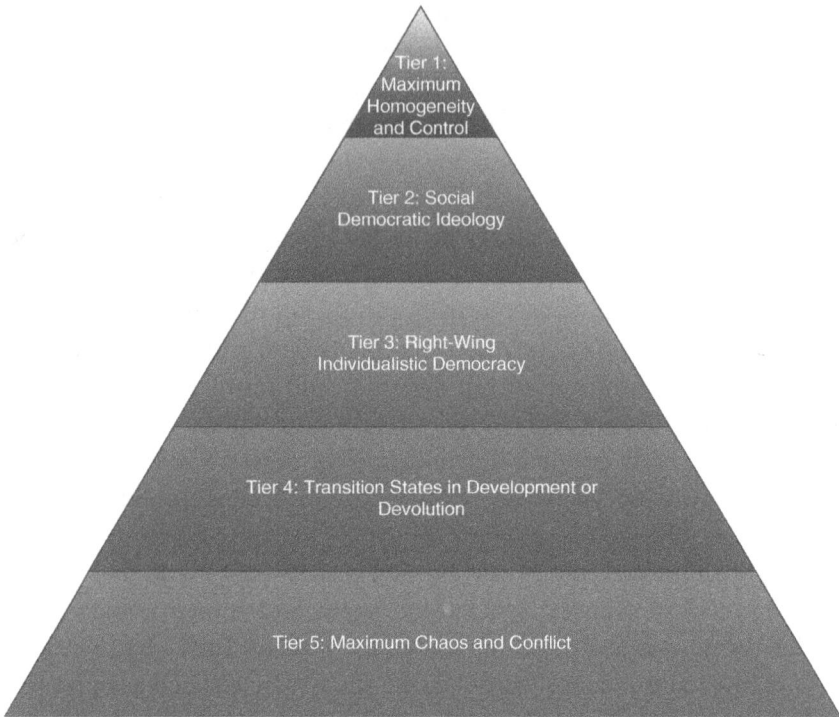

Note: The portion of the population involved in crime is represented within the
pyramid. The portion not involved in crime is outside the pyramid but within an
imaginary rectangle representing the whole population.

PYRAMID OF CRIME AND CHAOS

TIER 1: MAXIMUM HOMOGENEITY AND CONTROL

There is religious, ethnic, and/or ideological homogeneity and a dictatorial or tyrannical political system. Crime usually originates because
of factors that are *idiosyncratic*—because of mental deficiency, psychosis, psychopathy, or situations inducing crimes of passion—or they are
categorically outgroup directed (e.g., directed at Gypsy, Arab, or African
targets not considered "real" citizens).

TIER 2: SOCIAL DEMOCRATIC IDEOLOGY
Enshrining individual rights allows the exploitation of society by some deviant individuals but also most basic needs are taken care of, so many potential criminals are siphoned off by the welfare system. There is less likelihood of differing categories of predatory groups as there are no official outgroups.

TIER 3: RIGHT-WING INDIVIDUALISTIC DEMOCRACY
Societies with a combination of strong individual rights, and the assessment of winners and losers result in those with psychopathic tendencies expanding their influence in street-gang and white-collar crime, recruiting losers, and using to their advantage entrenched individual rights, which constrain the powers of police and government. A significant portion of the population engages in crime. A prime theory accounting for this situation is Merton's strain theory, which emerged during the Depression to account for gang, street, and white-collar crime in the 1930s. Central consensus is tenuous in these societies but can be buttressed by a country's political constitution if it is strong and there is minimal immigration, or, if immigration is significant, by the successful assimilation of newcomers. Another tactic to increase consensus is to emphasize threats from outsiders (e.g., from other states or ideologies). A prominent example is the response by the United States to the 9/11 terrorist strikes and foreign terrorists in general, which seems to be effective as crime has dropped in the ensuing years.

TIER 4: TRANSITION STATES IN DEVELOPMENT OR DEVOLUTION
Such states are developing or devolving. When devolving, they experience a loss of superordinate consensus (e.g., constitution, ideology, dictatorship, elite, religion). The general responses are a reversion to primary group membership—e.g., ethnic, tribal, or religious—and the rise of a struggle for control. Yugoslavia, Ukraine, Kazakhstan, and Romania are examples. There is little public order, ambiguity is high, and there are great opportunities for demagogues to marshal their primary group or unite various groups under a cause such as the exploitation of historical injustice. Corruption among police and politicians is widespread, and, in some respects, underworld elements have a great deal of influence. The gulf between the "haves" and the "have-nots" becomes huge.

TIER 5: MAXIMUM CHAOS AND CONFLICT

These societies are experiencing civil strife; tribal, religious, or socio-economic conflict; or civil war. The opportunity for rational reflection and rational decision making based on idealistic principles does not exist. Such societies are characterized by maximum moral and legal ambiguity and violence. The only relative safety net is decisive group affiliation: you are either part of the ingroup or part of the outgroup. Be aware that if you are anything other than part of the ingroup—that makes you a target. Even neutrality is not acceptable unless protected by extreme geographical isolation. I once visited the melancholy ghost town of a small community on the Kola peninsula in the Russian Arctic. It was a stunningly beautiful spot where a major salmon river flowed into the sea. But I discovered a chilling detail. The well-preserved log cabins were peppered with holes from machine-gun fire. The residents had lived for several years through the Russian Revolution oblivious in their splendid isolation. One day, an expedition of Bolshevik military arrived. The residents greeted the party according to tradition, "May God bless the Tsar!" Wrong salutation. They were immediately gunned down. Thus few individuals (those on the margins in small triangles outside the pyramid) remain unaffected. Psychopaths and demagogues have maximum free reign as high fear, ambiguity, and the need for affiliation maximize conformity recruitment processes to one cause or another.

As this outline demonstrates, tier 5 is the opposite of tier 1. In tier-5 countries, there is near-total fragmentation into situationally defined, primary membership groups: families, clans, and tribes. No super-ordinate unifying principle exists, no sentiment such as "We are all Canadians, Americans, Germans, Rwandans, Christians, Muslims, Iraqis." Ironically, colonial governments can provide that unifying principle within their empires; historically, for instance, the Roman, British, Russian, Portuguese, and American versions unified when they could impose their will or win the hearts and minds of the people. Very often, the easiest route away from the chaos of tier 5 is unlimited civil strife and even war and then the imposition of dictatorship, leading back to the oppressive security of tier 1. Some recent surveys suggest that majorities in many South American countries now prefer reverting to a dictatorship rather than continual economic strife. Hence, Vladimir Putin is popular as a strong man, just short of a totalitarian dictator, in Russia.

Ironically, tier-1 governments can marshal genocide against a minority (Jews, Kurds, Armenians) most effectively, and tier-4 circumstances can lead to those experienced by tier-5 countries, as disintegration produces maximum fear and so opportunities for splinter groups. Societies categorized as tier 2 and 3 are the least likely to produce genocide, as they are based on the incorporation of outgroups either at the group or individual levels of rights and are constantly, though perhaps never totally efficiently, adjusting.

IN SUMMARY

The structure of society determines what percentage of people engage in severe criminal behavior, ranging from a tiny minority in tier-1 societies to the vast majority in tier-5 societies.

Tyranny usually dominates tier-1 societies, whereas social democratic government provides significant protective factors to keep criminality at a minimum in tier-2 societies. The introduction of unbridled competition and individualism promotes more crime in tier-3 societies. Tier 4 heralds the devolution of society as civilization recedes into more basic identity groups and, with weaker central government, more violence is prevalent. In tier-5 societies, civilization has evaporated and to survive people must choose a side, a group to gain protection, or be considered a member of the other side and be killed.

CHAPTER NINE

VIOLENCE IN AND OF THE FAMILY

This chapter examines the related phenomena of partner or spousal abuse and child abuse.

In this chapter, there is a discussion of the traditional theories identifying men in patriarchal society as the perpetrators. However, some research over the last thirty years suggests that once the data get beyond incident reports to police and hospitals, victims of domestic violence and aggression may often be male as well as female. It also suggests that homosexual relationships may have more highly elevated levels of domestic violence than do heterosexual relationships. The causes of domestic violence—individual, cultural, and societal—are evaluated, and explanations based on social learning paradigms as well as individual predilections are considered.

Child abuse is covered historically as well as analyzed within the same framework of individual idiosyncrasy, cultural values, and the transmission of accepted punitive regimes dealing with children across generations.

THE FAMILY: CRADLE OF LOVE, ABUSE, AND PERVERSION

A close friend of mine once told me an incredibly sad story. She had been working very hard at two jobs to support her husband and his two children from a previous marriage. To make it almost unbearable, she had contracted mononucleosis, which saps one's strength. Still just recovering, she arrived home absolutely exhausted and told her spouse that she had to lie down for a few moments before she could cook dinner, which she did daily. Her spouse, who was unemployed, became infuriated, shouting that he had been trapped all day with two demanding kids and was himself tired and at the end of his rope. He had been drinking.

She lay down on the bed. Moments later, she felt something land on top of her, and opened her eyes to see her spouse straddling her, screaming obscenities and brandishing a butcher knife. She pushed him off averting a potentially lethal blow, but as he fell, he stabbed her in the thigh. Bleeding profusely, she called 911 and, gratifyingly, two officers appeared in only a few minutes as she kept her spouse at bay behind the kitchen door she held shut with her shoulder, the children screaming at the tops of their lungs. When she opened the door, her partner, still holding the bloody knife claimed he was only defending himself. The police arrested my friend, took her to the station, booked her, and put her in jail without taking her to a hospital or administering first aid. Hours later, she had to make her own way to the hospital where she received medical attention.

That blood-chilling story is true except for one small detail, gender: my friend is a man, and the assaultive spouse was his wife. It is hard to believe that authorities would respond in such a callous way to someone who was almost murdered, but the reality is that many constituencies in North America now have legislation in place that gives the police no choice when called to the scene of a "domestic." Without questioning anyone, police must arrest the male involved in the dispute and put him in jail.

"But," you may object, "you are giving an example that is so unusual as to be ludicrous, and the legislation was put into place so no discretion would be required by the police in the 99 percent of cases where the assaulter is male and the victim female." Let us examine that premise.

It is ironic that the place spouses may be most at risk for assault or even homicide is in the matrimonial home. It is the one place that such disparate testaments as the Bible and the *Ladies Home Journal* would

192 · Crime and Criminality

both identify as symbolic of peace and security. And sociobiology, the discipline that explains the existence of social phenomena in terms of their evolutionary survival value, should argue that the home is where the person most important in perpetuating one's gene pool—one's spouse—should be safest from threat. Why then would some of us assault and even kill our spouses?

Dutton (2006), in his paradigm-altering book *Rethinking Domestic Violence*, argues that the existence of such violence is a weak point of sociobiology since domestic homicide is counterintuitive to its premises. For instance, in a study of domestic homicides in Detroit, the sociobiologists Daly and Wilson (1988) found jealousy to be a motive in only 13.6 percent (25/183) of the murders committed by men, whereas 31 percent (9/29) of the murders committed by women were jealousy driven; but, in a Canadian study, 24 percent (195/812) of male-perpetrated homicides and only 7.6 percent (19/248) of female-perpetrated homicides were jealousy driven. Since the US cases involved African Americans and the Canadian ones involved white couples, Dutton argues cultural differences outweigh sociobiological explanations. Buss (2013) acknowledges that some human universals may have spread through cultural transmission but argues that jealousy, especially sexual jealousy, is a basic human emotion whose adaptive value promoted its perpetuation and similar universality. That is, sexual jealousy defends initially against infidelity by one's mate through intimidation and even violence; second, it defends against mate poaching (i.e., by threatening the interloper who may want to have sex with your spouse); and third, it also defends against mate defection, namely the loss of one's mate by their departure. The response is restriction—of interaction with family, friends, and travel alone, for example—and isolation may be the consequence. The goal is to monopolize the mate's reproductive ability and to make certain the paternity (fatherhood) of any children in the case of men.

One could argue that one cannot compare the Canadian and American studies in that way, because in Detroit not only did 18 women kill males but another 11 women killed females. Also, the jealousy-driven rate for female-perpetrated homicides in Detroit is four times that of the Canadian rate while males in Detroit were found to kill for reasons of jealousy at about half the rate of the males in Canada (Dutton, 2006). Walsh, Ellis, and Davis (2007) contend that because male mortality is so high among young African American males, they are in short supply, so females are very competitive with one another, which would account for females killing both males and females out of sexual jealousy at a high rate—even though male insecurities over paternity would seem to give them a stronger motive for violence occasioned by sexual jealousy.

Dutton outlines a long history of wife beating that became somewhat tempered in England, in the late middle ages, by the "rule of thumb," which allowed the husband, should he have to discipline his wife, to use a stick no thicker than his thumb. Nevertheless, perhaps wife beating was the norm in France and England as village festivals were mounted in which men were mocked and abused by painted revelers if they were beaten by their wives, but no such admonition was mounted against wife beaters. However, in the seventeenth century, Puritans in both England and the United States condemned wife assault.

And so too, eventually, did the British Parliament in response to the philosopher John Stuart Mill's famous 1869 essay, "The Subjection of Women." In that treatise, he attributed abuse to the savage nature of men, a tendency kept in check in public (again, community standards of tolerance come into play) but unleashed in the home where women, no longer protected by societal disapprobation of male brutality, were too often regarded merely as possessions. Of course, most of the abuse was attributed to men of lower class, the presumption being that better bred men would not resort to such primitive behavior. Buss would disagree, arguing it would be as frequent among the upper classes where an important goal, a blood heir to a fortune, was at stake. Mill's work sparked a report to parliament, and by the end of the century, all violence against women, including that regulated by the rule of thumb, was rendered illegal, although Dutton suggests it was merely overlooked by the authorities unless murder was committed. In early 1900, President Theodore Roosevelt, an extremely progressive intellectual, suggested whipping posts for assaultive husbands (Brinkley, 2010). Progressive means different things in different eras, apparently.

When patriarchal norms preside, the male is required to be head of the household and the source of all strength and protection for the family. Thus, he would be shirking his duty and seen as a failure were he to report to authorities that he had lost control and that his spouse was physically assaulting him. And so few did report. Thus, the conception of the problem of domestic violence as the assault of women victimized by men was eminently reasonable, and, as Dutton points out, the studies that confirmed that belief derived their statistics from women's shelters that were created to provide sanctuary for abused women and their children or from police intervention or arrest reports that documented calls coming from assaulted women. That was the situation until studies by Richard Gelles and Murray Straus of the University of New Hampshire in the late 1970s through the 1980s contradicted those beliefs. Their research culminated in a monumental work that studied 8,142 families, titled *Physical Violence in American Families* (Gelles & Straus, 1992). Their approach was to interview men and women separately and ask them whether they had engaged in physical assault of their partners (intimate partner violence or IPV); then assaults were ranked using a ten-point scale of severity.

As Dutton has shown, surveys of national crime and violence against women and measuring the frequency of police calls have obtained ratios of male assault of women versus women of men ranging from 1.4:1 to 13:1; assaultive men clearly predominate. On the other hand, Straus and Gelles's studies using the **Conflict Tactics Scale**, an instrument that measures conflict ranging from rational discussion to slapping with an open hand to assault with deadly weapons, found that the perpetrators, interviewed alone and admitting their own involvement as aggressors, revealed a rate of assault, severity of assault, and bodily injury that is virtually identical for men and women.

Those results, replicated in many studies in the United States, as well as by Dutton and Kennedy in Alberta (Dutton, 2006), were met with shock, disbelief, and even threats of violence against the researchers from audience members—not surprisingly, but perhaps ironically, from militantly feminist women (Murray Straus, personal communication). Those skeptics claim that patriarchy—the control of women by men in society—is the cause of violence against women. Findings by various researchers (Campbell, 1985, 1992; Smith, 1990; Sorenson & Telles, 1991) agree with Dutton that although patriarchy might be a main cause of violence against women in some societies, especially in fundamentalist religious societies, for example, in Nigeria (Abayomi & Kolawole, 2013) and in Nepal (Sapkota, 2011), such attitudes are no longer dominant within North America and Western Europe.

Those same critics of a more gender-balanced view of domestic violence point to the **misogynistic** motivation of the murder of 13 women at the École Polytechnique in Montreal in 1990 as an example of "violence against women" sustained by patriarchal society. But, as I pointed out in *Canadian Psychology* (Boyanowsky, 1991), the killer, Marc Lépine, was lashing out at a society that accepted women into engineering school on merit; he wanted preference for males as had existed traditionally. Lépine, with his successive failures, felt himself disappearing. So he, who was out of step with the way society was evolving, chose to lash out against women who had succeeded where he had failed in the emerging meritocracy, that is, in a society wherein status obtained was based on achievement, not gender. In other words, the motivation for Lépine's horrendous crime underlines his pathology, his deviation from the norms of Canadian society. Had patriarchy *sustained* his violence, he would have been perceived as a champion rather than a pathologically deviant individual.

This movement toward a more egalitarian society bodes well for the reduction of domestic violence. For instance, Coleman and Straus (1986), who studied married couples' power-sharing arrangements in terms of who had the "final say" on family decisions, report that the couples they classified as "equalitarian" had the lowest level of conflict, the highest level of consensus, and the least "minor violence." Only 11 percent of egalitarian (equalitarian) couples experienced violence. By contrast, they report that 27 percent of "male-dominant" couples and 31 percent of "female-dominant" couples experienced violence. Couples in "divided power" relationships also experienced less violence than either female- or male-dominant couples.

Furthermore, early research on lesbian relationships indicated that they were twice as assaultive as male homosexual relationships (Bologna, Waterman, & Dawson, 1987, cited by Dutton, 2006, p. 124) and significantly more assaultive than heterosexual relationships (Lie, Schilit, Bush, Montague, & Reyes, 1991). Recent studies suggest that violence occurs at similar rates in female and male same-sex relationships (Laskey, Bates, & Taylor, 2019), is related to "internalized sexual minority stressors" (Carvalho, Lewis, Derlega, Winstead, & Viggiano, 2011), and is underreported (Sylaska & Edwards, 2015). Thus, violence exists within relationships of all sorts, irrespective of gender and sexuality. However, for North America at least, the good news may be that with egalitarian relationships increasing, spousal assault is declining. There are, nevertheless, too many men who assault their spouses, and surprisingly, a similar number of women who assault their partners. A study of 55,000 US military families found that among those that experienced violence at all, 63 percent of intimate partner violence was mutual (Neidig, 1993). Why would bilateral violence be so common?

For one, Moffitt, Caspi, Rutter, and Silva (2001) found that negative emotionality and attachment factors predicted assault in the birth cohort they studied. Again, the theorizing of Bowlby and Harlow (chapter 4) regarding attachment or lack thereof clearly relates to the issue of which families become violent families. And even more fascinatingly, individuals with a disposition toward violence could be identified in early teen years and were attracted to partners who were similarly violently disposed. Dutton (2006) believes Gunderson's idea of borderline personality organization is relevant here. Borderline personality organization is a dimensional, less serious form of the borderline personality type that goes through extreme personality shifts from intense love and affection to implacable rage. Such a person has an unstable sense of self and, as a result, experiences intense, unstable relationships characterized by anger, impulsivity, and major shifts in perception of the partner, which in all probability are the precursors to aggressive behavior.

SO WHERE DOES IT COME FROM?

Straus et al. in their 1975 national survey found that husbands whose parents had been violent toward each other were three times as likely to have hit their wives. Daughters of violent parents had a much higher rate of hitting their partners (26.7 percent) than daughters of nonviolent parents (8.9 percent), just as Bandura's vicarious learning paradigm would have predicted. Sons of the most violent parents had wife-beating rates 10 times that of sons of nonviolent parents, and daughters had six times the rate of assault. The lesson these children learned is that those who love you hit you, that hitting family members is acceptable, and that hitting is permissible when things don't work. And so on, to the next generation and the next. Temple, Shorey, Tortolero, Wolfe, and Stuart (2013) found that teenaged dating violence for girls was related to viewing both mother against father violence and father against mother violence, but oddly for boys it was related only to viewing their mothers engaging in violence against their fathers. Perhaps for violence to be imbued in girls, their early life had to be rife with it, requiring two violent role models; for boys, dating violence might be attributable to resentment toward violent women.

Many effects of witnessing parent-parent violence have been noted, including diminished social competence and magnified behavioral problems—with boys experiencing more severe consequences than girls (Jaffe, Wolfe, Wilson, & Zak, 1986). In fact, the research revealed that witnessing the violence was as significant in producing future violent assault against partners as suffering abuse at the hands of a parent. That supports Douglas and Straus's (2006) finding from 9,549 university students in 19 countries that those who had been corporally punished were much more likely to engage in aggression during dating. More females assaulted their dating partners than did males, although more male students than female students inflicted an injury on a dating partner, leading Douglas and Straus to conclude that "current policy ignores the fact that violence is an interactive event" (p. 313).

Bandura (1976) would concur that aggression is learned behavior; for these students who had experienced corporal punishment, physical violence had proved to be a successful strategy. When I polled classes on whether corporal punishment had ever been used against them about half put up their hands. And when I asked whether they would use it against their own children, many agreed: "It worked for me" was the consensual reply.

In a recent presentation to a Senate committee of the Canadian parliament, Dutton (2016) displayed a table of several large-scale studies comparing the violence rates of men and women in both cohabiting and married relationships. If there was violence at all, it was mutual (bilateral) in 38 percent to almost 60 percent of the physically aggressive couples. Male violence predominated in 14.3 percent to 21.6 percent of the couples, and, in a higher percentage of couples, female violence predominated: 25.6 to 35.6 percent. Altogether, those studies had compiled data from over 22,000 subjects, so sample error was obviously not a problem.

How then to explain the focus on women as the victims of intimate partner violence? In part, it is about the number of reported incidents.

Table 9.1. Comparing Past-Year Incidence of Reported IPV by Men and Women in Relationships

	% of IPV Reports	Male more severe[a]	Female more severe[b]	Bilateral
Stets & Straus, 1989 National FV Survey (n = 5,242) Married	15%	15.6%	35.6%	38.8%
Cohabitating	35%	14.3%	34.9%	45.2%
Whitaker et al., 2007 National Longitudinal Study on Adolescent (18–28) Health (n = 11,370)	24%	14.8%	35.6%	49.7%
Williams & Frieze, 2005 National Comorbidity Study (n = 3,519)	18.4%	21.6%	28.7%	49%
Caetano et al., 2008 National Survey of Couples (n = 1,635)	13%	14.6%	25.6%	59.7%
Morse, 1995 National Youth Survey 1992 (n = 1,340)	32.4%	16%	30%	47.4%

Source: Don Dutton (2016). Used with permission.

[a] Males use more severe acts of violence (e.g., male minor, female none; male severe, female none; male severe, female minor)
[b] Females use more severe acts of violence (e.g., female minor, male none; female severe, male none; female severe, male minor)

For example, in 2016, 79 percent of the 93,000 Canadians who reported intimate partner violence to the police were women (Burczycka, 2016). Nevertheless, the same study indicates that intimate partner violence against men was more likely to include major assault, weapons, and injuries. An even more significant finding is that men rarely report being abused to the police, even if that abuse is severe, and are much more dissatisfied with police responses to their reports (Lysova, Dim, & Dutton, 2019).

The conclusion of those studies is that domestic violence is not gender specific and not solely a product of a patriarchal society in North America. Rather, such studies suggest that domestic violence is engaged in by both genders and may be related to personality disturbance and the mutual attraction experienced by the perpetrators to similarly violent partners. Lysova et al. (2019) do point out that part of the reason victim studies and policy have focused on the victimhood of women is that women do often experience serious injuries and are the more frequent victims of homicide committed by their partners. What the new generation of research underlines, however, is that both genders are equally capable of violence and aggression. And, until recently, women have been more financially dependent on men, leaving them fewer options to deal with the situation.

IN SUMMARY

Throughout history, violence against wives and other partners in relationships was a serious issue, not even challenged until the eighteenth century and not widely condemned until the nineteenth century.

The study of domestic violence assumed from its inception that women were overwhelmingly the victims, and in fact sexual jealousy, according to evolutionary psychology, gives men a special impetus to control their mates and even to use aggression to defend paternity and to prevent infidelity, poaching by predators, and defection (leaving). Those suffering abandonment issues tend to be more likely to engage in violence to prevent the departure of their mates, which may explain the higher rate of intimate partner homicide among some African American women for whom there are fewer available potential mates (due to the relatively higher mortality rate of African American men).

Police and hospital records confirmed that women were many times more likely to be the victims, and policies to eliminate violence against women were developed to achieve that outcome, including the automatic arrest of any male involved regardless of who called the police.

Not until the national surveys by Gelles and Straus using the Conflict Tactics Scale was it suggested that women engaged in at least as much violence as men and at a comparably severe level (e.g., using weapons).

While those studies remain controversial in some circles, they do challenge the gender paradigm, namely, that men are brutal and women are the sole victims in domestic disputes, suggesting there may be other explanations for engaging in violence in relationships. Those include having viewed it in one's family as a child, finding it acceptable, suffering from borderline personality disorder, and suffering severe abandonment anxiety and other mental illnesses. As it turns out, some research suggests that violent boys and girls seek each other out in their teen years.

The encouraging sign is that domestic violence against intimate partners has diminished in Canada and the United States (Kaukinen & Powers, 2015; Ibrahim, 2019).

SUFFER THE CHILDREN: VIOLENCE AGAINST OFFSPRING

In 1874, a health nurse on her rounds in New York City was horrified to find a little girl chained to her bed, naked, covered in bruises and cuts, and covered in her own filth (Markel, 2009). When she informed the police and district attorney, it was soon discovered that the authorities had no jurisdiction over how parents treated their children. Then someone had a brilliant idea: Darwin (1871/1981) had recently published his sensational book *The Descent of Man*, which argued humans were descended from apes. So concerned New Yorkers went to the American Society for Prevention of Cruelty to Animals and made the case that the girl, Mary Ellen, was an animal, which allowed the society's officers to apprehend her (in order to protect her).

We like to believe that the world progresses inexorably toward a more just state, but in 1989, Joel Steinberg was convicted of murdering his child by forcing her to drink gallons of water until her kidneys gave out. And his wife did nothing to protect her daughter. How could that be? In fact, Steinberg was well educated, a lawyer, and like Mary Ellen's guardians, living in New York City (Tumulty & Drogin, 1989).

It was not until John Caffey (1972), a physician who had seen many hematomas and other injuries in children, began to wonder whether there was a common disease or injury-prone environment producing them, that the specter of parents rose as perpetrators in the consciousness of society, culminating in the Child Abuse Prevention and Treatment Act of 1974. For a while, the solution was to remove the child for its own protection without probing the cause. In 1959, many authorities decided to gather detailed medical histories, and from those records and his own survey, conducted in the 1960s, C. H. Kempe coined the phrase "the battered child syndrome" (Kempe, Silverman, Steele, Droegemueller, & Silver, 1962). He argued it comprised two types: commission of physical injury and pain, which required charges being laid and/or treatment of parents, and neglect, requiring treatment and care for the child.

Why does it occur to children (usually designated as under 18 years of age)? As discussed above, it often involves the acceptance and endorsement by parents of physical punishment as an appropriate measure, which is transferred from the spouse to the children.

Helfer has suggested three interesting discrete concepts and related factors (Helfer & Kempe, 1976):

1) *Potential for abuse.* Parents' potential for abuse begins with how they were raised, with those raised in violent homes having more potential. Next, this potential is intensified by the reluctance of parents to seek out societal resources whether because they are not aware of what is available or are too ashamed to admit they need help. Also important is the relationship between the parents. Conflict can make the children pawns in the ensuing war. Finally, and perhaps most important, is how those parents see the child.

2) *The special child.* If the child is disfigured or mentally handicapped or somehow different from the other children in the family, he or she is more likely to be abused. A few years ago, while living nearby, I heard that social workers found a male child dressed in rags wandering the streets of Vancouver, British Columbia. He led the workers to a pleasant middle-class house in Kitsilano where they discovered a model family with two other children, well dressed and well behaved. The runaway boy, unlike the others, lived in the woodshed in the backyard where he was usually confined and fed scraps. No one in the family seemed to think anything was amiss. Thus, a norm can develop in a family wherein a child is relegated to a lesser status, sometimes one more akin to an animal than a human.

3) *Economic or emotional crises.* These trigger abuse and neglect. Some people, fearful for the survival of their marriages, try to salvage them by buying a house, getting a pet, or worst of all, having a child (all of which actually massively increases responsibility and stress). When these plans don't work out, they do not have the resources to cope. So too a crisis ensues when the economy plummets and stress permeates the household. "Special" children are especially at risk, as parents become preoccupied with the struggle for mere survival—and can lash out at the most vulnerable target available as an outlet for their distress, a form of displaced aggression.

Studies of the characteristics of abusing parents reveal two very simple causes. The first is a lack of warmth on the part of the parents who may be not only unable to show their feelings but also immature for their age (Kempe & Helfer, 1968). Second, as Gerald Patterson (1993) and his colleagues have discovered (chapter 7), there is very often a lack of basic knowledge of child rearing and what to expect of children at different ages. One heartrending example involves a child who was beaten to a pulp by a father for crying incessantly and another who was sat on a hot stove for soiling itself. Frequently, such parents have no idea what a two-year-old is capable and not capable of.

A LICENSE TO PROCREATE: A THOUGHT EXPERIMENT

A solution is needed given the cost of domestic child abuse to the child and to society as well, in the form of a cycle of violence that spans several generations (Widom, 1989). Other costs include the emergence of sadistic behavior among severely abused children (consider the example of the Romanian orphan who became a student at Simon Fraser University and was convicted of animal cruelty). Therefore, it is my strong contention that so much grief could be averted by not allowing people to procreate without a "reproduction license." We do not allow anyone to drive a car or aircraft, practice medicine or law, or own or shoot a firearm without that individual's demonstrating mental and skill-based competence. But the one act that has the gravest implications not only for individuals and their progeny but for society as well—procreation—we allow anyone to engage in, at will. And some unfit parents go on to abuse and neglect children, born and unborn, without any compunction on their part. That has to change. And with this change we would ameliorate so much of society's greatest heartache: what to do with the damaged, the dangerous, and the doomed children that can be the result of mindless child bearing. A prominent Canadian example is the young glue-sniffing woman who produced two brain-damaged children but refused contraception, abortion, or sterilization (Global Health and Human Rights Database, 1997). Do you agree or disagree that requiring a license to procreate could go a long way toward eliminating such vexing and heart-breaking cases?

IN SUMMARY

Children have been abused throughout history, especially when they were viewed as owned by their parents. As recently as 150 years ago, a child neglected and abused to the point of serious injury and death could not be taken away from its parents. Even now, when sensitive cultural issues come into play, social workers may have their hands tied. In British Columbia, the case of Matthew Vaudreuil, a five-year-old boy repeatedly abused by his mother and her companions and suffering from multiple fractures but not removed from his drug-addicted mother was asphyxiated by her to squelch his screaming (Gove, 1995). The child welfare agency was excoriated for its lack of action in the case, and the public outcry prompted a demand for the seizing of children at risk. The next day, 49 children were taken from their homes, all aboriginal (Native American), which created a political crisis and protests from aboriginal leaders. Perhaps education and training would succeed where draconian measures did not.

In the 1960s, medical practitioners coined the phrase child abuse (through active mistreatment or neglect) and began to study the factors leading to its occurrence.

Factors leading to child abuse include the child's being challenged mentally or physically, the child's being unwanted, and the parents being under severe social or economic stress. Most important is that many parents grew up in a society without the contact with children that traditional villages allowed, so they know nothing about what children are and are not capable of at different stages of development.

SEXUAL ASSAULT AND MURDER

For male assaulters, Dutton (2006) reports, the main contributing factor appears to be abusive and rejecting fathers and lack of warmth in the mothers. Gerdes's (2000) study of serial killers (individuals who have killed at least two or three people with a "cooling off period" separating the murders) builds on that notion, delineating an intricate web of parental rejection and physical and sexual abuse, although from first appearances, the families might appear "normal" or at least conventional. Very often, the "loner" turns inward and develops deviant fantasies that provide empowerment. Those fantasies, with repetition and eroticization, become the dominant interest in the teenager's life. For most killers studied, the amount of abuse and rejection discovered by the therapist or researcher is overwhelming.

A case in point is serial killer Henry Lee Lucas, whose mother raised him as a girl until the school objected, after which she subjected him to serious abuse (Levin & Fox, 1985). According to Lucas, his mother was the first of his many dozens, perhaps hundreds, of victims. The most common characteristic among assaulters is mediocrity—if not successive and debilitating failure in life and relationships—*coupled with psychopathy*. Sometimes psychopathy is primary (genetic), sometimes secondary (a product of extreme abuse, neglect, and rearing conditions comparable to those suffered by Harlow's monkeys or the Romanian orphans).

More puzzling are the handful of violent predators who are not only successful in life, and even in love, but also leaders in their field and without any obvious psychopathic personality. One of the most prominent is former Colonel Russell Williams who completed an economics degree at perhaps Canada's most prestigious university, the University of Toronto, and within 10 years of entering the Canadian Forces to become a pilot had shot to near the top as commander of Canada's largest military base. Apparently, Williams was happily married to an attractive professional who worked for a nongovernmental organization and who, with him, owned not only an expensive condominium but a charming cottage in eastern Ontario. Williams suddenly (it appears) embarked on a bizarre campaign of fetishistic, digitally recorded Peeping Tomism, of breaking and entering various houses, and of the theft of many undergarments of young girls and women— and the wearing of this underwear in meticulously arranged videos in which he starred. Within months, his obsession escalated to abduction and sexual assault of different kinds, including oral, vaginal, and anal rape, finally culminating in the murder of two victims.

Upon being caught because of an unusual tire tread noticed at a roadblock, he confessed to his crimes and showed contrition and concern for his wife. Although there was no obvious abuse in his background and he claimed to have begun his fetishistic pursuits— including cross-dressing—only in adulthood, experts consulted by journalist Timothy Appleby (2011) for his book *A New Kind of Monster* believe his tendencies must be partly genetic and were triggered in childhood, perhaps by his parents' divorce and his subsequent living arrangements with his mother. She was extremely attractive but both seductive (walking about scantily clad in front of her teenaged son) and cold and withdrawn. Apparently, sex games with other couples had predated the divorce, and perhaps a young Russell had been witness to those games. Psychiatrists speculate that he experienced Freud's oedipal complex, which resulted in lust for his mother combined with **malignant narcissism**, a condition not quite psychopathy but characterized by grandiosity, a sense of entitlement, interpersonal exploitation, poor empathy, arrogance, and ruthlessness. Someone diagnosed with a narcissistic personality disorder accepts her or his own sadistic tendencies without regret, hence Russell's taking photos of his victims propped up after their murder in close proximity to his erect penis.

In psychology, very often pathology is not a Dr. Jekyll–Mr. Hyde complete transformation but merely personal tendencies that go far beyond the normal range in their expression. Two things might have tipped the balance for Williams. The first was his mind-boggling rate of rising stardom; for instance, he advanced rapidly from a mere pilot in the air force to soon chauffeuring VIPs around in military aircraft, celebrities that ranged from the minister of defense to Queen Elizabeth of Britain. Those circumstances may have overfed his ego, and in reaction, he may have felt something very much like the instability that young athletes or rock stars experience when massive sudden success and multimillion dollar contracts come their way (consider the tribulations of pop star Justin Bieber or any number of NBA basketball rookies).

Second, that personal egocentric euphoria may have been further accelerated by the use of the arthritis drug prednisone, known to have, in a minority of people, a bizarre effect on their personalities so that they begin to believe they are practically immortal and experience a huge increase in their libidos, that is, their sexual appetites. On the other hand, the most common complaint among some patients on prednisone is a loss of sex drive.

Once again, the conclusion must be that, as Aichhorn suggested many years ago, there are latent qualities in certain individuals that life events, not necessarily traumatic, bring to the surface, leading to tragic criminal consequences.

IN SUMMARY

Many serial killers have been raised in horrendous conditions and, like Ed Gein and Robert Pickton and Henry Lee Lucas, have suffered from low cognitive functioning in addition to those traumatic early experiences. Others, however, like Russell Williams, are exceptionally bright in the Hannibal Lecter mold. That character from *The Silence of the Lambs*, written by Tom Harris, was based on an elegant doctor, Alfredo Balli Trevino, whom Harris had met in a Mexican prison. Trevino had murdered and chopped up his lover, but unlike Lecter, the doctor was released in 2000 and spent the last nine years of his life tending to the poor. Colonel Williams did not act out until middle age, so although he perhaps had the genetic disposition to offend, one can speculate that life stresses or the powerful drug he took for severe arthritis may have triggered, that is, disinhibited, his deviance and aggression.

The history of human sexuality is rife with violence, torture, and brutality. As discussed, feminist theorists and others have argued that the patriarchy and inegalitarian relationships within society are causes of the widespread horror too often found in heterosexual relationships. However, others suggest that violent aggression in those relationships is either bilateral or as likely to be instigated by females and that lesbian relationships are more violent than heterosexual ones. So the task is not solely reforming any elements of toxic masculinity that continue to exist in our society. Rather a restructuring of aggressive, criminogenic culture may be the solution. Do any examples exist in either the animal or human world?

To cite one example, we seem to have inherited our most unfortunate characteristics from our closest animal relations: the chimpanzees. According to Jane Goodall and other researchers cited by de Waal (2005), chimps are loners, their social unit comprising a mother and baby. Chimps are male dominated, flesh eating, and have a great capacity for violence and aggression, attacking monkeys and other apes for food and even eating one another, although the hierarchy is so well defined that aggression is rare. The alpha male has strict first dibs on sex and food and in fact anything he should take a fancy to. If animal patriarchy is the cause of human aggression, there is the original example.

But I recall a very different type of example, one that astounded me. At a meeting of the International Society for Research on Aggression, a wonderful organization whose stimulating biennial meetings I always looked forward to, Frans de Waal, a behavioral ecologist from my old graduate school the University of Wisconsin–Madison, wowed the crowd with a presentation and video about **bonobos**.

Bonobos are pigmy chimpanzees and, in fact, endangered. In part, they are at risk because they are hunted by humans in Africa for "bushmeat." Interestingly, in contrast to chimpanzees, bonobos are very gentle, eat a mostly vegetarian diet, engage in little or no warfare, and use sex rather than aggression to achieve their desired outcomes. Confronted by an irate male, a female will calm him by fondling him to orgasm or engaging in fellatio, or if she is not in the mood, pass him on to a sister. Thus an irate male bonobo is always pacified and coopted by a female, rather than gaining any traction in upward social mobility. Not surprisingly then, the dominant bonobo in a colony is always a female, and the only way a male can gain any status is to form a friendship with a superior female, usually his mother, although I do not believe incest is practiced. Unlike chimpanzee society, the bonobo colony is characterized by sexuality, empathy, caring, and cooperation.

As de Waal (2005) says when comparing chimpanzees with bonobos, "One resolves sexual issues with power, while the other resolves power issues with sex" (p. 19).

Perhaps there is a lesson for us humans in there somewhere. In *Sexual Personae*, Camille Paglia (1991) claims that men created sky gods, whom they could never be certain they pleased, in order to displace in knowledge the high rank of women; up until then, it seems, women possessed all the secrets of the earth goddesses. Thus, according to Paglia, men competed and aggressed and created trade and technological advances, but if women had remained in control, we would "still be living in grass huts." Let's hope those are not the only two choices open to society. In fact, my personal approach is to practice eclecticism, taking the best from different systems, rather than orthodoxy, that is, adhering slavishly to one system or paradigm. But that grass hut is looking more tempting lately.

CHAPTER TEN

CLIMATE, AGGRESSION, AND CRIME: EFFECTS OF TEMPERATURE ON HUMANS AND HUMAN REACTIONS TO ENVIRONMENTAL THREAT

This chapter may startle the reader by arguing, as Darwin emphasized, that we are creatures of our environments and that the physical environment determines a great deal of our reactions, emotionally, cognitively, and socially. Specifically, it looks at violence and aggression as a function of ambient temperature, especially heat stress. Some of the findings are among the oldest and most robust in the study of crime and criminality. Causal theories have ranged from geographic, sociological, and cultural to psychophysiological. Recent work on the neurophysiology of aggression and violence has found that brain function changes caused by both heat and cold can be precursors to antisocial behavior and sexual arousal. Cross-cultural findings in the United States, Canada, Europe, and the Far East reveal that violent crime increases as temperature increases. Implications for dealing with crime and climate change are discussed.

The attempts of critical criminologists to reduce the analysis of crime to a series of dialectical concepts or "the conflict of opposites" has proven inadequate (e.g., Arrigo, 1999). By contrast, the science of the study of the causes and execution of crime has revealed those phenomena to be governed by the same scientifically observable and measurable factors as genetics (Mednick, Moffitt, & Stack, 1987) and developmental psychology (Moffitt, 1993).

Paramount among those factors is the environment itself, which is perhaps the most powerful force operating in Darwin's theory of natural selection and in other theories that predated it, for example, Quetelet's 1833 thermic theory of delinquency and Kropotkin's idea that not only environmental temperature but humidity was an important cause of violent crime (Cohen, 1941). Lombroso, the father of biological criminology, conducted elaborate statistical analyses of climate and crime, and Dexter (1899) completed a monumental study of unrest among prisoners, mental patients, students, and others during times of elevated daily temperature, for which Gaedeken (1909) posited a direct physiochemical effect. Alas, some climatic determinists such as Huntington (1945) arrived at conclusions regarding ethnic groups living near the equator that were perceived to be racist so that, with the rise of sociological environmental egalitarianism and the rejection of recent Nazi racial supremacy theories, such levels of analysis fell into academic and political disfavor.

Nevertheless, when the United States National Advisory Commission on Civil Disorders (1968) pointed out that the majority of recent incidents of mass urban violence occurred on days when the temperature rose above 80 degrees Fahrenheit and Goranson and King (1970), in an unpublished report, noted that 15 of 17 cities suffering riots in 1967 had prolonged abnormally hot temperature during the days of unrest, academic interest in the issue was once again piqued. Although some sociologists criticized those studies as attempting to dismiss societal problems with simplistic biological determinism rather than accepting the social inequities that were their true cause, such political criticism missed the point: no one denied that the poor or the discriminated against were the first to experience the harshest brunt of environmental stresses—few riots occur in posh neighborhoods even during heat waves.

As with most significant social phenomena, especially crime, however, it is not biology versus social factors—an either-or reality—that prevails other than, perhaps, in the minds of simplistic ideologues. In this worrisome era of apparent and significant climate change one must weigh carefully the contribution of all relevant factors, and it is incumbent upon researchers to ignore none. Ironically, the tables have turned: now left wingers appear to be espousing the relative importance of environmental factors and right wingers are accused of denying them or at least being skeptical to the point of obtuseness. Meanwhile, researchers beaver on learning much more about the phenomenon of temperature-associated violent crime and its underlying causes.

GEOGRAPHIC EFFECTS

Studies in the nineteenth, twentieth, and now twenty-first centuries have shown that cities closer to the equator, in the United States and other countries, have greater rates of violent crime, specifically assault and homicide, than do those of a more temperate nature. Van de Vliert and Simister in various studies (e.g., Simister & Van de Vliert, 2005) have shown that murder and attempted murder and political violence increase in many countries as a function of climate as represented in daily temperatures. They have argued that the alleged curvilinear function—suggesting that violence is reduced at very high temperatures—can be accounted for by the fact that, in many countries, rain occurs as a certain temperature is experienced, reducing both temperature and human interaction. A second hypothesis is that countries closer to the equator are characterized by "machismo"—masculine aggression (Simister & Van de Vliert, 2005)—or southern violence cultures that produce more aggressive behavior and violent crime (Anderson, Anderson, Dorr, DeNeve, & Flanagan, 2000). Statistical analyses by Anderson et al. (2000) suggest, however, that the machismo factor, though possibly contributing, is not a major cause of the phenomenon.

TEMPERATURE EFFECTS

Among the most robust of criminological phenomena is the positive relationship between average daily and monthly temperature and violent crime. Although most of the research has been done on American cities ranging from Dallas to Minneapolis, studies have also been conducted on British cities (Field, 1992), Pakistani cities (Simister & Van de Vliert, 2005), and now Canadian cities (Boyanowsky &Yasayko, 2007, 2011). Some researchers have argued that the strong relationship between temperature and violent crime is best explained by **routine activities theory (RAT)** (Cohen & Felson, 1979). That hypothesis posits that, as the weather becomes more pleasant, people interact more and so more perpetrators and victims have access to each other, and consequently, on a probabilistic basis, more crime occurs.

Baron and Bell (1976) and others have also argued that the relationship is curvilinear, so that at temperatures above 80 or so degrees

Fahrenheit, aggressive behavior and its consequence, violent crime, drop. They have suggested that the reduction in violent crime is prompted by people's desire to escape the heat. Although few researchers question that at some high temperatures people's highest priority would be to escape if possible in order to avoid collapse from heat exhaustion, in the most careful statistical reanalysis undertaken, Anderson et al. (2000) have concluded that the curvilinear finding of Baron and others is due to statistical artifact and that the linear relationship persists to very high temperatures.

Cohn and Rotton (1997) have contrarily pointed out that, when days are partitioned into sections, in some American cities, the hottest part of the day is accompanied by a drop in the crime rate. That time, however, encompasses the hours from four to six pm when many Americans are in their cars or on buses and trains, commuting, so that potential rates of interaction are actually much lower. Yet Kenrick and MacFarlane (1986) have shown that horn honking at intersections where cars did not budge on the change to a green light (a suggested aggressive behavior) increased dramatically as temperatures rose, but only for cars without air conditioning. Nor can the routine activity or **negative affect escape hypothesis** account for the dramatic relationship between increasing temperature and domestic violence, which, by definition, occurs within the confines of the home (Michael & Zumpe, 1986), or for the finding that baseball pitchers are more likely to hit batters with a pitch on hot rather than cool days (Reifman, Larrick, & Fein, 1991). Obviously, something else is going on.

ENVIRONMENTAL TEMPERATURE, BRAIN TEMPERATURE, AND INTERPERSONAL AGGRESSION

In his book *The Stranger*, Albert Camus (1946, pp. 38–39) describes the distress of his protagonist:

> The heat was beginning to scorch my cheeks; ... I had the same dis-
> agreeable sensations—especially in my forehead, where all the veins
> seemed to be bursting through the skin. ... I was conscious only of

the cymbals of the sun clashing on my skull … of the keen blade of
light flashing up from the [Arab's] knife.… Then everything began
to reel before my eyes.… Every nerve in my body was a steel spring,
and my grip closed on the revolver. The trigger gave.…

In a series of studies inspired by the riots of the sixties that Baron and
his colleagues conducted (e.g., Baron & Bell, 1976), those researchers
found that subjects given the opportunity to retaliate against another
person in a laboratory situation (where the provocateur was actually
an accomplice of the experimenter) gave more electric shocks to their
antagonist under conditions of heat than they did when tested under
normal laboratory temperature conditions. But only in moderate heat:
when the dry bulb temperature rose above approximately 80 degrees
Fahrenheit (26.7 Celsius) or the subjects were provoked by personal
verbal attacks on them, their levels of retaliation actually dropped. To
account for those results, the authors invoked the curvilinear or inverted U relationship between temperature and aggression. They argued
that the combined distress of heat and anger led to attempts to escape
from the heat rather than engage in aggression, a rather puzzling metaphorical explanation as no escape was physically possible—the only
response available to them was pressing the button to deliver more or
fewer shocks.

By contrast, in a parallel series of studies conducted by my colleagues
and me (Boyanowsky, 1999; Boyanowsky, Calvert-Boyanowsky et al.,
1981), we found that there was a direct linear relationship between
environmental heat and retaliatory aggression that increased as provocation was added to the procedure even to the level of 95 degrees
Fahrenheit (dry bulb) or 90.5 effective temperature (combining heat
with humidity), that is, 32.5 degrees Celsius. How to account for those
different results?

For one, we felt that Baron and Bell's procedure of informing subjects that the purpose of the experiment was to study the effects of
heat was a fatal flaw. Baron felt subjects would be suspicious of the
heat if they were not informed, but we found that they didn't notice,
and other researchers in thermoregulation (Benzinger, 1969) have also
commented on how unaware people are that ambient heat is not only
causing their distress during kinesiology experiments but also leading

to great irritation and anger expressed toward others. (This lack of awareness that heat is increasing is analogous to the frog in the slowly heating water who fails to leap out.) On the other hand, telling subjects that researchers were studying heat made these subjects increasingly acutely aware of its effects as the heat rose, and they perhaps noticed themselves becoming increasingly irritable and compensated for it. So we replicated their experiment changing some conditions. For half the subjects, conditions included a large thermometer prominently placed on the subject's control panel; for the other half, however, conditions were the same as in the original testing procedure, and there was no monitoring of the temperature by the subject.

Using the original experimental conditions, we replicated our results: aggression increased as temperature increased. But under the thermometer-monitoring condition, subjects, now aware of the source of their irritability, reduced the intensity and duration of shocks delivered to their provocateur to the levels administered in control conditions (20°C or 68°F). Our conclusion was that if individuals under heat stress and interpersonal provocation become aware that the source of their extreme physiological and psychological stress, their anger and hostility, formerly attributed solely to the attacks upon them by their antagonist, is in fact caused by the environment, their hostility will be reduced, and they will modulate their potentially antisocial responses. That would account for the results of Baron and colleagues when stress was highest. But how does heat stress translate into human aggression and violent crime?

THE PSYCHOPHYSIOLOGICAL BASES OF THERMALLY FACILITATED HUMAN AGGRESSION—THE ECS-TC SYNDROME

The hypothalamus has long been implicated not only in thermoregulation (Benzinger, 1969) but in emotional modulation (Zajonc, Murphy, & Inglehart, 1989). In fact, the neurotransmitter released by the anterior hypothalamus to reduce core temperature is the same as that released to prepare the individual for fight or flight: adrenaline. (In scientific literature, this hormone and neurotransmitter is called **norepinephrine** or **noradrenaline**.) As Benzinger (among others) and my colleagues and I have noticed, hot subjects become increasingly irritable, hostile, angry, and less discriminating, developing a sort of tunnel vision of the situation, especially in terms of what is the true source of their distress and provocation. Consequently, that release of adrenaline activates aggression toward the most salient or prominent social source of distress: their antagonist. And as Anderson has pointed out, a rising, vicious cycle begins if their antagonist reacts to the display of anger and, in turn, lashes back: if violence is met with violence, the aggression escalates. The pattern is similar among intimate partners in the home and among young men in bars, on street corners, or in encounters with the police that become enflamed and erupt into widespread riots.

So too, our subjects tested in the heat experienced increases in brain (core) temperature (measured by a **tympanic thermometer** that provides an index of temperature at the **anterior hypothalamus**), an accelerated heart rate, and feelings of anger, which resulted in their administering heightened levels and duration of painful shock to their antagonists (these shocks did not actually occur; numbers were merely being recorded on the experimenter's instrument panel). That aggression occurred after a significantly larger latency of response time (i.e., they took longer to respond) that we concluded was a product of emotional-cognitive stress and thermoregulatory conflict. By contrast, for subjects who, in viewing the thermometer, were made aware of the major environmental contribution to their arousal (the hot room), we found, to our amazement and delight, reductions in brain temperature, heart rate, angry feelings toward the provocateur, and concomitant aggression (i.e., reductions in latency, intensity, and duration of shocks delivered), though the ambient temperature in the laboratory remained high and unchanged.

Our conclusion was that people affected by heat stress are experiencing conflict between the body's attempts to thermoregulate and their motivation to respond to perceived threats or attacks in their environment and that, under the conditions of reduced cognitive discriminatory powers (the reduced ability to think clearly) created by such heat stress, they lash out, at least initially. If the response they experience is retaliatory or equally provoking, even more aggression follows that then contributes once again to emotional and physiological disequilibrium and an escalation of aggression. That phenomenon, emotional and cognitive stress under thermoregulatory conflict, we call, in shorthand, the **Ecs-TC syndrome**. Thus it is clear that significant causal psychophysiological processes underlie the correlations repeatedly obtained between heat and crime.

CLIMATE, CULTURE, SOCIAL INTERACTION, AND CRIME

Wilhelm (2003) has argued that, in the cultures he studied, high average temperature is associated with gender inequality, the dominance of religion, corruption within national governments, and crime. Although Nisbett (1993) suggested southern culture is associated with a propensity for settling differences violently, possibly based on the frontier mentality of protecting one's herds from thieves and predators, Anderson (2001) found little evidence that this attribute ("southernness") was associated with violent crime. Temperature, on the other hand, was significantly correlated with violent crime when population and low socioeconomic status were controlled for. In fact, it is widely noted that cultures closer to the equator are friendlier and have more elaborate courtesy rituals and formal systems of dealing with matters of honor. Perhaps those rituals of "politesse" evolved in compensation for a greater propensity, caused by heat stress, to overreact to perceived slights or insults.

On the other hand, as originally observed by the philosopher and traveler Montesquieu (1748/1989) in the eighteenth century, northern Germanic and Scandinavian cultures are noted for their relative bluntness. Such characteristics are strikingly in keeping with the mental state observed in our subjects tested in cold, who responded aggressively much more quickly but only to appropriate provocation and with much less simmering malice and hostility. For these subjects, the presence and monitoring of the thermometer had no effect on brain temperature, heart rate, anger, or the intensity or duration of the shock they delivered. To risk a metaphor: they behaved in a much more appropriate and "cold-blooded" manner. As Montesquieu first stated and Darwin might have affirmed, we and our cultures are creatures of our environments—of long-term physical environments.

IMPLICATIONS FOR CLIMATE CHANGE

It is thus vitally important that we take note of the changing climate of our planet. Although we may sometimes temporarily ameliorate the violent aggression stoked by high temperatures by alerting people to the environmental source of much of their distress through education and communication programs, our research indicates that the effect of heat is insidious, especially for escalating violence and aggression under conditions of social provocation (i.e., in the heat of the moment). And, as always, those on the margins of society who have the least insulation from social and environmental stressors will be affected most. Anderson (2001) has estimated that, within the United States, a 2 degree Fahrenheit increase in average temperature would translate into an increase of more than 24,000 murders and assaults per year. As figures 10.1, 10.2, and 10.3 (Boyanowsky, 2007) demonstrate, the same relationship between average monthly temperatures and recorded assaults holds for Vancouver, Toronto, and Montreal. Field (1992) has shown the same relationship even in wet, soggy, temperate Britain. Of course the effect is greater in the south where temperatures climb higher and will become worse in northern countries as their climates heat up.

With climate change undeniably underway, the concern it has prompted has led to a flurry of studies on the possible effects. One of the most thorough is a review of 60 studies of the effects of climate change, specifically the effects of increasing temperature on crime and conflict (Hsiang, Burke, & Miguel, 2013). The results are not encouraging. Hsiang et al. found that, with every standard deviation increase in temperature and deviation from the norm in rainfall, interpersonal violence increased by 4 percent and group conflict increased by 14 percent.

A further worrisome factor is the synergistic potential produced by toxic pollutants and other substances we ingest, perhaps inadvertently, but that relationship has not received the same degree of scrutiny. For instance, from our own research, we do know that alcohol raises brain temperature, thereby lowering the threshold for violence (thereby increasing the likelihood of violence and aggression), especially for individuals who are inordinately affected by alcohol ingestion.

Figure 10.1. Vancouver assaults related to mean monthly high temperature,
2001–2005

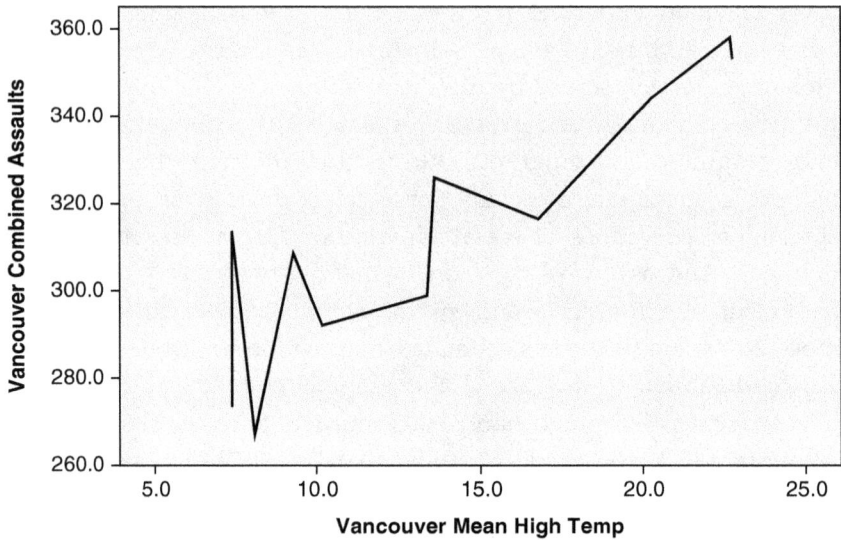

Source: Boyanowsky (2007).

Figure 10.2. Toronto assaults related to mean monthly high temperature,
2001–2005

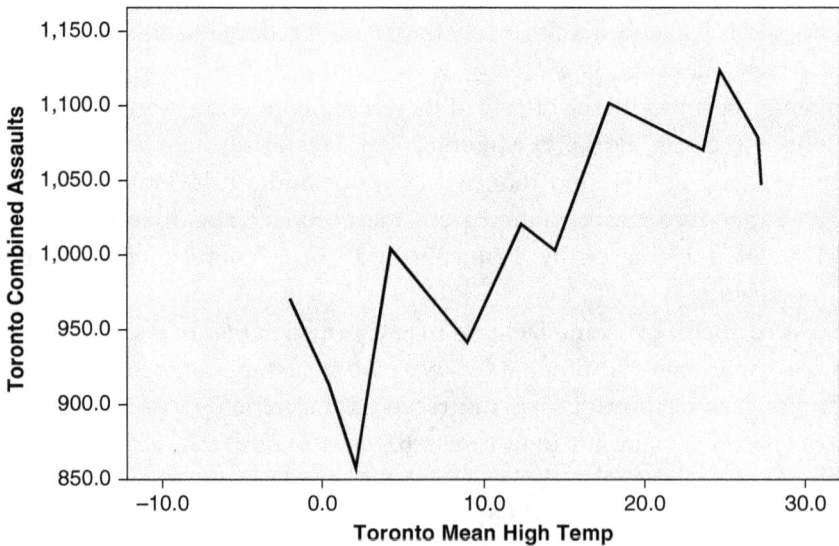

Source: Boyanowsky (2007).

Figure 10.3. Montreal assaults related to mean monthly high temperature, 2001–2005

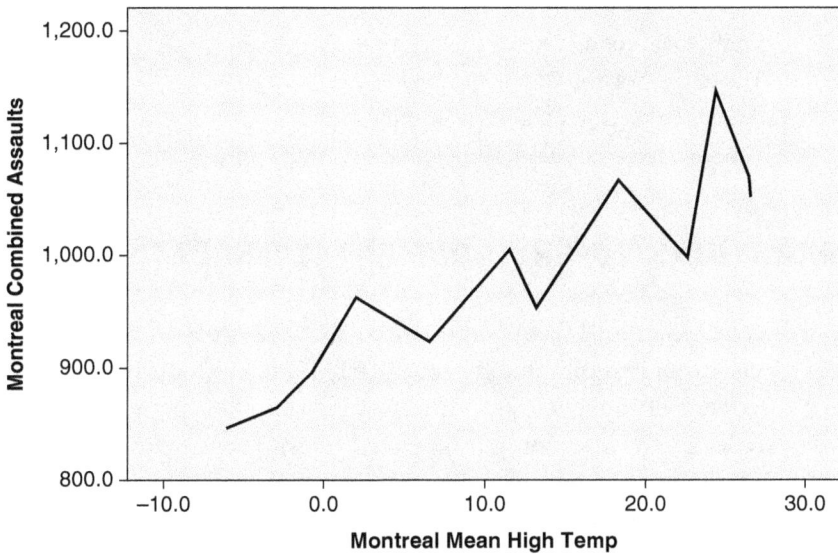

Source: Boyanowsky (2007).

WHAT CAN WE DO?

Ironically, the answers have a ring familiar to those who have addressed society's ills in the past, prior to the concern regarding escalating climate change: adequate housing, information, education, socialization, and conflict resolution processes that exclude violent solutions. But now they become more urgent. Analyzing 20 years of accumulated crime and climate data, Mares (2013) found that the 20 percent most disadvantaged neighborhoods in St. Louis, Missouri, experienced more than half of the increased violent crime produced by temperature increases. Once again, those who can least cope with adverse effects are most drastically affected by them in our society.

But perhaps most importantly, we must act to reduce environmental degradation and rising environmental temperatures. The "right to be cold," as the Inuit put it, is a condition allowing nature to regain its curative powers. Otherwise the outlook is not very promising, as Shakespeare cautioned in *Romeo and Juliet* (3.1.1–5):

> I pray thee, good Mercutio, let's retire;
> The day is hot, the Capulets abroad,
> And if we meet, we shall not 'scape a brawl,
> For now, these hot days, is the mad blood stirring.

REACTIONS TO ENVIRONMENTAL THREAT—RET

For several decades, I have been involved in the study of community **reactions to environmental threats (RET)**. One case study involved the discovery of dioxins, by-products of the pulp and paper process's use of chlorine to bleach pulp (macerated trees). Those toxins had been dumped into watersheds, oceanic and freshwater, by pulp mills. When their presence was detected in the late 1980s, people became adamantly opposed, as **dioxins** are perhaps the deadliest poisons known to humankind. To my surprise (but in retrospection, not so much), the upscale populace of West Vancouver became very militantly opposed to the pulp mill effluent flowing from two mills in Howe Sound, and after the provincial government reneged on its agreement to pass legislation demanding zero tolerance, direct action was planned. At the eleventh hour, the minister of environment, a West Vancouver resident, resigned in protest, and in the election that followed, the new provincial government brought in legislation banning dioxins thereby obviating massive protests and even the sabotage threatened by some militant groups.

In a second case study, the new government disallowed the diversion of 87 percent of the Nechako River that would have threatened the Fraser River, BC's paramount salmon stream, even though Rio Tinto Alcan (formerly the Aluminum Company of Canada) held permits to do so in order to increase its independent power production massively. Again, direct action, including armed rebellion on the part of northern residents, was imminent. Distilling the most prominent behavioral reactions to such impending threats in several case studies in North America and worldwide, I created a theoretical flow chart, an algorithm that predicted the outcome in environmental threatening circumstances.

Figure 10.4. Public reactions to environmental threat

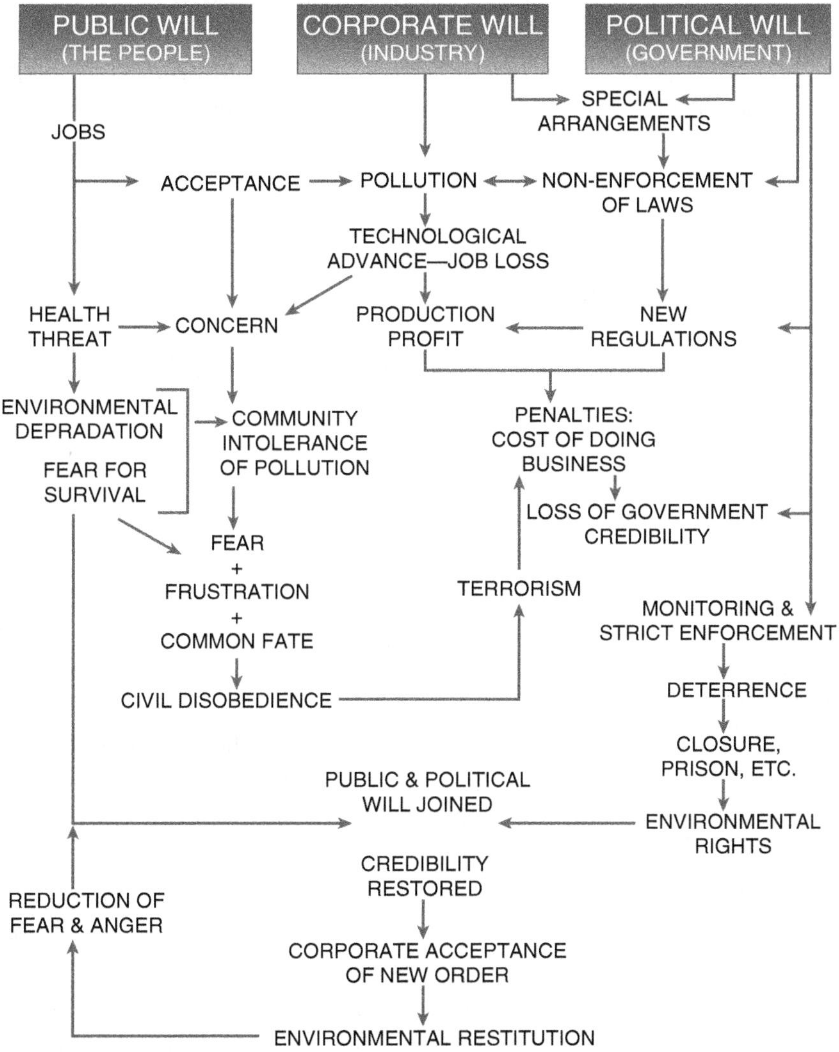

It begins with the premise that there are three sources of social influence and change in democratic society—political will, corporate will, and public will—and that two of them must be marshaled in order for change to occur. (See figure 10.4.) If one follows the path of potential events, the outcome should be predictable, whether it results in corporate advantage, protest or sabotage, or public resolution of its fears.

In two separate studies, Omi Hodwitz (2010) tested the concepts associated with the RET theory (Boyanowsky & Hodwitz, 2010, 2011). The first was conducted in Vancouver and found that willingness to engage in more activism increased as the threats to health and livelihood increased. In the second, conducted in North America and Europe, feelings of personal threat, feeling a need to respond, and degree of activism determined willingness to engage in illegal protest.

However, willingness to engage in violence was stronger for young men and for those with lower levels of education, as found in most other research (see chapter 7).

It is clear that people respond to environmental threat and that the closer to home the threat, the greater the willingness to engage in protest and even illegal activities. Wise governments should take note.

AN OVERVIEW OF THE PATHWAY OF RET

In society, there are three sources of initiative and power: public will, corporate will, and political will (government). In order to create employment (or sometimes in corrupt societies just to receive a financial kickback), government or significant figures in government will cooperate with business in a special arrangement to allow an activity that puts the environment, wildlife, or human health at risk: for example, a mine extracting minerals, a steel or leather factory, a dairy processor or pulp mill dumping toxic effluent into waterways used for drinking and holding fish. The rationale is that environmental damage is the cost of doing business. The public historically has accepted the pollution generated so long as good jobs are made available.

However, if health threats arise (e.g., dioxins in fish or carcinogens in the air), concern is raised and pollution is tolerated less, especially if technological advances such as automation lead to job loss, making the public less willing to absorb the health threat or sickness resulting. The government may bring in new regulations that do not eliminate the threat entirely but appear to be doing something on behalf of the public. Penalties for pollution are imposed but are seen by the corporation as merely the cost of doing business and by a cynical public as trivial measures.

As environmental degradation becomes more apparent, the public's fear for its health increases, eventually leading to fear for actual survival and to increasing intolerance of the situation. As the corporation achieves higher profits, the government loses credibility in its fiduciary responsibility to act on behalf of the people and the environment. At the tipping point, civil disobedience and even environmental terrorism (e.g., sabotaging equipment, factories, vehicles) arises among the more militant of the populace (often young men) who are supported by the more passive majority.

However, if the government realizes the gravity of the situation and increases environmental regulations and their enforcement, prosecutes corporate lawbreakers, and reasserts the importance of environmental values and rights (to a healthy existence), public and political will become joined, and the corporation accepts the new order. Eventually, environmental restitution leads to the reduction of fear and anger and the reunification of public and political will.

Those are the stages in the flow chart that occurred during the dioxin crisis in Howe Sound. The pulp mills went to oxygen rather than chlorine delignification or went bankrupt and shut down, and the environment eventually recovered (Hagen, Colodey, Knapp, & Samis, 1997). Government credibility was restored. But during the protests, civil disobedience came very close to the threshold for industrial terrorism; only the resignation of the environment minister when the premier reneged on zero tolerance for dioxins averted direct action by militants.

IN SUMMARY

The effect of increasing ambient temperature on public disorder, violent crime, and aggression is one of the most robust findings in criminology over the last century. Hotter climates are associated with greater violent crime.

Two alternative explanations—routine activities theory and a curvilinear relationship between temperature and crime—have been considered and found not to have major explanatory value for the general phenomenon, though both may contribute.

Laboratory research has revealed that the Ecs-TC syndrome—emotional-cognitive stress leading to thermoregulatory conflict—is occurring. The processes of Ecs-TC are as follows: core temperature rises, the anterior hypothalamus releases adrenaline to cool the body, but if a provocation occurs, the adrenaline may be redirected to aggression unless the individual recognizes that the increased physiological distress experienced is coming from a neutral source—the high ambient temperature—and assuages the arousal, thereby leading to a lowering of temperature at the hypothalamus, less anger, faster responses, and lower aggression.

Many studies have now confirmed the effects of rising temperatures on conflict and crime in many different geographic locations, from near the equator to temperate zones in Europe and North America

The RET algorithm begins with the premise that there are three sources of the will to produce outcomes in society: public, corporate, and political will. Societal action and change usually require the enlisting of two of the three. When corporate and political will collude to produce pollution, the public will tolerate it so long as jobs are involved, but if public health is threatened and if jobs disappear, then civil disobedience and other forms of rebellion can lead to violent reactions unless the government acts in the best interests of the people, pollution is abated, and public confidence restored.

CHAPTER ELEVEN

HAZARDOUS WASTE AND ORGANIZED OR CORPORATE CRIME

This chapter explores the relatively new and, in regards to academic study, **inchoate** criminological phenomenon of crimes against the environment.

Part one describes how coping with toxic waste produced locally has led to destruction of natural resources such as fish and forests as well as to contamination of the environment upon which people depend. Case studies of pulp mill pollution of the ocean and of hazardous waste dumped in landfills demonstrate that disease and death can be prevalent even in the allegedly sophisticated and democratic countries of United States and Canada. And we examine the problem of how to evaluate the actions of corporations and governments as they cut economic corners or regard potentially deadly situations as mere misdemeanors versus outright criminal acts.

Part two traces the trafficking of hazardous waste in Canada, the United States, and internationally, as corporations and even countries try to rid themselves of the poisonous detritus of industry. Although a north-south axis of movement of waste is hypothesized and poignantly disturbing case studies exist in support of this hypothesis, there appears to be hope as countries such as the United States and Canada create facilities for dealing with their own waste, ironically making it more profitable for traffickers to follow the law than to engage in nefarious, illegal activities.

PART ONE: HAZARDOUS WASTE AND CORPORATE CRIME

When I was a teenager in Red Lake, the richest gold-mining area in North America, our class was hosted by the local mine managers to a careers promotion night. During the evening, they encouraged us to pursue careers in mining. At one stage the presenter asked whether there were any questions. I popped up and challenged the rationality of digging up tons of ore; refining it to extract minute amounts of gold and, in the process, dumping tons of the cyanide-contaminated waste into a nearby lake, killing all the fish and other life in it; and then shipping off the bullion—only to reinter the gold bars underground in depositories at Fort Knox, Kentucky, and the Royal Canadian Mint in Ottawa, Ontario.

I recall our school's athletic director blanching; the mines were very generous in funding our athletic programs. But to their credit, the mine managers merely chuckled and jokingly inquired whether I was a 16-year-old "communist." They went on to somewhat lamely explain how gold has many uses in industry, medicine, dentistry, and jewelry in addition to its use as a stored testament to the financial strength of the country. In those days, dollars were backed by the gold standard, requiring vast reserves of gold. Even today, gold reserves serve to buttress the economic stability of many countries.

Although the mine managers continued to fund our sports teams very generously, they didn't even bother to address the contaminated waste problem that to me as a young sports fisherman seemed especially concerning. In that time, waste was seen as the "cost of doing business." Since then, I have learned from local physicians that the town closest to the polluted lake had a much higher incidence of cancer and infant maladies than the main town of Red Lake. Gold mines and other mineral mines continue to require contaminated waste depositories, usually an isolated lake that is dammed at the outlet or a natural dry land basin. The water is dumped in the lake and the polluted material settles to the bottom to be covered by sediment eventually. Often, by the time this sedimentation process is over, the authorities consider the wastewater as not requiring treatment, so it is pumped into a local waterway.

That traditional treatment of "pollution by dilution" is the object of scorn of many environmental groups such as Greenpeace, the organization formed in Vancouver in the late sixties to protest nuclear atmospheric testing in Amchitka, Alaska. (Greenpeace went on to world prominence and is now headquartered in Amsterdam, Netherlands). In fact, the practice of using water to dilute waste continues unabated. In 1985, a tailings dam near the village of Stava, Italy, was breached, sending a wall of polluted water roaring down the valley and killing 268 people. Locals had expressed concern about the dam, and the government's response was to have the mining company that owned the dam inspect and sign off on it. Eventually, 10 people, including mine management, regulatory officers, and members of local government, were convicted of manslaughter. The criminal responsibility in that case was clearly evident.

However, as George Santayana (1905) noted, "Those who cannot remember the past are condemned to repeat it" (p. 284). And so, after having declared its dam safe despite repeated concerns expressed by government inspectors and its own shift supervisor, who quit his job when unheeded, Imperial Metals in British Columbia ignored all warnings until the dam on the tailings pond of Mount Polley mine burst on the morning of August 4, 2014, releasing 17 million cubic meters of water and 8 million cubic meters of toxic **slurry** into Polley Lake (British Columbia, n.d.). The polluted water then carried mud and debris into Quesnel Lake, formerly the cleanest of the deepest lakes in the world. BC's Liberal Party (actually a conservative coalition), which formed the government at that time, had been generously supported by donations from the owners of the Mount Polley mine; the party refused to agree with mine safety officials and environmental groups that the tailings dam breach was one of the greatest mining disasters in Canadian history (Boyanowsky, 2015).

So much for the self-regulation that right-wing governments, like BC's at the time, favor. They repeatedly cut the budgets of environmental protection agencies, as did the newly elected president of the United States, Donald Trump, on February 26, 2017, while increasing the budget of the military. As idealist German philosopher Georg Hegel (1770–1831) quipped in a lecture, "But what experience and history teach is this—that nations and governments have never learned anything from history" (Hegel, 1822–1828/1975, p. 21). Of course, to be realistic and fair, some of the most polluted places on earth exist where communist regimes once ruled, for example, in parts of Romania, Ukraine, Russia, and most poignantly China. Fifty percent of China's rivers have completely disappeared from the earth, and the remaining 50 percent still flowing are polluted to varying degrees (Boyanowsky, 2015). In those jurisdictions, polluters are not seen as criminals but rather as making decisions that allow the greatest good for the greatest number, as urged by the utilitarian philosopher John Stuart Mill (1806–1873). Of course, the problem is that the benefits are often immediate and self-evident, as occurred with the building of the great Three Gorges Dam on the Yangtze River, allegedly to halt the depredations of flooding—whereas the dangers and consequences of pollution are often insidious and long term.

On the flipside, we are horrified by a visually vivid but, in terms of societal impact, relatively insignificant crime such as a home invasion or the rape or murder of an individual (recall the Amanda Knox trial in Italy from chapter 1). But we regard the contamination of a whole neighborhood or state as "the cost of doing business," as mentioned previously, and do not identify the perpetrators as criminals, though their actions may condemn or damage not only an individual but a whole population or generation. Hence the algorithm developed in chapter 2 incorporates the idea of dissemination (D), or how many experience the effects of a crime, ranging from one person as victim to a multitude:

$$C = K\,[F + I + (H \times D)]$$

Many people are often affected by pollution and other corporate crimes. Witness one lawsuit filed as a class action (referring to whole groups of people affected) and settled by American tobacco companies for US$100 million, wherein the case was argued to the satisfaction of the judiciary that the companies were aware of the **carcinogenic** elements in their products (Reuters, 2015).

Much of the credit for sounding the alarm must go to whistleblowers: courageous men and women who take on corporations and governments when they discover crimes being committed against the public. Although very determined and even troubled, they have a resolve that is almost frighteningly strong. I remember taking a burly, quiet fellow fishing on a favorite steelhead river one spring morning. I didn't know him well; a friend had asked me to be his host. As we chatted, the steely resolve and suppressed anger that seeped out of him inspired me to ask the extra question about his past. He said he was a chemist and anti-smoking crusader, head of an institute at Rockefeller University in New York. I had met a few academics from Rockefeller and his name sounded vaguely familiar, but the light went on when he washed his hands in my kitchen sink—just as Russell Crowe did in the film *The Insider*. He was Jeffrey Wigand, who at great personal cost (loss of job, wife, family, position, and potential fortune) blew the whistle on the tobacco industry. He could not salve his conscience once he learned that the tobacco company he served as vice president of research and development knew that additives that made cigarettes more addictive and carcinogenic (e.g., coumarin) were nevertheless purposely put into cigarettes to increase sales.

He was one of the brave few who valued the life of millions more than his own personal comfort, security, and status in the corporate world. That day on the river, he didn't catch a steelhead (a highly prized anadromous "rainbow trout" of the Pacific salmon family), but he commented how immersing oneself in nature heals open wounds in one's soul for things one had done in the past. Most whistleblowers can appear arrogant, but that may be because they have to grow a Teflon panoply (shield) in order to withstand the condemnation of their peers in business and even of their families, who worry about security. Very often the public itself condemns them, as people don't want to be told the bad news about a favorite habit. Whistleblowing means rejecting the norm operating in the reference group demanding conformity (e.g., the nation, city, corporation, or university), and, usually, it means standing alone—a personal version of the community standard of tolerance (actually intolerance of culpability) takes over (i.e., I can't live with myself if I do nothing). Those are people operating at stage 6 of Kohlberg's theory of moral development, and they are not only brave but rare, perhaps, ironically, rarer than psychopaths, who in their obliviousness to public disapprobation they somewhat resemble. Perhaps they, like psychopaths, must necessarily be rare or society would not function smoothly.

So why do we tend to dislike whistleblowers and overlook crimes affecting many, such as pollution, while at the same time reacting strongly against crimes affecting the individual? One reason is that we identify with the individual victim because "a single death is a tragedy, a million deaths is a statistic" (O'Brien & Bartlett, 2014, p. 636). That quotation is attributed to the incomparably brutal dictator Joseph Stalin who not only engineered the deaths of 8 million Ukrainians in 1932 but an estimated 20 plus million of the best and brightest Russians in peacetime (Conquest, 1986). Rationalization comes in many forms.

In the 1940s, Hooker Chemical and the US Army used an abandoned waterway known as the Love Canal in Niagara Falls, New York, as a dumpsite for hazardous chemicals. By the time of its closure in 1952, 21,800 tons of hazardous chemicals had been buried on a 16-acre site. The site was covered with a layer of clay. Then the school board approached the company to purchase the site for a new school. And the company's executive responded:

> The more we thought about it, the more interested Wilcox and I became in the proposition and finally came to the conclusion that the Love Canal property is rapidly becoming a liability because of housing projects in the near vicinity of our property. A school, however, could be built in the center unfilled section (with chemicals underground). We became convinced that it would be a wise move to turn this property over to the schools provided we could not be held responsible for future claims or damages resulting from underground storage of chemicals. (Colten & Skinner, 1996, p. 158; Glaberson, 1990)

And so the land was deeded to the school board for $1. Members of the board could not have been more pleased as they touted the saving of taxpayer dollars. Two schools were eventually built on the site and 800 houses and 240 apartments adjacent to it. Alas, some of the land soon collapsed creating deadly puddles that children enjoyed playing in. Then the sewage-line building breached the layer of clay, and the toxic sludge spread even farther, sometimes appearing in people's basements. By 1978, an investigation by journalist Michael Brown of the *Niagara Gazette* (who wrote 100 articles about Love Canal) and subsequent testing by health agencies revealed a mind-boggling deadly swamp of chemicals leaking from the site, including hydrocarbons and dioxins, and many children were found to have massive, multiple birth defects and serious diseases such as leukemia.

Nevertheless, the mayor insisted nothing was wrong with the dump. President Jimmy Carter, however, rose to the occasion and chose to act, forming the "**Superfund**," a tax on chemical companies to create what was hoped would be an adequate amount of financial resources to deal with future disasters (Rahm, 1998). The government demolished the homes and reimbursed those who were willing to move (only 90 chose to stay), and the company was sued by the EPA and agreed to pay $129 million in compensation. One can see how difficult it is to pin blame on individuals in such cases, as discussed in chapter 2 and illustrated in figure 2.1. For pollution is like poison in that it is frequently insidious rather than blatant and violent and visual, so the harm done by the poisoner or the polluter can be difficult to assess. But unlike the poisoner, the polluter usually has no intention to harm; rather, the purpose is merely to make money. Thus, perhaps greed, measured by relative profit obtained by allowing the pollution versus doing the right thing, should be worked into an even more sophisticated model and measured as a dimension of crime.

Right wingers (ironically also referred to as "conservatives") argue against government regulation, claiming that market forces rather than central planning—which cannot possibly consider all the elements at work in the world before imposing economic and even conservation policy—should determine the fate of the economy and even of the environment. (See Hayek, 1991.) That could prove disastrous as pollution and overconsumption could lead to significant environmental degradation before a correction based on the market would naturally occur. We might experience illness and death from burning coal for electricity or from waste disposal, as discussed, or our overharvested trees and other resources could require decades, if not millennia, to recover. Or a tipping point could be reached. Some argue, for instance, that "**fracking**" (injecting water and chemicals into the earth under extremely high pressure causing underground rock strata demolition to release natural gas or oil), if continued unabated, will irreparably contaminate, damage, or deplete the Ogallala Aquifer, the mammoth underground lake that supplies the American Midwest with water. And that is precisely why Hayek, unlike some of his supporters, differentiated between economic knowledge and scientific knowledge.

As a longtime conservationist, I favor government regulation on the "precautionary principle"—the same one the US Food and Drug Administration (FDA) adopts in making most of its decisions: if the purely beneficial evidence is not incontrovertible, do not approve a new drug. For example, the FDA did not approve thalidomide, an anti-nausea drug for pregnant women, but its Canadian counterpart did, and the Canadian government has had to deal with the fallout of a generation of people born with stunted limbs as a side effect of thalidomide. As another example, British Columbia and the Pacific Northwest of the United States are very dependent economically on forest products and so vast harvesting of trees has been the norm. However, in some areas, Theodore Roosevelt, the amazingly prescient Republican president of over 100 years ago, defied the fury of exploitation-mad timber barons, ranchers, and railroad tycoons—owners of millions of acres of forest land—to establish federal forest reserves, national parks, and monuments, a "conservative" and conservationist approach (Brinkley, 2010). And today, most of those reserves form a buffer against the pressures of population explosion and exploitation besetting the Northwest.

British Columbia had no comparable "wilderness warrior" or guardian angel, and so pulp mills were established right on Howe Sound, the inlet whose magnificently verdant and fecund shore is home to most of BC's urban population, including the people of Greater Vancouver and other communities. So the surrounding mountains were **clear-cut** in the early 1900s. Fishermen and conservationists and biologists soon noticed that the once almost limitless resident fin and shellfish populations had begun to plummet as the pulp mills came on stream in the mid-twentieth century, but they had already been affected by the toxic effluent from the Britannia Beach copper mine. No specific lethal levels of toxins could be detected in the deep waters of the sound nor in the flesh of resident fish to account for the decline. Then in the 1990s, tests were, for the first time, made available for the presence of dioxins and furans, the deadliest carcinogenic chemicals known to humans (merely sixty grains in an Olympic-sized swimming pool are harmful to fish). Those chemicals are the by-products of the delignification and bleaching process of wood fiber by chlorine.

As a resident of West Vancouver and a member of Save Howe Sound, I was witness to at least one instance where government regulation did not remedy a situation but market forces did. I examined Department of Fisheries and Oceans (DFO) test results that had been completed but merely allowed to sit on DFO shelves rather than being used to sound the alarm (a good reason for having at least a passing familiarity with statistical methods, by the way). Shades of communist governments? Not exclusively: unpalatable scientific research collected by other democratically elected governments has been allowed to molder on the shelf; consider the actions of New York state authorities in the Love Canal case. Those tests I examined at the DFO revealed that furans existed at many times the allowable limit in the flesh of shellfish such as crabs and prawns, which both aboriginal and other residents harvested regularly. The well-heeled communities of Howe Sound formed a lobbying group and held a headline-grabbing press conference. The next day, DFO shut down harvesting shellfish in Howe Sound, but the pulp mills claimed that if compelled to convert to the benign **oxygen delignification** process, they would go bankrupt, and so the conservative (Social Credit) government of BC relented and allowed them to continue polluting the environment. Environment Canada did not impose significant fines, and, as the flow chart "public reactions to environmental threat" in chapter 10 predicts (figure 10.4), violent protest against the pulp mills was being planned by the more radical elements of the organization.

The situation was very tense. Then an unexpected announcement was made. Greenpeace had been lobbying with European customers not to purchase pulp or paper from Howe Sound Mills that contained trace elements of dioxins and furans. And the European Union agreed. Suddenly there was no market for tainted paper. Perhaps Hayek was right? The recently renovated Woodfibre Pulp Mill near Squamish announced it was shutting down. Having wrongheadedly spent hundreds of millions in retrofitting for the cheaper chlorine bleaching process, it couldn't afford another renovation. The Howe Sound Pulp and Paper Corporation's mill at Port Mellon was much older and on the verge of renovation, so it transitioned to oxygen delignification and continued to be profitable. Thus, the outcome, as the RET flow chart outlined, was a reunion of public and political wills, corporate acceptance of the new order, and finally environmental restitution. By the year 1997, dioxins and furans were vastly reduced and fish populations rebounded so that safe harvesting could be restored (Hagen et al., 1997). And herring by the billions were in evidence for the first time in many decades.

As I have argued elsewhere on these pages, an eclectic approach, in this case to containing and neutralizing the industrial waste we produce locally, seems to be the most effective, ultimately. We need to adjust the balance of regulation, enforcement, and allowing market forces to operate if we want to achieve the ultimate beneficial effect.

PART TWO: THE INTERNATIONAL TRAFFICKING OF TOXIC WASTE AND ORGANIZED CRIME

For at least four decades, organized crime has been recognized internationally as a serious problem in the illegal dumping of toxic waste. Although much of the attention has been focused on Europe and especially on Italy, few countries have been spared from the potentially grave operations of unscrupulous or criminal organizations in this endeavor as the opportunities are widespread and the financial rewards are comparable to or exceed those of the drug trade, without the attendant violence or threat of long-term imprisonment (Boyanowsky, 2015). A review of the literature in the area revealed problems with consensus, even on the definition of hazardous waste, and disagreement among nations regarding the prohibitions stated in the Basel Convention and the Bamako Convention against sending hazardous waste to developing countries. Most traders internationally appear to be legitimate companies usually operating within the international agreements but sometimes taking advantage of opportunities to cheat on the regulations.

TRAFFICKING IN HAZARDOUS WASTE AS A WORLDWIDE PHENOMENON

To begin, here are some snapshots of the situation:

> In 1988, the cargo ship *Khian Sea* began a two-year journey trying to dispose of fly ash from the City of Philadelphia, Pennsylvania,

which had engaged a company to dispose of this waste safely. Instead, that cargo was partly unloaded on a Haitian beach until the ship was driven off by the army. After changing its name twice, the ship arrived back at port mysteriously empty. (This incident was cited by many authors as a portent of an impending catastrophe in toxic waste trafficking.)

Now consider two Canadian examples:

Twenty-three years later, on Monday, March 28, 2011, this was reported in the *Vancouver Sun*: "A [British Columbia] Lower Mainland asbestos removal and demolition contractor is facing a possible jail term after being charged by WorkSafeBC [formerly the Workers' Compensation Board] with allegedly putting employees lives at risk by letting them work unwittingly on homes that contained asbestos" (Bellett, 2011).

Two Toronto *Globe and Mail* reporters, Mitrovica and Mittelstaedt, wrote a series of articles in 2000 on a leaked secret study titled *Organized Crime and the Environment: A Strategic Report.* The study was prepared for the Criminal Investigation Services of Ontario (CISO) and detailed how reputed mobsters had engineered slews of scams to dump toxic waste illegally in the United States and Canada rather than legally disposing of it. In the process, those individuals were said to have garnered millions in profits. The CISO study was conducted in 1993, but it has never been revealed to the public officially.

Those snapshots give some indication of the difficulties involved in studying the illegal trafficking of hazardous waste. First, what is hazardous waste? Its widespread use as an example notwithstanding, the *Khian Sea* incident might not be about hazardous waste disposal at all; Montgomery (1995) has questioned whether the cargo of the *Khian Sea* would qualify as "hazardous waste." A perusal of the literature on the illegal disposal of hazardous waste reveals a curious phenomenon. Very often writers begin by discussing "hazardous waste" then lapse into the transportation and disposal of industrial and municipal waste in general (e.g., Clapp, 1994, 1997). Sometimes the discussion begins to focus on the hazardous material itself (e.g., **asbestos**), rather than on its disposal. And often information about illegal trafficking in hazardous waste is kept secret, especially if criminal investigations are involved. To address the issue of how to define hazardous waste, let us turn next to the definitions prevalent in various countries.

DEFINITIONS OF HAZARDOUS WASTE

THE UNITED STATES OF AMERICA

In the United States, the Environmental Protection Agency (EPA) defines hazardous waste as liquid, solid, contained gas, or sludge wastes that comprise properties that are dangerous or potentially harmful to human health or the environment. EPA, which has blown the whistle on many polluters but come under attack by the US presidency in 2017, cites specific characteristics of hazardous waste. These characteristics include ignitability, corrosiveness, reactivity, and toxicity. It is noteworthy that discarded electronic devices are not classified as hazardous wastes but rather are dubbed "recyclables," except for cathode ray tubes (CRTs). That classification is significant because the average US household possesses 24 electronic (e) devices. Nevertheless, **e-waste** is one of the largest issues confronting industrialized, middle-income, and developing nations (Interpol, 2009).

BRITAIN

By contrast, Britain, although following similar principles, has "localized" or fine-tuned the definitions so that criteria vary among England, Wales, and Scotland based on local context and conditions. That approach has apparently evolved from the philosophy originating with the Conservative government of Margaret Thatcher that a "results-based" system when dealing with business, rather than a strictly regulation-driven system, be put in place (O'Neill, 1997). Thus yet another conservative government has shied away from strict overseeing control through regulatory measures.

CANADA

A Canadian parliamentary background paper defines hazardous wastes as "those wastes which, due to their nature and quantity, are potentially hazardous to human health and/or the environment and which require special disposal techniques to eliminate or reduce the hazard" (Meakin, 1992).

However, in a follow-up statement, the paper states that no universal consensus on a definition has been reached, even among the provinces of Canada, so each tries to harmonize its definition with the federal version. Currently, more than 20 years after the Canadian Environmental Protection Act of 1999 came into effect, the definition of hazardous waste remains problematic. And the issue of harmonized definitions, ones that are accepted by all stakeholders, complicates the regulation of waste disposal nationally and internationally, even when these definitions are more precise and comprehensive (see, for example, Environment and Climate Change Canada, 2017).

It is a situation similar to the use and definition of the term "violence"—now so overused that it has ceased to have any distinct meaning other than as something the writer or speaker of the moment opposes. Again we addressed that issue in chapter 2.

ILLICIT TRAFFICKING OF HAZARDOUS WASTE

Waste is something we all produce as by-products of cooking, eating, building, traveling, and, often, doing business. Some of that waste can be disposed of easily through sewage, incineration, recycling, and burying in a landfill. In some especially fastidious jurisdictions, for example, in Germany, one can be charged with an offense merely for putting the wrong waste in a blue box. That is defined as illegal disposal, and it is hazardous waste disposal if the material in question is a battery, for example, or another product containing lead. But it becomes illegal trafficking only if one disposes of the waste for monetary gain.

The vast majority of industrial waste in Canada that is moved from the generating site is done through contracts with transporters. Contractors have a duty to collect and move the waste safely and to deposit it in an appropriate treatment, transfer, or safe landfill facility. All those options are expensive, especially if the waste is deemed toxic, so as the cost of permits and safe transport goes up, the temptation to dispose of the material cheaply in order to increase one's profit increases commensurately. Legally, the waste generator's liability is usually yielded once the contract has been signed. In the United States, it is slightly different in that the Resource Conservation and Recovery Act gives the Environmental Protection Agency control over the substance "from the cradle to the grave." The intention was to make certain there was commitment throughout the process to safe disposal. The upshot is that the United States maintains greater control over waste than does Canada.

Now that the laws regarding the disposal of hazardous waste have been outlined, we can turn to the matter of illegal disposal. Some questions arise. What is the true situation regarding the illicit disposal of hazardous waste? Is organized crime involved, and what is being done about it?

THE DEFINITION OF ORGANIZED CRIME

In Canada and the United States as well as within many other countries, criminal organization means a group, however organized, that

1) is composed of three or more persons in or outside the country and
2) has as one of its main purposes or activities the facilitation of one or more serious offences, that, if committed, would be likely to result in the direct or indirect receipt of a material benefit, including a financial benefit, by the group or by any of the persons who constitute the group.

   It does not include a group of persons that forms randomly for the immediate commission of a single offence. (Criminal Intelligence Services Canada, 2009, p. 9)

Organized crime that meets that definition is well established in many parts of the world, and there is a huge market in the hazardous waste disposal field according to Liddick (2009), comprising 500 million tons per year, of which 45–50 million tons crosses international borders (Clapp, 1997).

JURISDICTIONS OF REGULATIONS IN CANADA

Hazardous waste management is the responsibility of the provincial and territorial governments (Meakin, 1992) in Canada. According to the Constitution Act, the federal government is responsible for regulating the international and interprovincial or interterritorial movements of hazardous waste (Environment Canada, 2011b).

INTERNATIONAL AGREEMENTS

The Basel Convention (1989) set the standards for handling hazardous waste internationally. The original convention set the rules for member countries of the Organisation for Economic Co-operation and Development (OECD) in dealing with the export of waste to non-OECD countries, which are usually developing and middle-income countries (defined by the per capita average income of citizens). Because some parties were circumventing the intent of the convention by exporting "recyclable materials," a follow-up ban extended the convention to that category as well (OECD, 2001).

The United States, however, has never ratified the convention, and creating the means of enforcement of the convention's principles did not even come up during the convention's development. As with all United Nations declarations, without an enforcement instrument, most of what is passed is meaningless, providing only a feel-good effect for the delegates who must file a report upon returning to their home states. That is my conclusion from having spent two weeks as a participant in a UN conference on violence in 1983 in Milan, the last one I accepted an invitation to attend: boring, cloying, and a brutal waste of time other than watching self-important bureaucrats swan about shaking hands and networking, the charms of Italy notwithstanding.

After the highly publicized *Khian Sea* episode and other incidents, the Bamako Convention (1991) banned the importation of hazardous waste into African, Caribbean, and Pacific countries. The convention was demanded by African countries that felt the Basel Convention was not strictly protective enough and could be easily circumvented, given its regulatory nature. The Bamako Convention was devised with Greenpeace serving as a close advisor. A related declaration, the Montreal Protocol is an international agreement that bans the use and importation of these substances, such as **chlorofluorocarbons**, by any signatory country, including Canada (United Nations Environment Programme, 2006). And finally, the Canada-US Agreement Concerning the Transboundary Movement of Hazardous Waste (1986) has served as the model for regulating the significant traffic between the countries. What are the consequences?

Some criminologists (e.g., Szasz, 1986) have, in fact, insisted that such "soft" international agreements are criminogenic, actually promoting the development of international criminal activity by clarifying how to circumvent the regulations (e.g., by falsifying manifests or mixing cargoes) while, in any event, not enforcing them, as I noted earlier. Cusack (1990) and Wasserman (1981) have emphasized that the phenomenal increase in the cost of disposal in developed countries combined with the economic vulnerability of poor countries creates a path of least resistance, resulting in the victimization of those less fortunate countries.

Montgomery (1995) has a very different take on the transboundary shipment of hazardous waste. Using Greenpeace's own compilation of data, he points out that the vast majority of transboundary shipment proposals to developing countries have been rejected by those countries and that most such shipments take place between highly developed, industrial countries such as Canada and the United States, which are well equipped to handle them. His conclusion is that the alarm sounded regarding the so-called north-south trend—rich countries exploiting poor countries as hazardous waste dump sites—is fueled by a few prominent incidents such as the notorious *Khian Sea* episode and that reporting of these incidents encourages the confusion of ordinary waste with hazardous waste, a trend observed in the current review of the literature. (Indeed, the Pan American Health Organization claimed that the *Khian Sea* was not carrying hazardous waste, merely waste.) In a way, Montgomery's conclusion is reassuring, although even ordinary waste is hardly a desirable commodity for importation.

What of the situation regarding Canada and the United States? Rabe, Becker, and Levine (2000) point out that the rate of hazardous waste production in Canada, in contrast to the predictions of the 1980s, has actually been dramatically reduced to 6 million metric tons. In the United States, only 10 percent of hazardous waste is now dealt with off the generation site. Those are very encouraging trends, although the latter one is probably not matched in Canada, where greater use of landfills and lower standards of environmental regulation, compared to the United States, remain in force. On the other hand, the Canadian Environmental Protection Act of 1999 (that, alas, the Harper Conservative government worked to weaken) has partly reduced the gap in regulation between the two countries. Of course, the Trump government is running amok, removing environmental regulations in the United States, as monitored by the Harvard Environmental Law oversight project.

CANADIAN FEDERAL REGULATIONS

Until the Canadian Environmental Protection Act (CEPA) was passed in 1999, the main environmental legislation at the national level was the federal Fisheries Act, a powerful piece of legislation that, however, was confined to prosecuting individuals and corporations for the introduction of deleterious substances into bodies of water bearing fish. With the boilerplate enforcement possibilities provided by CEPA and the concomitant provincial statutes regarding toxic waste harmonized with it, significant penalties were introduced, characterized by fines of up to $1 million per day and prison sentences of up to three years or both. Because most offenses are detected by provincial environmental enforcement officers, provincial penalties and enforcement capabilities must be comparable or they will produce motivation to operate in those jurisdictions where the deterrent is lower. Girard, Day, and Snider (2010) point out that after the Harris government in Ontario reduced the size of the enforcement service, charges under the CEPA dropped dramatically from 1,640 in 1994 to 724 in 1996, and fines against corporations went from $3.6 million to $1.2 million according to Szasz (1986). This deregulation once again created a potentially criminogenic situation.

One could posit a similar decrease in detecting financial crime if regulators were reduced in number, traffic offenses if highway patrol officers were reduced in number, and street crimes in inner cities if city officers were reduced in number. But as I have pointed out, because crimes against individuals are experienced more personally and empathy is inspired by the suffering of an individual victim, there is much more of a hew and cry when those measures are taken versus measures reducing the potential for detecting and prosecuting environmental crimes that have the potential to harm millions (the D in the algorithm proposed in chapter 2).

Few countries have enacted legislation to fulfill the obligations of international conventions. Among those that have, Canada, through the federal Canadian Environmental Protection Act (CEPA) and congruent regulations in each province, dictates the handling and disposal of hazardous waste. The enforcement division oversees compliance with CEPA. Provinces also have conservation officers who enforce compliance with both provincial and federal regulations.

As mentioned above, Girard et al. (2010) report that the enforcement and conviction rates under CEPA have actually *declined* over the last 20 years despite their opinion that there has been an *increase* in the trade and trafficking of hazardous waste in Canada. They lay the blame at the feet of government, which seems not to have the political will to deal with the problem, and they include as a cause of the problem's escalation the massive reduction in the number of provincial enforcement officers in the late 1990s (by almost 30 percent across the provinces), a reduction felt most keenly in Ontario.

OTHER SPECIFIC COUNTRIES

Unlike other countries that dispose of their hazardous wastes (produced by steel and cement factories, tanneries, chemical and pharmaceutical industries) entirely overseas, Italy retains a significant portion of its hazardous wastes within its borders. According to Massari and Monzini (2004), much of that traffic is handled by large criminal organizations such as the Cosa Nostra (Sicily), Camorra (Naples), and 'Ndrangheta (Calabria). The environmental destruction has been colossal, perhaps best characterized by the scene in the docudrama *Gomorrah* in which the Mafia boss is offered vegetables by an elderly lady whom he thanks profusely; then, as his chauffeured limousine pulls away, he throws the offering into the ditch professing that he would never eat anything from that area as he sold fertilizer mixed with hazardous waste to the farmers there.

Mazzari and Monzini cite medical authorities who claim certain cancers in those areas have increased by 400 percent (Senior & Mazza, 2004). Other criminal disposal options they have noted include contaminated brick making, surfacing highways, and merely dumping huge amounts of acid and tannery sludge, transformers, and de-oiled earth by the roadside. The amount dumped in 1999 was depicted as a mountain 1,120 meters high (over 3,500 feet) with a base of three hectares (Massari & Monzini, 2004). According to the environmental organization Legambiente, 15 to 20 percent of Italy's hazardous waste merely disappears between production and disposal. The profit gleaned approaches 2.6 billion euros. The whisper of good news is that, since the passing of legislation in 2001 specifically targeting such waste trafficking, convictions are now more probable (Massari & Monzini, 2004). The illegal trafficking of hazardous waste takes place at all three points in its existence: origin, transit, and disposal. Here is an outline of that process:

- Origin: Producer pays for removal, perhaps choosing an unrealistically low bidder to do the job.
- Transit: Agent mislabels, underweights, or merely dumps material falsely identified as recyclable.
- Disposal: The disposal site relabels the material as its own and passes it off as nonhazardous.

And so it proceeds.
Common illegal operations include

- dumping in unauthorized sites outside legal regulations;
- recycling centers that process waste only on paper and produce fraudulent documentation mislabeling the material as recyclable (e.g., even for fertilizer);
- recycling centers that collect huge amounts of waste then declare bankruptcy without processing anything;
- use of ordinary municipal waste incinerators; and
- illegal dumping on roadsides or into rivers, natural caves, or mine shafts.

WHO ARE THE PERPETRATORS?

According to a "desktop study" conducted for the United Nations (Soyland, 2000), participants in those types of crimes range from the traditional Mafia-type members of crime organizations to legitimate corporate individuals and even farmers. Unlike other criminal endeavors, violence is almost never resorted to and conflict is usually limited to undercutting the competition. The sad irony is that, as regulations become more stringent, the incentive to cheat and thereby gain wealth escalates. In addition, very often organizations will be formed ephemerally to take advantage of especially lucrative opportunities and then evaporate. Over several years, the Interpol Pollution Crime Working Group has undertaken phased research on the disposal of hazardous waste by organized crime. In the first phase, it consulted with law enforcement agencies in the United Kingdom, Netherlands, Sweden, Canada, and the United States. Thirty-five case studies were collated. Details were sparse in the working group's report, but the conclusion was that organized crime was indeed involved.

Conducted by Bureau Veritas, the second phase of the **Interpol** study concluded that, even considered on its own, the British problem in dealing with electronic waste (old computers, stereos, and TVs) is immense. Four million tonnes of e-waste is generated each year by only eight countries with whom the UK deals. A Michigan State University research team began by examining the activities of registered hazardous waste disposal corporations and recyclers. Unlike their counterparts in Europe, the US researchers did not have access to closed cases of pollution crimes as the export of hazardous electronic waste is not heavily regulated, so not much was concluded.

Consequently, very little data regarding violations of environmental regulations exist. Second, it was deemed useful to examine the corporate ownership structure among apparently legitimate companies, as the literature suggested that connections among legitimate and illicit organizations existed at least in some states (Rebovich, 1992). Third, it was regarded as potentially heuristic to interview the managers of legitimate companies to determine whether they knew of illicit operations. Finally, interviews conducted with members of various regulatory agencies to obtain their opinions on the degree to which legitimate corporations engage in illegal activities revealed that those companies do commit criminal acts but not exclusively. Thus, these companies act illegally in a way similar to the pulp mills in BC that released toxic sludge from time to time or that exceeded their pollution permits, raising the question of at what point one should shut down a local corporation that is providing hundreds of jobs.

In 2005, the United States generated around 2 million tons of e-waste alone. Of especial note is that Canada, at over 11 million tons of hazardous e-waste, was, after Malaysia, the world's second largest importer of e-waste into its facilities (i.e., Falconbridge, Swan Hills, and Horizon).

That statistic may surprise many individuals who presume Canada would be much more part of the north (producer) not the south (recipient) when it comes to toxic waste. It is, however, a cautionary tale as we may ask, "What really happens to the toxic waste both produced and imported into Canada?"

The conclusion of the Interpol report (2009) is that there appears to be evidence of organized crime involved in the United States and so by extension in Canada (much of that conclusion is derived from literature reviews). This organized crime, however, differs from the hierarchical Italian mob organizations in that loosely related individuals and organizations will form corporations for short-term profits and then reorganize or even vanish, thus making it difficult for law enforcement to track the development and evolution of hazardous waste disposal as a criminal activity.

In fact, the *National Post* reported on May 28, 2019 that not only the Philippines, whose controversial leader, Rodrigo Duterte was threatening to "declare war on Canada," but also Malaysia was demanding that Canada repatriate dozens of containers of garbage that were falsely labelled as recyclable materials by companies that have since dissolved (Associated Press, 2019). So the problem is far from solved.

ORGANIZED CRIME AND ENVIRONMENTAL CRIME IN CANADA

It is ironic that the most definitive study of the involvement of organized crime in the trafficking of hazardous waste in Canada still, to date, remains a classified 93-page study completed in 1993 for Criminal Intelligence Service Ontario and titled *Organized Crime and the Environment: A Strategic Study*. According to Mitrovica and Mittelstaedt (2000), that secret study actually names various crime organizations involved in the trafficking and disposal of hazardous waste. It claims that the main activity is the widespread practice of fake recycling services: companies registered as recyclers who actually merely dump the refuse they acquire. Part of the blame for the problem is attributed to the laxer regulations regarding the importation of hazardous waste into Canada compared to the United States, which provides a significant incentive for illicit operators to import waste, allegedly to recycle it, and then to dump it in landfills or on aboriginal reserves. Another tactic it describes is to get laboratories to fake results for hazardous substances so as to allow cheap disposal methods without the required treatment. Criminal organizations target isolated farms as dump sites or mix PCBs with oil to be sprayed on rural roads as dust suppressants.

The report makes several recommendations:

1) A new ... federal offence, crime against the environment, should be added to the Criminal Code.
2) Intelligence should be gathered on "radical environmental activists who have the potential of participating in violence [a recommendation that appears a nonsequitur in view of the reports overriding mandate]....
3) [I]nstead of a large number of squads operating in an uncoordinated fashion, there should be one central unit with surveillance and investigative capabilities to oversee the enforcement of [provincial] regulations that would oversee the enforcement of the regulations. (Mitrovica & Mittelstaedt, 2000)

Again, the need for enforcement by dedicated groups, in other words, police, as is true of other forms of crime, is paramount. "A concerted effort must be exerted by enforcement authorities to prosecute violators who allow their by-products to poison our environment" (Mitrovica & Mittelstaedt, 2000).

THE PRESENT STUDY

Because almost no empirical research exists on this important issue, I will describe my efforts to conduct an exploratory study and, in doing so, get a grasp of the situation at least in Canada, a situation that seems very vague in the literature. Of course, the situation and findings, as you will see, overlap a great deal with those in the United States.

To obtain information on the state of knowledge regarding the involvement of organized crime in hazardous waste disposal, I contacted the agencies and individuals who might be best placed to provide vital information.

Once formalities were completed and I gained the confidence of the informants, I posed five questions from an inventory derived from talking to a sample of six government officials, members of non-governmental organizations (NGOs), and journalists. The interviews ranged in time from 15 minutes to two hours depending on how much relevant experience and information the informant had. That protocol comprised the following questions:

Do you know:

A. Of groups who conduct illegal businesses on a repetitive basis in related areas (e.g., transport)?
B. Whether ownership of different companies involved in dumping often includes the same persons?
C. Of anyone who has been charged with such offenses more than once?
D. Or can you give an opinion regarding the seriousness and widespread proliferation of such activities?
E. Whether the rumors involving dumping on Indian reserves have any credence?

KEY INFORMANTS

ENVIRONMENTAL NONGOVERNMENT ORGANIZATIONS Lawyers at Ecojustice (formerly the Sierra Legal Defence Fund) were interviewed regarding the issue. Their mission is to sue governments for noncompliance with the law. None seemed to be aware of organized crime but pointed out that enforcement is so lax and underfunded by government that enterprising legitimate organizations can operate at will. They gave examples of various construction and demolition crews observed dumping special wastes into general landfills, especially in the interior of BC where supervision is low or nonexistent. That view is supported by the work of Girard et al. (2010)

Representatives of the conservation group Fraser Riverkeeper, including one longtime former prosecutor, were not aware of the involvement of organized crime. They reported that the hazardous waste they observed appeared to be dumped, with little impunity, on the banks of or even right into the Fraser River (BC's largest and most important salmon river) by regular construction companies or truckers hired to clear demolition sites. They also mentioned seeing hazardous wastes such as oil barrels and drywall dumped on reserves. They assumed that this was the work of "midnight dumpers."

GOVERNMENT ORGANIZATIONS In the course of conducting this investigation, I contacted 25 individuals in the following organizations: Environment Canada, Criminal Intelligence Service Canada (CISC), Canadian Intelligence Service Ontario (CISO), the Ministry of the Environment of Ontario Enforcement Branch, Six Nations Police, and the departments of the environment in Quebec, New Brunswick, Alberta, British Columbia, Nunavut, and Manitoba. Both former and present members of the environmental departments responsible for the environment were contacted. Finally, I contacted the undersecretary responsible for the environment and fisheries in the United Kingdom, who was very interested in the study. Then I was passed on to the Department for Environment, Food and Rural Affairs that handles matters of enforcement. So far the Interpol study has been the most useful information that government organizations have provided.

FINDINGS
Few respondents were willing to go on record, but following are some of the conclusions gleaned from the interviews and exchanges:

- No organized crime activity appears to be operating in the Far North, probably because there are few mines to date in Nunavut and no road or rail links with southern Canada.
- Enforcement informants in Manitoba report that illegal dumping does take place but to their knowledge on a smaller scale than existed during the 1990s when biker gangs were deeply involved in the illegal disposal of waste. One point made was that, with the state-of-the-art facilities available in Swan Hills, Alberta, and Sarnia, Ontario, it was much easier to profit by following regulations as the supply grew with the economy.
- Organized crime is reported to be operating in Quebec and to be increasing with the movement from New York State of waste disposal companies associated with organized crime. There is at least one hazardous waste disposal site that is highly suspect. One informant reported that gangsters have always been involved to some extent and that he had even been involved in charging perpetrators

and appearing as a witness in several cases. Some had received short jail sentences, but he did not recall anyone ever serving any time. He appeared to know of one company that was, to his knowledge, originally from New Jersey; it was now operating in Quebec.

- Several of the informants interviewed were very helpful and experienced. They spoke of small organizations that would bid on disposal contracts and then disband or go bankrupt if there was any surveillance or enforcement pressure, a finding similar to that of studies I have noted previously. Organized crime appears to be well established in Ontario and increasing, especially with the incursion of American waste disposal companies. Some individuals have been repeatedly convicted and reportedly have even served jail time. Some sources lamented the lack of more resources, especially to track individuals who were involved in hazardous waste disposal and had previous convictions.

- No hard evidence exists for the involvement of organized crime in the dumping of toxic waste in British Columbia, but there appear to be opportunistic individuals who have been involved in questionable activities on more than one occasion. The model appears to involve entrepreneurial individuals forming a company, obtaining a contract by underbidding, and then declaring bankruptcy or dissolving the company as surveillance increases. They form another company in the future as opportunities arise.

- Dumping of toxic waste on aboriginal land, especially on reserves, is occurring and is probably increasing, but no one seems to have a grasp on the gravity of the problem. There are three types of dumping on reserves (known as reservations in the States): formal deals made with waste companies, illegal dumping by individual Native American entrepreneurs trying to make a fast dollar, and, finally, midnight dumping by unknown parties.

PRESS RELEASES AND NEWSPAPER REPORTS A survey of press releases by governments and journalistic reports uncovered charges laid against the exporting of toxic wastes to various countries (see, e.g., Environment Canada, 2011a), but the documentation makes no mention of whether the companies involved are legitimate or criminal organizations.

CONCLUSIONS

It is clear that the impetus for illegal dumping is financial. That is, illegal dumping occurs whenever profits can be increased dramatically by circumventing proper procedures and destinations. However, legitimate means of disposal aided by the existence of state-of-the-art facilities such as the one at Swan Hills (which is, moreover, strongly supported by the local citizenry) allow a handsome profit to be made easily by operating within the law. In the opinion of informants, a combination of lowered volumes of waste being produced by generating sites, onsite treatment, and accessible waste disposal facilities may be the biggest economic and convenience deterrent to organized crime. Conversely, lack of legitimate opportunities spawns the criminogenic situation extant in Italy and other constituencies. It is especially telling that the so-called garbage strikes in Naples appear to be at least in significant part motivated by the entrenched Mafia's objection to legislation promoting greater recycling rather than mere collection and landfilling, which it apparently controls (Newcomer, 2015).

WHAT CAN WE CONCLUDE?

Two conclusions are clear: there is a market in the illegal transportation and dumping of hazardous waste, and it varies dramatically from country to country, with perhaps the worst situation existing in southern Italy.

A review of the claims of the victimization of developing nations in the southern hemisphere suggests that some distressing situations exist, such as the Trafigura dumping in the Côte d'Ivoire in 2006, but these situations (and that incident) are unusual rather than the norm. In that case, a ship refused to pay high disposal charges for hazardous waste disposal in the Netherlands and ended up releasing its cargo in Abidjan. The cargo was then dispersed among various sites in the city, resulting in 17 deaths and thousands requiring immediate medical attention. Eventually, Trafigura ended up paying US$198 million to the Côte d'Ivoire government, but none of its employees or officers was charged, whereas local government officials were prosecuted for their complicity.

In fact, most transboundary movement of hazardous waste is legitimate and occurs between equals or near equals with the recipient prepared to deal with the waste. One main issue is the very definition of hazardous or toxic waste itself, as there is little consensus even among European countries. For instance, the Netherlands has a very specific definition of hazardous waste with different degrees of chemical waste among other gradations. Britain, however, varies its definition according to the location of the waste within its own boundaries. The United States does not regard most e-waste as waste but rather as recycling material, perhaps with some justification, for it costs $25 to dispose of a computer there for which some Asian agents will actually pay $15. Thus the British have some justification in arguing for context when defining toxic waste.

Toxic waste is a growing problem in many parts of the world, but the main way it is being dealt with in North America is to reduce the output and to ship the rest to a few designated sites that can deal adequately with the waste, facilities such as those in Swan Hills or Sarnia. Regarding the involvement of organized crime, there is ample evidence that the large profits available have attracted organized crime's involvement worldwide. Most often, the organized crime involved in disposing toxic waste does not follow the traditional Mafia model.

International conventions and federal and provincial regulations have been established in the area of hazardous waste disposal, but very little political will to combat the immensity and gravity of the crime of illegal trafficking and dumping has manifested itself either internationally or in Canada. In fact enforcement capacity has generally diminished across Canada in the last 20 years, although some informants have said that the federal government has recently hired more enforcement officers. The Trump administration has announced massive cuts to follow in the United States.

Much more in-depth, empirical, on-the-ground research must be conducted to evaluate the extent of organized crime's involvement in Canada and the United States, as well as on the international scene.

IN SUMMARY

PART ONE: HAZARDOUS WASTE AND CORPORATE CRIME

Pollution has often been viewed as the price of doing business and creating wealth. Governments have repeatedly been in cahoots with corporations, resulting in both catastrophic disasters and the insidious contamination of food and wildlife, which threatens public health. Governments have been eager to take over unreclaimed and thus inexpensive contaminated sites to show the public how they are saving tax dollars. Too often, governments wish to cut a compromise between pollution and leaving pristine and healthy environments.

Market forces, in effect applying community standards of tolerance, will force corporations to cleanse their products or waste disposal in order to keep their major customers, but perhaps not soon enough to avoid considerable environmental damage.

PART TWO: THE INTERNATIONAL TRAFFICKING OF HAZARDOUS WASTE AND ORGANIZED CRIME

International disposal of waste is marked by terrible anecdotes of dumping in developing countries, but even the definition of hazardous waste shows no consensus among countries.

Organized crime is involved in Canada, the United States, and especially Italy, but the situation is improving in North America as legitimate toxic waste sites are established. In Italy, the situation is dire and appears not to be improving.

A mind-boggling slew of international regulations and agreements is basically ineffectual as no enforcement authority exists to back these up.

Governments in Canada and the United States have dramatically reduced enforcement capability.

Much of the organized crime operating in waste disposal appears to be ephemeral rather than generational; in other words, these operations are not like the Mafia's involvement in other crimes.

Few if any individuals have been incarcerated for committing environmental crimes.

CHAPTER TWELVE

CYBERCRIME: ADVANCING TECHNOLOGY IN AGGRESSION, WAR, AND CRIME

This chapter argues that computer crime is only the current, latest enabling instrument in the armament used by past leaders, criminals, and revolutionaries to win wars, rule the world, make the world better, or merely make a buck.

The year was 1229. The Mongols attacked on horseback, constantly firing arrows at the seemingly endless Chinese army assembled before them. The Chinese had never experienced such an onslaught of arrows. The Mongol horsemen seemed to be firing continuously rather than halting to reload their bows, but finally they were in retreat, so the leading Chinese squads gave pursuit. Unexpectedly, those Mongols in retreat unleashed another continuous volley of arrows, wiping out their closest pursuers. How was that possible if they remained seated in their saddles? Reloading always required stopping to maintain balance. The answer was a simple but revolutionary technological advance: the stirrup. The Mongols were able to stand on horseback, their feet securely inserted into stirrups that allowed them to shoot arrow after arrow in full charge and even to pivot and shoot at full gallop when retreating and beyond the reach of horsemen-wielding swords and lances or mounted archers without stirrups (Inglis-Arkell, 2017). So retreat also became a deadly tactic. The bow and arrow became the first rapid-fire cavalry weapon.

According to the historian Thomas Craughwell (2011), Mongol leader Genghis Khan founded the largest ever contiguous land empire and the second largest empire in history, in significant part thanks to that "small" technological advance, the stirrup, which made the Mongol cavalry practically unbeatable on the battlefield against more primitively equipped horsemen.

On the other hand, 500 years ago, the Chinese Ming Dynasty had the greatest navy in the world, about 3,500 great warships, far outnumbering the navy of any other country (currently, the United States has about 480). China's giant warships were also up to 120 meters long, five times the size of any European country's vessels. But they conquered nobody though they repeatedly made huge merchant voyages to Africa and other destinations. Why, with such technological superiority, did they not rule the world?

One oft-quoted explanation is that, having completed many voyages to other parts of the world, the Chinese emperor concluded that there was nothing worth pursuing beyond China's borders. Only primitive societies existed abroad, none comparable to advanced Chinese culture and technology, and so, it is said, given the monumental cost of maintaining such a huge fleet, the emperor ordered it burned. More recently, Nobel Prize–winning economist Angus Deaton (2013) in his book *The Great Escape: Health, Wealth, and the Origins of Inequality* disagrees, arguing that the world trade produced by the voyages of the great Admiral Zheng He was creating a wealthy merchant class that threatened the absolute power of the emperor and his ruling class. So they put an end to those voyages. By 1525 not one megaship remained.

Because of that self-imposed isolation, over the centuries China missed out on the rising tsunami of technological advances emanating from Europe and then North America, including the industrial and communications revolutions. It was not until the late twentieth century that, embarking on an economic revolution from within to overcome the cloying strictures of communism, China caught up and finally, after so many centuries, has become poised to surpass the rest of the world. Part of that lightning-speed progress has been prompted by its insistence that any high-tech trade with it includes giving China the trading partner country's intellectual property and patents, for example. That bargaining demand has allowed it to leapfrog to the front of world trade. It is an aspect of its trade that, in 2018, President Trump vowed to halt (Long, 2018).

Emerging from that strategy, China has sprung to the front in the **"cyberwars"** with a massive number of computer experts, hackers, and other tech whizzes whom some claim regularly and remotely pirate the industrial and technological secrets of the world and, even more sinisterly, perhaps attack its national security and military control systems (Clarke & Knake, 2010). So China, after 500 years and now with technological parity or even supremacy recouped, this time contemplates no withdrawal from the real world or the virtual world of **cyberspace**. China had learned the lesson well from history: not only is isolation a fatal choice but so is being even a step behind the emerging technology of the day. Indeed, falling behind could be disastrous economically and militarily in the twenty-first century. Thus, China has become a major player ready to do battle in the impending world of cyberwarfare.

> Cyberwarfare is the use or targeting in a battlespace or warfare context of computers, online control systems and networks. It involves both offensive and defensive operations pertaining to the threat of cyberattacks, espionage and sabotage. ("Cyberwarfare," 2019)

According to Andy Greenberg (2017), near catastrophic attacks have already happened in Ukraine, where the Russians in their unrelenting attempts to destabilize and reseize that country have unleashed thousands of cyber strikes derailing its media, power grid, and even its finance ministry's functioning. The most profound attacks occurred in December 2015 and 2016, when large parts of the Ukrainian electrical grid were plunged into blackout. But that was just a test run compared to what could follow.

It was not the first attack of this kind. According to Kim Zetter (2014, 2015), a joint Israeli-US attack against Iranian uranium enrichment facilities—insinuating the Stuxnet worm, a virus that targets programmable logic controllers through infected flash drives—caused hundreds of centrifuges to spin out of control and physically self-destruct. This attack set back the campaign to create nuclear weapons, which threatened Israel, given the Iranian regime's avowed intention to destroy that nation.

Thus the war is waged anonymously and remotely through malware-accessing computer systems. Those characteristics allow for a certain type of individual to enter the realm of war and crime. This person is a far cry from the Bill Miner type. Miner was a pioneer of an earlier technology, a gentlemanly American who coined the phrase "Hands up!" when robbing trains, which, like personal computers in the 1990s, were a new technology for transporting money and gold bullion in large amounts in my area near Ashcroft, British Columbia, during the late 1800s and early 1900s. So too, the Bonnie Parker and Clyde Barrow duo that robbed banks in the United States during the 1930s adopted the emerging technologies of ever-faster cars and automatic rifles to make their getaways.

And Ken Leishman, a fellow I knew who ran for mayor of my northern Ontario hometown of Red Lake, used small bush planes to fly to and from bank robberies that he perpetrated in southern Ontario (Robertson, 1981). Though armed, he never killed anyone, and after engineering the largest gold heist of bullion in Canadian history in Winnipeg, Manitoba, Leishman was captured and imprisoned. After serving his sentence, he became a model citizen in town and even ran for mayor. Ironically, given that it was a tough mining town that you fought your way into and out of, the only black man in town beat him in the election. Thus Leishman was a curious mix of the psychopathic renegade and the solid citizen; he died in a plane crash on a mercy mission flying a patient to hospital.

Common to Miner, Bonnie and Clyde, and Leishman was their willingness to show themselves publicly. Yes, they used the latest technology to facilitate their criminal careers and their cavalier attitudes. However, in the process, they exposed themselves in criminal situations that were risky, not to mention that possibly required them to injure or even kill, as did Parker and Barrow—anyone who stood in their way or tried to apprehend them. Not so cybercriminals.

Among the first high-tech, anonymous criminals were those who hacked the long distance telephone systems of large companies in order to make free calls during the 1960s to 1990s, when tone signals could be imitated (in some cases using special "blue boxes") to gain access to the lines. That phenomenon is known as **phreaking**, derived from phone and freak, perhaps a play on the word "frequency." It has come to mean any attempt to hack into a closed communication system. It is a testament to their history of innovation that the founders of Apple, Steve Jobs and Steve Wozniak, were in their youth among the first phreakers named by Steven Levy (1984).

Steven Levy, in his celebrated book *Hackers: Heroes of the Computer Revolution*, lionizes the brilliant, anarchistic students at Massachusetts Institute of Technology who, with makeshift computers, some made from parts salvaged from pinball machines that had primitive logic systems in them, began by **hacking** into a card-sorting machine and ended by trying to infiltrate the closed computer systems of corporations and the military in the 1960s. (Their "enemy" was the giant IBM computer at MIT.) They were the classic nerds, who in high school aced math and failed phys ed, characterized by "underdeveloped pectoral muscles" in short-sleeved plaid shirts and chino pants. Many went on to prominent roles in academia and industry. They were portrayed as idealistic, wanting to share all available information with the world, but the typical hacker, according to Rogers (2014), is a creature of lesser stature, literally and ideologically.

One hacker that runs true to type is Michael Calce, born in 1986 in Montreal. He was very distraught when his parents separated when he was five years old and his mother, who had custody and lived with him in the suburbs, would send him to stay with his father in the city, away from home and friends. To assuage the boy's unhappiness, his father bought him a computer, which became Michael's object of complete fascination, first with its sounds as it processed commands and then later as a way to communicate with others on the Internet. In the isolation created by that custody order, Michael quickly became an aficionado of the Internet, a lonely, unhappy boy for whom producing electronic mischief became an end in itself.

On February 7, 2000, Michael, now self-named "MafiaBoy," targeted Yahoo—a multibillion-dollar company—with an attack he dubbed Rivolta (riot or uprising in Italian). He shut down the company for an hour using a program he had downloaded from Hotline, a file-sharing platform. He then went on to shut down eBay, CNN, and Dell over the following week. One estimate, given in court when he was apprehended, calculated the damage he had wrought to be as high as US$1.2 billion; other estimates were much lower. He might never have been caught had he not bragged about his accomplishments to his online chat group, the virtual friends who had replaced any he might have made face to face at school. After serving eight months of open custody, one year of probation, having use of the Internet restricted, and paying a small fine, he was released. He went on to write a column for a Montreal newspaper and to found his own computer security firm (Calce & Silverman, 2008).

That story is almost charming; it's about a boy who was a brilliant user of a new technology and caused havoc—just because he could and to win the envy and esteem of his online peer group. This peer group resembles a gang in that both are reference groups. But even a virtual "gang" is rather different than the street corner or drug-economy-driven variety. There is no physical violence, no physical posturing, no actual meetings with living people. Virtual anonymity.

Today, some things about cybercriminals have changed but other aspects remain the same. Fast forwarding to 2018, we have another lonely boy, Karim Baratov, whose family moved to a Hamilton, Ontario, suburb from Kazakhstan in 2007, when he was 12 years old. He had few friends, couldn't speak the language, and was obsessed with his computer on which he spent too much time, to the point of almost failing high school for lack of attendance and interest. Then he did a job for a woman he knew, infiltrating an e-mail account, and though he insisted he wanted no reward, she gave him $200, a fortune to him.

A light came on. He could put his services on the web for hire. Within a short time, he created a multiplicity of websites, offering his services at the beginning for small amounts of money, for example, $60 to $90. He made his first million by the time he was 15. Soon, fancy cars, including a Lamborghini, and Armani clothes followed, so by the time he graduated, he was in a position to buy his own house, which he did down the street from his mum and dad for over $600,000 (Lista, 2018). And then he was sought out by some much bigger fish: Russian secret agents, hackers extraordinaire.

"Kim," as he preferred, created a Russian "**spearphishing**" website titled WebXakep, which in Cyrillic is pronounced "webhacker." For a modest sum, he offered to gain access invisibly to any account by spearphishing, that is, sending a notice pretending to be a missive from a company with which the target had an account and requesting a confirmation, including the password. He said it usually took five minutes, enabling him to make $1,000 per hour. Of course spearphishing gave Kim access to Visa accounts, bank accounts, and many more sources of funds that could be absconded with by Kim's clients. No estimate has been made of the vast economic hardship he, a professional gun for hire, created.

When Yahoo, one of the world's largest Internet companies, was infiltrated in 2012 and had 450,000 accounts compromised, it appeared to be a humanitarian gesture intended to serve as a warning. Unfortunately, Yahoo did little to strengthen security. According to the FBI, however, a second attack in 2014 was launched from the Lubyanka building in Russia, home to that country's secret service, now known as the FSB. Though it was denied by the Russians, the FBI identified Dmitry Dokuchaev and his boss Igor Sushchin, Russian espionage agents, as the perpetrators. They then added a notorious computer criminal, the Latvian Alexey Belan, who had fled to Russia after defrauding many individuals and corporations, was captured, and then recruited rather than imprisoned.

The spies went on to obtain the computer files of prominent people across the world, but especially of Russians who were known to be critical of Putin. So like the Russian KGB and the Stasi (the East German secret police) in communist times, they were tracking the activities of, rather than merely listening in on, their countrymen—thanks to that cyberspace advance in technology. And when they hacked Yahoo, it lost 6 percent of value in one day, and a potential buyer, Verizon, lowered its offer of $4.8 billion by $350 million.

Baratov did very little for them, but when the FBI net descended, he was entangled, and when a grand jury indicted the four men, Baratov was arrested. Dokuchaev was likely a double agent for the FBI and was charged by the Russians with treason. Baratov was the only one arrested in North America, as the rest were in Europe or Russia. He was found guilty on several counts of identity theft and one count of intent to commit computer fraud and abuse. He claims not to have known he was working for a network of top Russian espionage agents. His prosecutors were asking for a prison sentence of seven to nine years (Lista, 2018); eventually, he received five years and a $250,000 fine.

How does this new breed of cybercriminal differ from our examples of criminals who embraced previous crime-facilitating technological advances: the train and airplane and fast car and machine gun? All the "old-school" criminals attained folk hero status. Several things characterizing these "old school" criminals leap out at once: physical risk taking, use of firearms, willingness to risk killing innocent victims, and, most of all, lack of anonymity. In fact, the bank and train robbers experienced its opposite: public notoriety. No "wanted" handbills are posted with likenesses of cybercriminals, though. Computer crime allows shy or socially isolated, physically underdeveloped, and clearly cerebrally gifted but nonviolent or even cowardly individuals to engage in criminal activity and to obtain accolades for a virtual persona from a virtual rather than a physical reference group. But the biggest differences are avoiding physical risk and maintaining anonymity.

In my estimation, however, the biggest similarity to the other criminals is faulty or lack of moral development—barring one type of exception, tantamount to the homicidal and/or suicidal terrorist who is involved for idealistic or religious reasons. Now let us examine that parameter.

Rogers (2011) has made an attempt to identify and differentiate among cybercriminals in a taxonomy within which most of our case studies can be located. In his system, they were originally labeled "script kiddies, cyber-punks, hacktivists, thieves, virus writers, professionals, and cyber-terrorists" (p. 218).

Script kiddies are young, immature, and do not truly appreciate what they are involved in. They have little technological knowledge and, according to Rogers, download software to create mischief. Sometimes they are not even aware of what the malware is creating, as occurred when MafiaBoy set it into motion and then went to school, leaving it alone to wreak its mayhem. Rogers speculates that they operate in Kohlberg's system at stage 2: naïve instrumental hedonism. To them, attacking a system is a "thrill ride" with the additional benefit of bragging rights. If they exercise those rights, they are most easily identified and caught by law enforcement individuals.

Rogers's second category is cyber-punks, who have a disrespect for authority and its norms and target its symbols. He believes they are driven by a need for notoriety and recognition by their peers and, in their virtual persona, by society. They are teenagers, so slightly older than script kiddies, and like other teenagers, they are dominated by a lust for status. They are also aware that, as minors, should they be caught, they will receive little more than a "slap on the wrist" from the courts, so they almost welcome detection as a portal to fame. Although Rogers refers to them as merely having a "faulty morality," they are also in stage 2 but with the added element of powerful adolescent peer influence that Moffitt (1993) refers to as **adolescent limited criminality**. Bandura would agree, pointing out that, as adolescents, they are at the height of susceptibility to modeling or vicarious learning. Most cease mayhem-wreaking hacking as they mature.

Among the cyber-punks, Rogers identifies a group that embellishes its activities with a patina of self-righteousness: the hacktivists. That group embraces the previous group's motivations: members hack because they can, and they also seek recognition and notoriety, although in a much more clandestine reference group. However, hacktivists purport to act not for self-gain but for the benefit of society. The first recorded incident of hacktivism occurred in 1989 when Worms Against Nuclear Killers (WANK) infected a network shared by NASA and the US Department of Energy to protest the launching of a plutonium-powered spacecraft given the concerns about radioactive fallout after the *Challenger* disaster (Karagiannopoulos, 2018). That attack merely communicated some protest messages.

Another early group—the Critical Art Ensemble—took pains not to damage media sites other than the one members were targeting. The attacks took several forms, most notably, the virtual sit-in that rendered a targeted site inoperable, often by flooding it with incoming e-mails. Another group of hacktivists, the Electronic Disturbance Theater, aimed to "translate and express the unbearable weight of physical beings into the immaterial informational channels"; members used software to automatically reload error pages condemning the host, for example, with an error message such as "Human Rights not found on this server" (quoted in Karagiannopoulos, 2018, p. 19). One of the principals, Dominguez, sees himself as an artist enhancing activist goals through artistic performance. The UK Electrohippies organized a major online disruption—a virtual sit-in during the World Trade Organization's meetings in Seattle in 1999. The harsh UK law enforcement response led the group to desist activities.

Perhaps the best capsulation of another hacktivist group's raison d'être is in the name of one of its most notorious and successful movements: **Anonymous**. That group started as a chat room rather than a collective of activists, originating from imageboard 4chan's random board /b/ to celebrate geekdom. The word "**geek**" originally referred to carnival freaks but now refers to experts in some fields, such as computers or other forms of pop culture. Since its politicization, Anonymous has been referred to as a collective, but in actuality it is not. Karagiannopoulos (2018) claims it is an umbrella identity that includes many factions with differing ideologies but common goals embracing a "humorous deviant outlook, an anticelebrity ethic," diverse tech tools, and well-planned political intervention techniques (p. 26). Some elements wanted more activism, some more irreverence—so splinter groups have appeared. Its activities include information hacks; "doxing," or releasing private information; virtual sit-ins; and even public demonstrations with participants wearing Guy Fawkes masks.

A prime target has been the Church of Scientology. Others include Mastercard, PayPal, and Amazon, for refusing to process donations to Julian Assange. Assange, the founder and editor of *WikiLeaks*, received and published US diplomatic cables from Chelsea (Bradley) Manning, a CIA operative who was sentenced to 35 years for revealing classified information and then pardoned by President Obama. Anonymous has also taken on the Islamic State of Iraq and Syria (ISIS), the Ku Klux Klan, and more recently US President Donald Trump. Several members of Anonymous have been uncovered and pleaded guilty to misdemeanors and even felonies. One who did not plead guilty was given two years probation and ordered to pay $183,000 in restitution. Another got two years in prison. The movement seems to have waned since.

Rogers (2011) argues that very often petty criminals adopt the sobriquet hacktivist because it is more respectable, though their actions have base motives such as revenge, power, greed, marketing, or media attention. Those motivated largely by money and greed, he labels "thieves" as they are common criminals engaging in wire transfer fraud and the fraudulent use of credit card numbers though their livelihood is not dependent on criminal acts. So like the script kiddies, their moral development is also at stage 2; they leave their hapless victims to bear the brunt of their nefarious activities. Like the drug dealer or the bank robber, they take advantage of the skills they possess to line their pockets, caring little for whom they victimize.

Rogers argues that virus writers may comprise several types paralleling cyber-punks who wish to show off their technical expertise, but I submit there is a very good possibility that virus writers may in some cases be working in concert with companies that sell antivirus software, although no solid evidence exists.

In that sense, they are like those he labels "professionals" who may be involved in corporate swindles or espionage. Or like the Russians referred to earlier, some professionals may have segued from being government operatives to mercenaries after the fall of the Eastern Bloc countries. And of course those he categorizes as cyber-terrorists are no different than any terrorist whose aim is to instill fear and loathing in the target group.

IN SUMMARY

Again, like the traditional terrorist or warrior or criminal, cybercriminals can inflict destruction and even death on a target using superior technology. However cybercriminals, unlike traditional criminals, operate without the element of personal physical risk. In the final analysis, like the stirrup or machine gun or airplane, the computer in the hands of a criminal is merely an instrument for carrying out the destructive actions and campaigns that have always motivated or even obsessed humankind throughout the course of history.

POSTSCRIPT

Not everyone embraces new technology. In 1811 to 1816, when mill owners used knitting machines to circumvent labor laws, gangs of deadly serious, but mischievous and even violent, protesters smashed machines and burned textile mills and got themselves killed by the authorities. Known as Luddites after a mythical young rebel who smashed a knitting machine two decades before, they came to symbolize those who protest new waves of technology that produce not only change but hardship for the masses.

So too, a brilliant young mathematician, a former professor at the University of California–Berkeley, began a campaign of bombings by mail in the late 1970s that terrified the United States for 17 years, culminating in over 20 victims seriously injured but, almost miraculously, only three deaths. For instance, a bombed airliner managed to land safely. To end the devastation and fear and the longest, most expensive manhunt ever undertaken by the FBI, he demanded that his essay "Industrial Society and Its Future" be published in the *New York Times* and the *Washington Post*. Under duress, Attorney General Janet Reno agreed (McFadden, 1996).

Theodore Kaczynski was born to a working-class couple of Polish origin in Chicago, Illinois. Although somewhat traumatized by a week's hospitalization in isolation as an infant, Kaczynski was doted over by his parents, as was his younger brother, David. He was shy and retiring but brilliant and entered Harvard on a scholarship at age 16. Despite an undistinguished undergraduate career, and a personal life on campus spent in isolation and misery, he was admitted to the mathematics graduate program at the University of Michigan where his academic talents burgeoned with his publishing several papers in prestigious journals and his doctoral thesis winning an award. At 25, he became an assistant professor at the University of California–Berkeley, where he was disliked by his students. He quit after two years to return to Chicago to work for a company under his younger brother in a mundane job. His brother was forced to fire him for harassing a fellow worker whom Theodore had briefly dated.

Kaczynski drifted west, ending up in a tiny cabin in the mountains of Montana where he lived a subsistence existence subsidized by his family. There, he read widely and wrote endless letters and tracts decrying technology's destruction of humanity's freedom and the natural world as he watched logging and mining devastate the countryside around him. And then he started making and mailing bombs: first to university faculty and airlines—hence the name Unabomber—and then to random individuals associated with genetics, computers, timber lobbying, public relations, and other aspects of industrial society. His manifesto argued that humanity was becoming enslaved by technology and would soon be controlled by it, enthrall to it, unless a revolution could be mounted. And that was in the 1980s and 1990s, before cellular phones became the center of one's existence.

As the FBI had hoped, someone close to the Unabomber (in point of fact, his brother's wife) read the manifesto and pointed out its chilling similarity to Ted's rants in his letters to his brother David. David turned him in. Ted Kaczynski is now serving a life sentence without possibility of parole.

Reading Kaczynski's history was a bit chilling for me as well—much in the same way that medical students worry they might have the disease they are studying that week. His background and career parallel mine even to the timeframe and his obtaining his doctorate at the University of Michigan, a university neighboring my own University of Wisconsin–Madison.

Kaczynski's mother said he had been a happy child and then suddenly changed, becoming quiet and withdrawn though not antisocial. His unhappiness intensified when he was sent to Harvard at the tender age of 16 where he should have blossomed. His housemates barely knew him. He seemed surly, perhaps terrified.

Why did we end up so differently? I, too, was a happy child even when difficulties arose in my family, but I had a sister and brother-in-law who embraced me and kept me afloat until those difficult times passed. Thus, I never ended up unhappy or isolated. I had never been in isolation as an infant, which we know from a previous chapter (again, regarding Harlow's monkeys and Romanian orphans) can be severely damaging. Ted's mum suspected he was autistic but withdrew him from an assessment program as she found the world expert who was in charge, Bruno Bettelheim, to be too cold and withdrawn.

Autism can interfere with a person's ability to interact socially and can reduce her or his ability to gauge signs of reaction in others. Most important, if autism is comorbid with alexithymia, it can reduce even a person's ability to empathize with others. Despite my apoplectic rage at how individuals, corporations, and governments destroy wilderness and the environment around us, I could never contemplate deliberately blowing up someone, even inflicting severe pain and injury. The mental picture alone would be too horrifying. So I funneled my efforts into conservation organizations. On the other hand, Kaczynski had no problem dealing alone with the organizations he viewed as culprits. They were just targets in his overall plan. And his confidence in his abilities, as well as his feelings of superiority over others, overcame his social ineptness. Ironically, given his aversion to technology, like cyber-criminals, he could wreak havoc without revealing himself. But he used bombs, not computer viruses.

Sadly, like other, baser serial killers, Ted was imbued with the desire to be recognized, to make his mark, to make up for his ultimate failure in academe, in life, in never having had an intimate relationship with a woman, with anyone. During his capture, unlike the shy retiring nerd of his youth who avoided social interaction, even eye contact, he appears in the Unabomber documentary on Netflix to be glorying in the attention of the media and stares straight into the cameras.

He has finally achieved his métier, a public persona, previously so elusive, unobtainable. Like so many other revolutionaries, he appears to relish his role as the bomber, the killer—to demonstrate that he is the exception to mundane society. In his mind, he is a true visionary. That obsession trumps all other factors.

GLOSSARY

abortion The intentional premature termination of a pregnancy.

accommodation The effect that assimilation has on mental concepts as children develop.

attention deficit hyperactivity disorder (ADHD) A chronic condition afflicting some small children, especially boys, so that they cannot stand still or focus on any one thing. ADHD is sometimes a precursor to psychopathy.

adolescent limited criminality The hypothesis that most young offenders will mature out of their delinquent youth. See also **life-course persistent criminality**.

affective Emotional. In psychology, *affect* is a concept describing the experience of feeling.

ambient temperature Surrounding or environmental temperature.

amygdala An emotion processing and aggression center in the brain.

anaclitic depression The syndrome identified by René Spitz among children warehoused in orphanages who had little human contact and often did not develop speech and even died within several months.

Anonymous A movement that began as a computer chat room and moved on to disrupt and even damage major computer systems of government and commerce for ideological purposes.

anterior hypothalamus An area of the brain that contains temperature-sensitive neurons and responds to internal temperature changes by initiating thermoregulatory responses to restore a constant temperature.

asbestos A naturally occurring mineral used in fireproofing that is deadly when ingested.

assimilation The process by which children take new material into their minds from the environment.

Bayer's H Heroin legally marketed as a soothing drug at the turn of the twentieth century.

biogenetic constitutional theories Explanations of human behavior encompassing biological and genetic causes.

birth trauma Experiencing stress or damage during birth that is translated into behavioral or neurological issues.

blasphemy Speech, writing, or behavior that insults God or something considered sacred.

bonobos Pygmy chimpanzees whose leaders are always female and keep males under their control through sex.

callous-unemotional syndrome (CU) A condition in children who do not show significant emotion. CU is believed to be a precursor to psychopathy.

carcinogenic Cancer causing.

caudate nucleus A center of the brain involved in inhibiting aggression through potentiating strong feelings of affection.

chlorofluorocarbons Substances used in various appliances such as refrigerators and in spray cans that deplete the ozone layer of the atmosphere.

classical conditioning The process discovered by Ivan Pavlov that an association can be made between a neutral stimulus or object by pairing it with a following reward or punishment. The effect is mediated by high arousal (fear or pleasure) within the individual.

clear-cut To harvest trees by cutting down all the trees in an area, creating huge swaths of devastated land.

coercion theory The theory that authoritarian parents (those who rule through arbitrary authority—"Do so because I say so!") pass along to their children a style using force or threat.

cognition Thinking, usually referring to the process within the brain as it relates to other processes.

cognitive Descriptive of conscious intellectual activity (such as thinking, reasoning, or remembering).

cognitive restructuring A psychotherapeutic technique for identifying and altering irrational or stressful thought patterns and beliefs.

community standards Especially of tolerance—what degree of deviation from the norm the group or community will accept.

concrete operational stage The third stage in Jean Piaget's theory of cognitive development, at which the child can use logical thought but can only apply logic to physical objects.

Conflict Tactics Scale A ten-point scale that measures aggression from mild reaction (e.g., pushing) to severely aggressive (e.g., using a deadly weapon).

conformity Adherence to the consensus of a majority in a group.

conscience The product of a healthy superego wherein reside guilt feelings and the ego ideal.

conscious awareness The ability to understand the actual state of the world and the effects of your actions in it.

conservation In Piagetian theory, the phase in which the child can now recognize objects and people when seen from different perspectives.

conventional level of morality The second level in Kohlberg's six stages of moral development, encompassing stages 3 and 4. The individual in stage 3 is dominated by the tendency to get along and engage in reciprocity. Stage 4 is dominated by conformity to society and its laws.

counterphobic response The theory that people are drawn to media content that depicts behaviors they fear in order to reduce that fear.

CT scan A coaxial tomography scan that produces a three-dimensional picture of brain structures.

culpability Guilt or responsibility for a negative outcome of one's actions.

cyberspace The notional environment in which communication over computer networks occurs.

cyberwars The use of computer technology to disrupt the activities of a state or organization.

decentration The process of moving from one system of classification of objects in the world to another. Decentration enables an individual to consider multiple attributes or perspectives of a situation or an object.

determinism The premise that if one knew all the factors involved one could predict a person's behavior. More broadly, determinism is a theory that behavior and natural and social phenomena are determined by preceding factors and natural laws.

differential association The theory that crime is learned in small interaction groups, that is, from the people whom you hang out with.

dioxins Highly toxic by-product produced by the delignification (wood fiber breakdown) process in pulp production using chlorine.

dissemination How widespread the effects are, for example, the number of victimized people, animals, or ecosystems.

dissynchrony Out of step or not coordinated with one another.

Dr. Jekyll and Mr. Hyde A character in a story by R. L. Stevenson. This character's personality would switch from civilized and educated to a murderous brute and then back.

ecological Concerned with the world of living organisms in the physical world and their relation to one another.

Ecs-TC syndrome Emotional-cognitive stress produced by thermo-regulatory conflict.

egalitarianism Believing in and/or practicing equality, especially in regards to gender or race.

ego A sense of self and a grasp of social reality based on the normal development of the child. In psychoanalytic theory, the ego is the division of the psyche that mediates between the individual and reality.

ego disturbance The consequence of improper custodial care by the mother or other principal caregiver, thereby not permitting the child to develop normally through the stages.

ego ideal A model of perfection for which the ego must strive.

egocentrism An early stage of development in which the child presumes it is the center of the universe.

Eros The life or love instinct that motivates sexual behavior, love, and compassion.

ethnocentrism The judging of other cultures based on the values and mores of one's own culture, often leading to pride, vanity, the belief in one's own group's superiority, and contempt for outsiders.

evolutionary neuroandrogenic theory Its major premise is that the genes and prenatal environments promoting high testosterone levels in the unborn child are precursors for several neurological disorders.

e-waste Discarded bits of electronic devices, including cell phones, TVs, and computers.

extraversion The personality condition of being outgoing under-laid by and so to compensate for low central nervous system arousal.

fellatio An oral sex act performed on the penis of a male.

fight or flight A physiological response, also called hyperarousal, that prepares one either to stay and fight or to flee; it occurs in the event of a perceived harm, attack, or other threat to survival.

fixed action pattern An instinctive or learned series of movements following a specific sequence in order to accomplish a goal.

formal operational stage The fourth stage in Jean Piaget's theory of cognitive development, at which the child can work things out entirely in his or her mind without requiring physical markers.

fracking Injecting water and chemicals into the earth to force out oil and natural gas.

frustration Formally defined as having a goal blocked by an obstructing object or behavior while the individual is engaged to achieve the goal.

functional magnetic resonance imaging (fMRI) A diagnostic technique that produces computerized images of the internal body; fMRI is often used to reveal blood flow in various parts of the brain.

geek An individual who is obsessed with mastering a technology, usually to do with computers.

general adaptation syndrome (GAS) Hans Selye's three stages of reaction to stress: alarm, resistance, and exhaustion.

glioblastoma A brain tumor.

hacking Breaking into secure computer systems for personal, mercenary, or military purposes.

HIV-AIDS Human immunodeficiency virus–acquired immune deficiency syndrome. HIV is a sexually transmitted virus also contracted through blood transfusions from infected donors; if not treated, HIV can develop into AIDS and almost certain death.

hypothalamus An area of the limbic system below the thalamus vital to the regulation of body temperature, hunger, thirst, sex, and emotion.

id In psychoanalytic theory, a division of the psyche and the source of the primitive drive within the individual for gratification of any deprived need or aroused desire.

identity change process Boyanowsky's theory of how significant change in personality can be achieved by isolation, arousal, and reprogramming, as is found in many aboriginal, religious, and indoctrination procedures.

inchoate Unfinished or just begun.

ingroup Members of a group who identify themselves as sharing a valued characteristic, which is often physical, such as race or gender, or sociocultural, such as family or religion.

Interpol International Police Agency.

ISIL A terrorist group (also known as ISIS or Daesh) dedicated to creating a fundamentalist Muslim caliphate in the Middle East.

Ku Klux Klan An organization established after the US Civil War allegedly to promote Caucasian society and values but used to suppress African Americans in the United States and, in the early twentieth century, Eastern European immigrants in Canada.

labeling theory In criminology, stigmatizing a person by identifying that person as an offender, which leads to alienation from society and discrimination by the criminal justice system.

life-course persistent criminality The hypothesis that a subset of young offenders is so entrenched in criminal behavior through genetic causes, early influences, and/or traumatic experiences that, unlike the adolescent-limited group, these individuals will continue offending through adulthood. See also *adolescent limited criminality*.

Likert scale A rating system to measure people's attitudes, opinions, or perceptions that uses a scale ranging between two opposite poles: strongly disagree at 1 to strongly agree at 11.

mala in se An act that is intrinsically bad.

mala prohibita An act that is illegal only because of the existence of a law.

malignant narcissism Feelings of grandiosity, entitlement, and lack of empathy, among other characteristics; it is similar to but not quite amounting to psychopathy.

manie sans délire Philippe Pinel's description of the condition he observed in patients who repeatedly engaged in antisocial acts but did not exhibit any of the symptoms of mental illness, such as delusions or hallucinations.

Marxism A sociopolitical system described by Karl Marx that promotes an ideal world of equality wherein individuals are provided for according to their needs and contribute to society according to their ability. A conflict is hypothesized to exist between those in power and those who have none in capitalist society, and change is considered to be the result of a dialectical process of contradiction and resolution.

mens rea Guilt in the mind, the intention or knowledge of wrongdoing in having intentionally committed a crime (broken the law).

misogynistic Strongly prejudiced against women.

Molotov cocktails Bombs made from bottles filled with gasoline and a rag to ignite it.

monoamine oxidase A (MAO-A) An enzyme in people encoded by the gene of the same name. It is one of two genes that encode enzymes that catalyze dopamine, norepinephrine, and serotonin.

morbid sense of entitlement A feeling that an individual deserves positive outcomes based on her or his background or ethnic group and a state of being unwilling or unable to achieve these outcomes legitimately. Individuals with this condition delve into anything that will work for them, even crime, to reach desired outcomes.

motor (brain structures) Parts of the brain involved in activating the body.

narcotics Drugs or other substances, usually with an opioid base, affecting mood or behavior especially in a tranquilizing fashion.

natural selection Charles Darwin's concept that characteristics or behaviors are perpetuated because they contribute to survival of the species that manifests them. This concept developed into a theory of how nature produces many variations of organisms but only some are favored by the ecology in which they are produced and so survive, thrive, and multiply.

negative affect escape hypothesis The theory that as subjects get uncomfortably hot and irate, they choose to leave rather than aggress.

neuroticism The personality condition of having a very fluctuating, unstable emotional nervous system.

neutralization Using bland, mild, or at least noninflammatory words to make terrible events seem less disturbing, usually to minimize their political or social impact.

norepinephrine / noradrenaline A hormone and neurotransmitter that mobilizes the body for action.

norms The most common forms of some behaviors, attitudes, or characteristics in a group.

Nunavut A territory with its own government in Northern Canada.

oedipal complex Lust for the mother and jealousy even hatred toward the father on the part of a male child.

ontogeny recapitulates phylogeny Ernst Haeckel's theory that the development of an individual organism reproduces the course of human evolution from single-celled creatures to the complexity of humanity.

outgroup Individuals or groups that are distinctly perceived as not sharing a characteristic of the ingroup, for example, different gender, race, religion, family, or even team.

outgroup/ingroup loyalties and discrimination Differentiating between one's membership group and those who do not belong and affording allegiance to one's ingroup and aversion to one's outgroup.

oxygen delignification A more benign way of processing wood to make it into pulp, one that produces no toxic waste containing dioxins or furans.

paranoid schizophrenia A mental illness characterized by feelings and delusions that certain people surrounding you wish to do you grievous harm or even kill you.

pedagogical To do with teaching.

pedophiles In psychological terms, adults or older adolescents who are sexually attracted to prepubescent persons; in legal terms, individuals who manifest a sexual attraction to persons defined as legally underage.

phenomenology The philosophical argument that reality only exists within the perception of humans and the consensus of human social interaction rather than independently.

phreaking Activity of people who explore and manipulate communications systems such as telephones to escape user costs.

polymath An individual with talents in many areas of endeavor.

polymorphously perverse The Freudian notion that children, but not adults, have the undifferentiated ability to be sexually satisfied in many different ways.

pornography Visual or written material created for the purpose of producing sexual arousal.

postconventional level of morality The third and final level in Kohlberg's theory of moral development, encompassing stages 5 and 6; individuals make their decisions in stage 5 based on the social contract (e.g., that laws are determined democratically) and in stage 6 based on universal ethical principles.

preconventional level of morality The first level in Kohlberg's theory of moral development, encompassing stages 1 and 2. The individual's rationale is based in stage 1 on classical conditioning (e.g., fear of certain outcomes). In stage 2, it is based on operant conditioning (i.e., what is the outcome of an action), and thus on instrumental orientation in the sense of which outcome is in my best interest.

preoperational stage The second stage in Jean Piaget's theory of cognitive development, at which the child requires physical markers to conduct operations (e.g., counting on fingers).

primary psychopath An individual displaying all the behavioral symptoms of psychopathy but with no apparent disadvantaged early life. So primary psychopathy is hypothesized to have a genetic, in utero, or birth trauma cause.

Prohibition Refers to the period of history when the Volstead Act was in force in the United States and occasionally to a similar, slightly earlier period in Canada.

pseudopsychopathic schizophrenia A mental disorder characterized by alternating psychopathy and psychosis.

psychopaths Individuals who are hypothesized to experience no empathy with victims of their actions, are highly risk taking, do not learn well from previous mistakes, and lack a conscience or sense of morality.

Psychopathy Checklist (PCL-R) Psychopathy checklist revised edition developed by Robert Hare to diagnose psychopathy. This test is the first one to have high inter-tester reliability: that is, the same individual receives a similar score regardless of who does the testing.

psychoticism Within Eysenck's theory of personality, a condition typified by very antisocial, unfriendly, aggressive tendencies. The term is not to be confused with psychosis, which refers to mental illness characterized by delusion.

recidivism Being convicted of reoffending.

reciprocal determinism The theory that cognitive processes and social environment both affect the individual and one another. That is, cognitive processes and the social environment are in a feedback loop, so a cognitive effect experienced influences the environment and that environment, so changed, has an increasing effect on cognition and consequently behavior in the future.

repressing / repression Voluntary inhibition of normally desired behaviors that may be inappropriate or antisocial.

reactions to environmental threat (RET) An algorithm or model for determining public reactions to environmental threat.

routine activities theory (RAT) The hypothesis that crime occurs during times and in places where perpetrators and victims interact to the highest degree.

sadomasochistic sex Sex acts wherein one person derives pleasure from inflicting pain (sadist) and the other from experiencing it (masochist).

schizophrenia A mental illness characterized by delusions (e.g., hearing voices or even seeing visions that are not seen by others).

secondary psychopath A psychopath whose early history is marked by severe abuse and/or social deprivation. See also *sociopath*.

self-regulation Posited by some criminologists as the difference between law-abiding and criminal individuals.

sensorimotor stage The first of Jean Piaget's four stages of cognitive development, at which the child experiences the world through feeling by hand and mouth and skin.

serotonin A neurotransmitter that modulates mood.

slurry A semiliquid mixture of water and solid material (e.g., waste from a mine).

social construction Phenomena created by society rather than existing independently in nature and a theoretical approach positing that people acting and interacting with others in society create their understanding of reality.

sociopath Someone diagnosed with antisocial personality disorder (ASPD). See *secondary psychopath*.

spearphishing Contacting people by computer and posing as businesses with which they hold accounts in order to obtain their passwords and access their accounts.

stage 6 The last stage in Kohlberg's theory of moral development, in which moral decisions are based on universal principles of justice.

strain theory The hypothesis that tension is created by an individual's desire to obtain the status and wealth universally desired versus his or her inability to do so caused by social factors or individual inadequacy.

sublimating / sublimation Transforming antisocial desires (e.g., hate) into prosocial activities (e.g., music, literature, or illustration).

superego The faculty developed by the individual to experience consciousness of morality and so the ability to differentiate right from wrong and feel guilt if transgressing against that understanding.

Superfund A financial reserve created by President Jimmy Carter to fund cleanup operations of polluted sites.

symbolic model One observed through the media (e.g., an athlete or pop music star).

Thanatos The death instinct that produces aggression and violence.

toilet training The process by which the child learns to use a toilet seat or commode rather than expelling at will.

Turing machine One of the first calculating machines (early computers) invented by Alan Turing during World War II.

tympanic thermometer An instrument that measures core temperature by pressing a soft thermistor against the eardrum.

vaginismus The involuntary constriction of the sphincter muscle of the vagina caused by anxiety, which is sometimes the consequence of sexual abuse. Fortunately, this condition is usually easily alleviated by behavioral therapy.

vicarious learning Learning purely through viewing with no attendant reward or reinforcement given to the viewer.

violence The release of large amounts of force or energy (not necessarily antisocial or prosocial).

Volstead Act A law prohibiting the making, possession, selling, or use of alcoholic beverages in the United States, enforced from 1920 to 1933.

weaning Tapering the child from breastfeeding.

zero point The only moment during emotional collapse (hitting rock bottom and feeling suicidal) when, in Samenow and Yochelson's schema of criminal personality, change in the truly criminal personality is possible.

REFERENCES

Abayomi, A., & Kolawole, T. (2013). Domestic violence and death: Women as endangered gender in Nigeria. *American Journal of Sociological Research, 3*(3), 53–60.

Agence France-Presse. (2010, August 16). German pop star on trial for causing bodily harm after keeping HIV status secret. *National Post.* Retrieved from https://nationalpost.com/news/german-pop-star-on-trial-for-causing-bodily-harm-after-keeping-hiv-status-secret

Agnew, R. (1990). The origins of delinquent events: An examination of offender accounts. *Journal of Research in Crime and Delinquency, 27,* 267–94.

Agrell, S. (2010, April 26). Robot subs trying to stop oil leak deep below Gulf of Mexico. *The Globe and Mail.* Retrieved from https://www.theglobe andmail.com/news/world/robot-subs-trying-to-stop-oil-leak-deep-below-gulf-of-mexico/article4316468/

Aichhorn, A. (1951). *Wayward youth.* London: Imago Publishing Company. (Original work published in German in 1925)

Akers, R. L. (1985). Social learning theory and adolescent cigarette smoking. *Social Problems, 32,* 455–73.

Akers, R. L. (2000). *Criminological theories: Introduction, evaluation, and application.* Los Angeles, CA: Roxbury.

Alexander, B., Coambs, R. B., & Hadaway, P. (1978). The effect of housing and gender on morphine self-administration in rats. *Psychopharmacology, 58,* 175–79.

Alexander, F. (1962). *The criminal, the judge, and the public: A psychological analysis* (H. Staub & G. Zilboorg, Trans.). New York, NY: Collier Books. (Original work published in 1931 with G. Zilboorg as translator)

Allen, M. (2018, July 23). Police-reported crime statistics in Canada, 2017. *The Daily*. Retrieved from https://www150.statcan.gc.ca/n1/pub/85-002 -x/2018001/article/54974-eng.htm

Allen, V. L. (1975). Social support for nonconformity. In L. Berkowitz (Ed.), *Advances in experimental social psychology* (Vol. 8, pp. 1–43). New York, NY: Academic Press.

Anderson, C. A. (2001). Heat and violence. *Current Directions in Psychological Science, 10*(1), 33–38.

Anderson, C. A., Anderson, K. B., Dorr, N., DeNeve, K. M., & Flanagan, M. (2000). Temperature and aggression. In M. Zanna (Ed.), *Advances in experimental social psychology* (Vol. 32, pp. 63–133). New York, NY: Academic Press.

Appleby, T. (2011). *A new kind of monster*. New York, NY: Vintage Books.

Arbuthnot, J., & Gordon, D. (1986). Behavioral and cognitive effects of a moral reasoning development intervention for high-risk behavior disordered adolescents. *Journal of Clinical and Consulting Psychology, 54*(2), 208–16.

Aron, A., Fisher, H., Mashek, D. J., Strong, J., Li, H., & Brown, L. L. (2005). Reward, motivation, and emotion systems associated with early-stage intense romantic love. *Journal of Neurophysiology, 94*(1), 327–37.

Arrigo, B. A. (Ed.). (1999). *Social justice/criminal justice: The maturation of critical theory in law, crime, and deviance*. Belmont, CA: Wadsworth Publishing.

Ascani, N. (2012). Labeling theory and the effects of sanctioning on delinquent peer association: A new approach to sentencing juveniles. *Sociological Perspectives* [University of New Hampshire], 80–84.

Asch, S. E. (1951). Effects of group pressure upon the modification and distortion of judgement. In H. Guetzkow (Ed.), *Groups, leadership and men: Research in human relations* (pp. 177–90). Pittsburg, PA: Carnegie Press.

Askwith, R. (1998, September 13). How aspirin turned hero. *The Sunday Times*. Retrieved from https://www.opioids.com/heroin/heroinhistory.html

Associated Press. (2019, May 28). Malaysia becomes second country after Philippines to return Canadian trash. Retrieved from https://nationalpost.com/news/world/malaysia-to-send-back-plastic-waste-to-foreign-nations

Bahrampour, T., & Horn, B. (2014, January 30). A lost boy finds his calling [Article and video]. *Washington Post*. Retrieved from https://www.washingtonpost.com/sf/style/2014/01/30/a-lost-boy-finds-his-calling/

Bailey, I. (2010, April 20). Vancouver fights smokers at beaches and parks with new ban this fall. *The Globe and Mail*. Retrieved from https://www.theglobeandmail.com/news/british-columbia/vancouver-fights -smokers-at-beaches-and-parks-with-new-ban-this-fall/article4388954/

Bamako Convention on the Ban of the Import into Africa and the Control of Transboundary Movement and Management of Hazardous Wastes within Africa. (1991). Retrieved from https://au.int/sites/default/files/treaties/7774-treaty-0015_-_bamako_convention_on_hazardous_wastes_e.pdf

Bandura, A. (1976). Social learning analysis of aggression. In E. Ribes-Inesta & A. Bandura (Eds.), *Analysis of delinquency and aggression* (pp. 1–46). Hillsdale, NJ: Erlbaum.

Bandura, A., Ross, D., & Ross, S. A. (1961). Transmission of aggression through imitation of aggressive models. *Journal of Abnormal Social Psychology, 63*, 575–82. doi: 10.1037/h0045925

Bandura, A., Ross, D., & Ross, S. A. (1963). Imitation of film-mediated aggressive models. *Journal of Abnormal and Social Psychology, 66*, 3–11.

Baron, R. A., & Bell, P. A. (1976). Aggression and heat: The influence of ambient temperature, negative affect, and a cooling drink on physical aggression. *Journal of Personality & Social Psychology, 33*, 245–55.

Bartol, C. R., & Bartol, A. M. (2017). *Criminal behavior: A psychological approach* (11th ed.). Harlow, UK: Pearson.

Bartusch, D. I., & Matsueda, R. I. (1996). Gender, reflected appraisals, and cross-gender labeling: A cross-group test of an interactionist theory of delinquency. *Social Forces, 75*, 145–72.

Basel Convention on the Control of Transboundary Movements of Hazardous Wastes and their Disposal. (1989). Retrieved from http://www.basel.int/ Portals/4/Basel Convention/docs/text/BaselConventionText-e.pdf

BBC. (2002). Behind the mask of sanity: Psychopathy [Television series episode 2]. In R. Lindsay (Narrator), *Mind of a murderer*. London, UK: BBC Worldwide.

BBC. (2010, May 29). Malawi pardons jailed gay couple. *BBC News*. Retrieved from https://www.bbc.com/news/10190653

Beard, J. (2019, March 3). Leaving Katlyn behind. *CBC News*. Retrieved from https://newsinteractives.cbc.ca/longform/transgender-teen-ontario

Beccaria, C. (1985). *On crimes and punishments* (H. Paolucci, Trans.). New York, NY: Macmillan. (Original work published 1764)

Beck, S. G., & O'Brien, J. (1980). Lethal self-administration of morphine by rats. *Physiology and Behavior, 25*(4), 559–64.

Bellett, G. (2011, March 28). WorkSafeBC wants jail for asbestos contractor. *The Vancouver Sun*. Retrieved from http://www.fpoa.bc.ca/index.php?option =com_content&view=article&id=147:worksafebc-wants-jail-for-asbestos -contractor&Itemid=570

Benzinger, T. H. (1969). Thermoregulatory responses to heat and cold. *Physiological Review, 15*, 671–759.

Bologna, M. J., Waterman, C. K., & Dawson, L. J. (1987). Violence in gay male and lesbian relationships: Implications for practitioners and policy makers. Paper presented at the Third National Conference for Family Violence Researchers, Durham, NH.

Botelho, G., & Yan, H. (2013, July 14). George Zimmerman found not guilty of murder in Trayvon Martin's death. *CNN*. Retrieved from https://www.cnn. com/2013/07/13/justice/zimmerman-trial/index.html

Bowlby, J. (1951). *Maternal care and mental health*. World Health Organization Monograph No. 2. Geneva, Switzerland: World Health Organization.

Boyanowsky, E. O. (1977). Film preferences under conditions of threat: Whetting the appetite for violence, excitement or information. *Communication Research*, 4(2), 133–44. https://doi.org/10.1177/009365027700400201

Boyanowsky, E. O. (1984). Self-identity change and the role transition process. In V. L. Allen & E. Van de Vliert (Eds.), *Role transitions: Explorations and explanations* (pp. 53–61). New York, NY, and London, UK: Plenum Press.

Boyanowsky, E. O. (1991). Grains of truth in the wasteland of fear. *Canadian Psychology, 32*(2), 188–89.

Boyanowsky, E. O. (1999). Violence and aggression in the heat of passion and in cold blood. *International Journal of Law and Psychiatry, 22*, 257–71.

Boyanowsky, E. O. (2007). Climate, aggression and violent crime: Worrisome implications of the Ecs-TC syndrome for a changing environment. *Journal of Environmental Peace, 6*, 2007.

Boyanowsky, E. O. (2009, February 18). Violent Valentine's Days: There and here, then and now. *The Vancouver Sun*. Retrieved from https://www.pressreader.com/canada/vancouver-sun/20090218/282686158124923

Boyanowsky, E. O. (2011). *Knowledge reifying force, intention, harm: The nature and structure of crime: A multidimensional model*. Vancouver, BC: Western Society of Criminology.

Boyanowsky, E. O. (2012a). *Analyzing criminality: What it is, what it isn't, where it comes from*. Boston, MA: Pearson International.

Boyanowsky, E. O. (2012b). *Essays on justice: Natural, unnatural and criminal*. Dubuque, IA: Kendall Hunt.

Boyanowsky, E. O. (2015). A recipe for a toxic culture. *Ecopsychology, 15*(2), 1–3.

Boyanowsky, E. O., & Allen, V. L. (1973). In-group norms and self-identity as determinants of discriminatory behavior. *Journal of Personality and Social Psychology, 25*, 408–18.

Boyanowsky, E. O., Allen, V. L., Bragg, B., & Lepinski, J. (1981). The generalization of nonconformity produced by social support. *Psychological Record, 31*, 475–88.

Boyanowsky, E. O., Calvert-Boyanowsky, J., Young, J., & Brideau, L. (1981). Toward a thermoregulatory model of violence. *Journal of Environmental Systems, 11*, 81–87.

Boyanowsky, E. O., & Hodwitz, O. (2010). *Reactions to environmental threat: Testing a general model of activism*. Association for Environmental Study and Science, Portland.

Boyanowsky, E. O., & Hodwitz, O. (2011). *Violence in activism: Instigating factors and thresholds breached*. Vancouver, BC: Western Society of Criminology.

Boyanowsky, E. O., & McElveen, R. (2010). *Canadian trends in sex crimes*. Paper presented to the forum on sex crimes against children, American Consulate, Vancouver, BC.

Boyanowsky, E. O., Newtson, D., & Walster, E. (1974). Film preferences following a murder. *Communication Research, 1*(1), 32–43. Also reported in *Behavioral Science,* 1974.

Boyanowsky, E. O., & Yasayko, J. (2007). *The relationship between violent crime and temperature in major Canadian cities.* Unpublished manuscript, School of Criminology, Simon Fraser University.

Boyanowsky, E. O., & Yasayko, J. (2011, February). *Climate and crime: How temperature affects violent crime.* Vancouver, BC: Western Society of Criminology.

Brecht, B. (1980). *Mother Courage and her children.* In J. Willett and R. Manheim (Eds.), *Collected plays* (Vol. 5). London, UK: Methuen. (Original work written in 1939)

Brinkley, D. (2010). *The wilderness warrior: Theodore Roosevelt and the crusade for America.* New York, NY: First Harper Perennial Edition.

British Columbia. (n.d.). *Mount Polley Mine tailing dam breach: Incident report.* Retrieved from https://www2.gov.bc.ca/gov/content/environment/air-land-water/spills-environmental-emergencies/spill-incidents/past-spill-incidents/mt-polley

Brooks, R. (Director and Screenwriter). (1967). *Truman Capote's in cold blood* (Motion picture). United States: Columbia Pictures Corporation.

Brown, C. (1965). *Manchild in the promised land.* New York, NY: Touchstone.

Bull, R. H. C., & Green, J. (1980). Relationship between physical appearance and criminality. *Medical Science Law, 20*(2), 79–83.

Buss, D. M. (2013). Sexual jealousy. *Psychological Topics, 22*(2), 155–82.

Caetano, R., Vaeth, P. A., & Ramisetty-Milker, S. (2008). Intimate partner violence victim and perpetrator characteristics among couples in the United States. *Journal of Family Violence, 23,* 507–18.

Caffey J. (1972) The parent-infant traumatic stress syndrome. *American Journal of Roentgenology, Radium Therapy, and Nuclear Medicine, 114*(2), 218–29.

Calce, M., & Silverman, C. (2008). *Mafiaboy: How I cracked the Internet and why it's still broken.* Toronto, ON: Viking Canada.

Cameron, S. (2011). *On the farm: Robert William Pickton and the tragic story of Vancouver's missing women.* Toronto, ON: Vintage Books Canada.

Campbell, J. C. (1985). The beating of wives: A cross-cultural perspective. *Victimology, 10*(1–4), 174–85.

Campbell, J. C. (1992). Prevention of wife battering: Insights from cultural analysis. *Response to the Victimization of Women and Children, 14*(3), no. 80, 18–24.

Camus, A. (1946). *The stranger* (S. Gilbert, Trans.). New York, NY: Vintage Books.

Canada-US Agreement Concerning the Transboundary Movement of Hazardous Waste. (1986). Retrieved from http://www.ec.gc.ca/gdd-mw/default.asp?lang=En&n=EB0B92CE-1

Canadian Constitution Foundation. (2010, April 19). University of Calgary continues its war on free speech. *CCF Press Release*. Retrieved from http://www.safs.ca/newsletters/2010/april/uofcalgary.htm

Canadian Press. (2010, April 19). Nunavut fights back at bootlegging trade. *The Globe and Mail*. Retrieved from https://www.theglobeandmail.com/news/national/nunavut-fights-back-at-bootlegging-trade/article4315572/

Canadian Press. (2017, March 7). Ontario teacher pleads guilty after having sexual encounters with students, exchanging nude photos. *National Post*. Retrieved from https://nationalpost.com/news/canada/ontario-teacher-pleads-guilty-after-having-sexual-encounters-with-students-exchanging-nude-photos. (Article was in March 9 print edition, p. A5)

Capote, T. (1966). *In cold blood: A true account of a multiple murder and its consequences*. New York, NY: New American Library.

Carstairs, C. (2006). *Jailed for possession: Illegal drug use, regulation, and power in Canada, 1920–1961*. Toronto, ON: University of Toronto Press.

Carvalho, A. F., Lewis, R. J., Derlega, V. J., Winstead, B. A., & Viggiano, C. (2011). Internalized sexual minority stressors and same-sex intimate partner violence. *Journal of Family Violence, 26*(7), 501–9.

Castelman, M. (2016, November 3). Dueling statistics: How much of the Internet is porn? *Psychology Today*. Retrieved from https://www.psychologytoday.com/ca/blog/all-about-sex/201611/dueling-statistics-how-much-the-internet-is-porn

CBC. (2009). Former Vancouver bank exec jailed for possession of child porn. *CBC News*. Retrieved from https://www.cbc.ca/news/canada/british-columbia/former-vancouver-bank-exec-jailed-for-possession-of-child-porn-1.847634

CBC. (2017, May 19). Eastern Ontario teacher gets 2 years in prison for sex offences involving students. *CBC News*. Retrieved from https://www.cbc.ca/news/canada/ottawa/jaclyn-mclaren-teacher-sentence-prison-sexual-offences-1.4123322

Chambliss, W. J. (1975). Toward a political economy of crime. *Theory and Society, 2*(1), 149–70.

Chang, I. (1997). *The rape of Nanking: The forgotten holocaust of World War II*. New York, NY: Basic Books.

Charles Lee Smith. (2018, September 21). *Wikipedia*. Retrieved from https://en.wikipedia.org/wiki/Charles_Lee_Smith

Chase, S. (2010, May 25). General pleads guilty to misfiring weapon. *The Globe and Mail*. Retrieved from https://www.theglobeandmail.com/news/politics/general-pleads-guilty-to-misfiring-weapon/article4321054/

Cherry, P. (2018, October 30). Montreal's underworld: Mafia, Hells Angels, street gangs worked in concert. *Montreal Gazette*. Retrieved from https://montrealgazette.com/news/local-news/police-recordings-provide-rare-glimpse-inside-montreals-underworld. Article updated November 3, 2018.

Chung, F. (2017, March 25). "Bury them alive!": White South Africans fear for their future as horrific farm attacks escalate. *News.com.au.* Retrieved from https://www.news.com.au/finance/economy/world-economy/bury-them-alive-white-south-africans-fear-for-their-future-as-horrific-farm-attacks-escalate/news-story/3a63389a1b0066b6b0b77522c06d6476

CIA. (2010). *The world factbook.* Retrieved from https://www.cia.gov/library/publications/download/download-2010/index.html

CIA. (2014). *The world factbook.* Retrieved from https://www.cia.gov/library/publications/download/download-2014/index.html

CIA. (2019). *The world factbook.* Retrieved on January 25, 2019 from https://www.cia.gov/library/publications/the-world-factbook/

Cimino, M. (Director). (1980). *Heaven's gate.* Belfast, Northern Ireland: Partisan Productions.

Clapp, J. (1994). The toxic waste trade with less-industrialised countries: Economic linkages and political alliances. *Third World Quarterly, 15*(3), 505–18.

Clapp, J. (1997). The illicit trade in hazardous wastes and CFCs: International responses to environmental bads. *Trends Organized Crime, 3*(2), 14–18.

Clarke, R. A., & Knake, R. K. (2010). *Cyber war: The next threat to national security and what to do about it.* New York, NY: HarperCollins.

Cleckley, H. M. (1976). *The mask of sanity.* St. Louis, MO: Mosby.

Cohen, J. (1941). The geography of crime. *Annals of the American Academy of Social and Political Sciences, 217,* 29–37.

Cohen, L., & Felson, M. (1979). Social change and crime rate trends: A routine activities approach. *American Sociological Review, 44,* 588–608.

Cohn, E., & Rotton, J. (1997). Assault as a function of time and temperature: A moderator-variable time series analysis. *Journal of Personality and Social Psychology, 72,* 1322–34.

Coleman, D. H., & Straus, M. A. (1986). Marital power, conflict, and violence in a nationally representative sample of American couples. *Violence and Victims, 1*(2), 141–57.

Colten, C., & Skinner, P. (1996). *The road to Love Canal: Managing industrial waste before EPA.* Austin, TX: University of Texas Press.

Conquest, R. (1986). *Harvest of sorrow.* New York, NY: Oxford University Press.

Cooley, C. H. (1902). *Human nature and the social order.* New York, NY: Scribner's.

Cossman, B., Bell, S., Gotell, L., & Ross, B. (1997). *Bad attitudes on trial: Pornography, feminism, and the Butler decision.* Toronto, ON: University of Toronto Press.

Cowan, P. (Director and Producer). (1982). *The kid who couldn't miss* [Motion picture]. Canada: National Film Board of Canada. Available from https://www.nfb.ca/film/the-kid-who-couldnt-miss/

Craughwell, T. (2011). *The rise and fall of the second largest empire in history.* Beverly, MA: Fairwinds Press.

Criminal Intelligence Service Canada. (2009). *Report on organized crime.* Retrieved from http://publications.gc.ca/collections/collection_2009/sp-ps/PS61-1-2009E.pdf

Criminal Law Amendment Act, S.C. 1968–69, c. 38.

CTV News Staff. (2007, July 13). Black guilty on 4 charges, including obstruction. *CTV News.* Retrieved from https://www.ctvnews.ca/black-guilty-on-4-charges-including-obstruction-1.248554

Cullen, F. T., & Agnew, R. (2011). *Criminological theory: Past to present, essential readings* (4th ed.). New York, NY: Oxford University Press.

Curtis, M. K., & Gilreath, S. (2008). Transforming teenagers into sex felons: The persistence of the crime against nature after *Lawrence v. Texas. Wake Forest Law Review, 43,* 155–221.

Cusack, M. (1990). International law and the transboundary shipment of hazardous waste to the Third World: Will the Basel Convention make a difference? *American Journal of International Law and Policy, 15,* 393.

Cyberwarfare. (2019, March 24). *Wikipedia.* Retrieved from https://en.wikipedia.org/wiki/Cyberwarfare

Daly, M., & Wilson, M. (1988). *Homicide.* New York, NY: Aldine de Gruyter.

Darwin, C. (1981). *The descent of man* (J. Bonner & R. M. May, Intro.). Princeton, NJ: Princeton University Press. (Original work published 1871)

Darwin, C. (2005). *The origin of species by means of natural selection.* Africa: Elibron Classics. (Original work published 1859)

Dasen, P. (1994). Culture and cognitive development from a Piagetian perspective. In W. J. Lonner & R. S. Malpass (Eds.), *Psychology and culture.* Boston, MA: Allyn and Bacon.

Davenport-Hines, R. (2004). *The pursuit of oblivion: A global history of narcotics.* New York, NY: W. W. Norton & Company.

Davis, M. (2006). Crimes mala in se: An equity based definition. *Criminal Justice Policy Review, 17*(3), 270–89.

Dawkins, R. (1976). *The selfish gene.* London: Oxford University Press.

De Waal, F. (2005). *Our inner ape.* London, UK: Granta Books.

Deaton, A. (2013). *The great escape: Health, wealth and the origins of inequality.* Princeton, NJ: Princeton University Press.

Delgado, J. M. R. (1963). Cerebral heterostimulation in a monkey colony. *Science, 141,* 161–63.

Delgado, J. M. R. (1969). *Physical control of the mind: Toward a psychocivilized society.* New York, NY: Harper & Row.

Dexter, E. G. (1899). Conduct and the weather. *Psychological Monographs, 11*(10), 1–103.

Diamond, M., & Uchiyama, A. (1999). Pornography, rape and sex crimes in Japan. *International Journal of Law and Psychiatry, 22*(1), 1–22.

Dier, A. (2014, January 3). Report: Kim Jong Un fed uncle alive to 120 starved dogs. *USA Today*. Retrieved from https://www.usatoday.com/story/news/world/2014/01/03/newser-kim-jong-un-uncle-execution/4303319/

Dollard, J., Doob, L., Miller, N., Mowrer, O., & Sears, R. (1939). *Frustration and aggression*. New Haven, CT: Yale University Press.

Doob, A. N., & MacDonald, G. E. (1979). Television viewing and fear of victimization: Is the relationship causal? *Journal of Personality and Social Psychology, 37*, 170–79.

Douglas, E. M., & Straus, M. A. (2006). Assault and injury of dating partners by university students in 19 countries and its relation to corporal punishment experienced as a child. *European Journal of Criminology, 3*(3), 293–318. https://doi.org/10.1177/1477370806065584

Dutton, D. G. (2006). *Rethinking domestic violence*. Vancouver, BC: University of British Columbia Press.

Dutton, D. G. (2016, April 21). *An empirical approach to innovations in intimate partner violence policy*. Presentation at a panel discussion organized by the Senate of Canada. Retrieved from https://www.youtube.com/watch?v=9f5v1QgtFfo

Dutton, D. G., Boyanowsky, E. O., & Bond, M. H. (2005). Extreme mass homicide: From military massacre to genocide. *Aggression and Violent Behavior, 10*, 437–73.

Ellis, L. (1982). Genetics and criminal behavior. *Criminology, 20*(1), 43–66.

Environment Canada. (2011a). Enforcement notifications. Retrieved from https://www.canada.ca/en/environment-climate-change/services/environmental-enforcement/notifications.html

Environment Canada. (2011b). *Part I: Canada's National Implementation Plan (NIP) under the Stockholm Convention on Persistent Organic Pollutants*. Retrieved from http://www.ec.gc.ca/lcpe-cepa/default.asp?lang=En&n=3EEAC8B8-1&offset=2&toc=show

Environment and Climate Change Canada. (2017). Export and import of hazardous waste and hazardous recyclable material regulations – guide to hazardous waste and hazardous recyclable material classification. Retrieved from https://www.canada.ca/content/dam/eccc/migration/main/gdd-mw/a8d9e099-1122-4f06-abb2-9f36a09d0b28/guide-20to-20hazardous-20waste-20and-20hazardous-20recyclable-20material-20classification-202017.pdf

Eysenck, H. J. (1990). Biological dimensions of personality. In L. A. Pervin (Ed.), *Handbook of personality: Theory and research* (pp. 244–76). New York, NY: Guilford Press.

Eysenck, S. B. G., & Eysenck, H. J. (1977). Personality differences between prisoners and controls. *Psychological Reports, 40*(3_suppl), 1023–28.

Fact check: Letter to Dr. Laura. (2004, March 9). *Snopes.com*. Retrieved from https://www.snopes.com/fact-check/letter-to-dr-laura/

Faith, N. (2007). *Bronfmans: The rise and fall of the house of Seagram.* New York, NY: St. Martin's Press.

Farrington, D. P. (2006). Family background and psychopathy. In C. J. Patrick (Ed.), *Handbook of psychopathy* (pp. 229–50). New York, NY: Guilford Press.

Farrington, D. P., Piquero, A. R., & Jennings, W. G. (2013). *Offending from late to middle age: Recent results from the Cambridge Study in Delinquent Development.* New York, NY: Springer.

Farrington, D. P., & Welsh, B. (2007). *Saving children from a life of crime.* New York, NY: Oxford University Press.

Farrington, D. P., & West, D. J. (1981). The Cambridge Study in Delinquent Development. In S. A. Mednick & A. E. Baert (Eds.), *Prospective longitudinal research: An empirical basis for the primary prevention of psychosocial disorders* (pp. 137–45). Oxford, UK: Oxford University Press.

FBI. (2019). *Uniform Crime Reporting Program.* Retrieved from https://www.statista.com/statistics/191219/reported-violent-crime-rate-in-the-usa-since-1990/

Fenichel, O. (1946). *The psychoanalytic theory of neurosis.* London, UK: Routledge and Kegan Paul.

Fergussen, D., Poulten, R., Smith, P., & Boden, J. (2006). Drugs: Cannabis and psychosis. *British Medical Journal, 332*(7534), 172–75.

Field, S. (1992). The effect of temperature on crime. *British Journal of Criminology, 32,* 340–51.

Find Fun Facts. (2013). Retrieved from http://findfunfacts.appspot.com/world_atlas/canada.html

Finkelhor, D., Shattuck, A., Turner, H. A., & Hamby, S. L. (2014). Trends in children's exposure to violence, 2003 to 2011. *JAMA Pediatrics, 186*(6), 540–46.

Fisher, M. (2013, December 12). Even by North Korean standards, this announcement of Jang Song Thaek's execution is intense. *Washington Post.* Retrieved from https://www.washingtonpost.com/news/worldviews/wp/2013/12/12/even-by-north-korean-standards-this-announcement-of-jang-song-thaeks-execution-is-intense/

Fletcher, J., & Wolfe, B. (2009). Long-term consequences of childhood ADHD on criminal activities. *Journal of Mental Health Policy and Economics, 12*(3), 119–38.

Frankenstein, C. (1970). *The varieties of juvenile delinquency.* London, UK: Gordon and Breach.

Freud, S. (1927). *The ego and the id* (J. Riviere, Trans.). London, UK: Institute of Psycho-Analysis.

Freud, S. (1949). *An outline of psychoanalysis* (J. Stratchley, Trans.). New York, NY: W. W. Norton. (Original work published in 1940)

Friedlander. K. (1967). *The psycho-analytical approach to juvenile delinquency: Theory, case studies, treatment.* New York, NY: International Universities Press. (Original work published 1947)

Fuller, J., & Blackley, S. (Eds.). (1995). *Restricted entry: Censorship on trial.* Vancouver, BC: Press Gang Publishers.

Gaedeken, P. (1909). Contribution statistique a la reaction de l'organisme sous l'influence des agents meteorologiques. *Archives d'anthropologie criminelle et de medecine legale, 24,* 173–87.

Gelles, R., & Straus, M. (1992). *Physical violence in American families.* New Brunswick, NJ: Transaction Publishing.

Gerdes, L. (2000). *Serial killers.* Farmington Hills, MI: Greenhaven Press.

Gillespie, A. A. (2012). *Child pornography: Law and policy.* New York, NY: Routledge.

Girard, A. L., Day, S., & Snider, L. (2010). Tracking environmental crime through CEPA: Canada's environment cops or industry's best friend? *Canadian Journal of Sociology, 35*(2), 219–41.

Glaberson, W. (1990, October 22). Love Canal: Suit focuses on record from 1940's. *New York Times.* Retrieved from https://www.nytimes.com/1990/10/22/nyregion/love-canal-suit-focuses-on-records-from-1940-s.html

Global Health and Human Rights Database. (1997). *Winnipeg Child, et al. v. D. F. G. [1997] 3 RCS.* Retrieved from https://www.globalhealthrights.org/health-topics/controlled-substances/winnipeg-child-and-family-services-northwest-area-v-d-f-g/

Glueck, S., & Glueck, E. (1950). *Unraveling juvenile delinquency.* New York, NY: Commonwealth Fund.

Golding, W. (1954). *Lord of the flies.* London, UK: Faber and Faber.

Goranson, R., & King, D. (1970). *The effects of heat waves on race riots.* Unpublished manuscript, Department of Psychology, York University.

Gordon, R. M., & Foley, S. (1998). *Criminal business organizations, street gangs and related groups in Vancouver: The report of the Greater Vancouver gang study.* Victoria, BC: Ministry of Attorney General.

Goring, C. (1913). *The English convict: A statistical study.* Montclair, NJ: Patterson Smith.

Gottfredson, M. R., & Hirschi, T. (1990). *A general theory of crime.* Palo Alto, CA: Stanford University Press.

Gove, T. J. (1995). *Report of the Gove Inquiry into child protection in British Columbia.* Victoria, BC: Queen's Printer. See also under title *A Commission of inquiry into the adequacy of the services, policies and practices of the Ministry of Social Services as they relate to the apparent neglect, abuse and death of Matthew John Vaudreuil.* Retrieved from http://www.qp.gov.bc.ca/gove/

Greenberg, A. (2017, July 20). Russia's cyberwar on Ukraine is a blueprint for what's to come: How an entire nation became Russia's test lab for cyberwar. *Wired.* Retrieved from https://www.wired.com/story/russian-hackers-attack-ukraine/

Greenwald, G. (2009) *Drug decriminalization in Portugal: Lessons for creating fair and successful drug policies* (White Paper). Washington, DC: Cato Institute.

Retrieved from https://object.cato.org/sites/cato.org/files/pubs/pdf/greenwald_whitepaper.pdf

Gurney, M. (2013, January 4). Ian Thomson acquitted after shooting at his attackers. *National Post*. Retrieved from https://nationalpost.com/opinion/matt-gurney-after-two-years-judge-acquits-man-who-defended-himself-with-a-gun

Guttmacher, M. (1960). *The mind of the murderer*. New York, NY: Farrar, Straus and Cudahy.

Hagen, M. E., Colodey, A. G., Knapp, W. D., & Samis, S. C. (1997, March–April). Environmental response to decreased dioxin and furan loadings from British Columbia coastal pulp mills. *Chemosphere, 34*(5–7), 1221–29.

Hager, M. (2013, January 9). Former Vancouver private school teacher sentenced for child porn. *Vancouver Sun*. Retrieved from https://vancouversun.com/News/Metro/former-vancouver-private-school-teacher-sentenced-for-child-porn/wcm/7f70b0d6-1eec-40bd-9ab4-a82432187545

Hammond, P., Hutton, T. J., Allanson, J. E., Campbell, L. E., Hennekam, R. C., Holden, S., … Winter, R. M. (2004). 3D analysis of facial morphology. *American Journal of Medical Genetics A, 126A*(4), 339–48.

Hancock, D. (2004, June 1). "TV intoxication" killer freed. *CBS News*. Retrieved from https://www.cbsnews.com/news/tv-intoxication-killer-freed/

Haney, B., & Gold, M. (1973, September). The juvenile delinquent nobody knows. *Psychology Today, 7*, 49–55.

Hare, R. D. (1999). Psychopathy as a risk factor for violence. *Psychiatric Quarterly, 70*(3), 181–97.

Hare, R. D. (2003). *The Hare Psychopathy Checklist-Revised: PCL-R™* (2nd ed.). Toronto, ON: MHS Assessments. Available from https://www.mhs.com/

Hare, R. D., & Neumann, C. (2007). The PCL-R assessment of psychopathy: Development, structural properties, and new directions. In C. Patrick (Ed.), *Handbook of psychopathy* (pp. 58–88). New York, NY: Guilford Press.

Harlow, H. F., & Suomi, S. J. (1971). Social recovery by isolation-reared monkeys. *Proceedings of the National Academy of Sciences of the United States of America, 68*, 1534–38.

Harris, G., & Rice, M. (2007). Treatment of psychopathy: A review of empirical findings. In C. Patrick (Ed.), *Handbook of psychopathy*. New York, NY: Guilford Press.

Hayek, F. (1991). *The fatal conceit: The errors of socialism*. Chicago, IL: University of Chicago Press.

Hayward, J. (2010, May 10). "Prince of Pot" will be extradited. *The Globe and Mail*. Retrieved from https://www.theglobeandmail.com/news/british-columbia/prince-of-pot-will-be-extradited/article4318951/

Hegel, G. W. F. (1975). *Lectures on the philosophy of world history* (H. B. Nisbet Trans.). Cambridge, UK: Cambridge University Press. (Original first draft written between 1822 and 1828)

Heimburger, R. F., Whitlock, C. C., & Kalsbeck, J. E. (1966). Stereotaxic amygdalotomy for epilepsy with aggressive behavior. *Journal of the American Medical Association, 198*(7), 741–45.

Helfer, R. E., & Kempe, C. H. (Eds.). (1976). *Child abuse and neglect: The family and the community*. Cambridge, MA: Ballinger Pub. Co.

Hessick, C. B. (2011). Disentangling child pornography from child sex abuse. *Washington University Law Review, 88*(4), 853–902.

Hodwitz, O. (2010). *Violence in activism: Instigating factors and thresholds breached*. Saarbrucken, Germany: VDM Verlag Dr. Müller.

Holland, A. (Director). (2019). *Gareth Jones*. Warsaw, Poland; Kyiv, Ukraine; Glasgow, UK: Film Produkcja; Kinorob; Boy Jones Films.

Hooton, E. A. (1939). *The American criminal: An anthropological study*. Cambridge, MA: Harvard University Press.

Hsiang, S., Burke, M., & Miguel, E. (2013, September 13). Quantifying the influence of climate on human conflict. *Science, 341*, 1235367-1–1235367-14.

Huesmann, L., Moise-Titus, J., Podolski, C., & Eron, L. (2003). Longitudinal relations between children's exposure to TV violence and their aggressive and violent behavior in young adulthood: 1977–1992. *Developmental Psychology, 39*(2), 201–21.

Humphreys, K. L., McGoron, L., Sheridan, M. A., McLaughlin, K. A., Fox, N. A., Nelson, C. A., 3rd, & Zeanah, C. H. (2015). High-quality foster care mitigates callous-unemotional traits following early deprivation in boys: A randomized controlled trial. *Journal of the American Academy of Child and Adolescent Psychiatry, 54*(12), 977–83.

Huntington, E. (1945). *Mainsprings of civilization*. New York, NY: John Wiley and Sons.

Hyde, H. M. (1963). *Oscar Wilde: The aftermath*. New York, NY: Farrar, Straus & Giroux.

Ibrahim, D. (2019). Police-reported violence among same-sex intimate partners in Canada, 2009 to 2017. *Juristat*. Retrieved from https://www150.statcan.gc.ca/n1/pub/85-002-x/2019001/article/00005-eng.htm

Ignatieff, M. (1993). *Blood and longing: Journeys into the new nationalism*. London, UK: BBC Books.

Inglis-Arkell, E. (2017, May 19). The Mongols built an empire with one technological breakthrough. *Ars Technica*. Retrieved from https://ars technica.com/science/2017/05/the-mongols-built-an-empire-with-one -technological-breakthrough/

International Court of Justice. (2019). *Jurisdiction*. Retrieved from http://www.icj-cij.org/jurisdiction/index.php?p1=5&p2=1&p3=3

Interpol. (2009). Electronic waste and organized crime, assessing the links. *Trends in Organized Crime, 12*, 352–78.

Interpol. (2019). *Member countries*. Retrieved from http://www.interpol.int/Member-countries/World

Ishikawa, S. S., & Raine, A. (2003). Prefrontal deficits and antisocial behavior: A causal model. In B. B. Lahey, T. E. Moffitt, & A. Caspi (Eds.), *Causes of conduct disorder and juvenile delinquency*. New York, NY: Guilford.

Ivanovic, D. M., Leiva, B. P., Pérez, H. T., Olivares, M. G., Díaz, N. S., Urrutia, M. S., ... Larraín, C. G. (2004). Head size and intelligence, learning, nutritional status and brain development: Head, IQ, learning, nutrition and brain. *Neuropsychologia, 42*(8), 1118–31.

Jacobs, P. A., Brunton, M., Melville, M. E., Brittain, R. P., & McLemont, W. F. (1965). Aggressive behaviour, mental subnormality and the XYY male. *Nature, 208*, 1351–52.

Jaffe, P., Wolfe, S. K., Wilson, S., & Zak, L. (1986). Similarities in behavioral and social maladjustment among child victims and witnesses to family violence. *American Journal of Orthopsychiatry, 56*(1), 142–46.

Kandel, E., & Mednick, S. A. (1991). Prenatal complications predict violent offending. *Criminology, 29*(3), 519–29.

Karagiannopoulos, V. (2018). *Living with hacktivism*. New York, NY: Palgrave Macmillan.

Karpman, B. (1941). On the need of separating psychopathy into two distinct clinical types: The symptomatic and the idiopathic. *Journal of Criminal Psychopathology, 3*, 112–37.

Kaukinen, C. E., & Powers, R. A. (2015). The role of economic factors on women's risk for intimate partner violence: A cross-national comparison of Canada and the United States. *Violence Against Women, 21*(2), 229–48.

Keller, J. (2013, October 16). Kayla Bourque appeal: Animal killer's probation conditions remain intact. *Huffington Post, BC*. Retrieved from https://www.huffingtonpost.ca/2013/10/16/kayla-bourque-appeal_n_4109957.html

Kempe, C. H., & Helfer, R. E. (Eds.). (1968). *The battered child syndrome*. Chicago, IL: University of Chicago Press.

Kempe, C. H., Silverman, F. N., Steele, B. F., Droegemueller, W., & Silver, H. K. (1962). The battered child syndrome. *Journal of the American Medical Association, 181*(1), 17–24. doi:10.1001/jama.1962.03050270019004

Kennedy, R. F., Jr. (2004). *Crimes against nature: How George W. Bush and his corporate pals are plundering the country and hijacking our democracy*. New York, NY: HarperCollins.

Kenrick, D. T., & MacFarlane, S. W. (1984). Ambient temperature and horn-honking: A field study of the heat/aggression relationship. *Environment and Behavior, 18*, 179–81.

Kernberg, O. (1998). Aggression, hatred, and social violence. *Canadian Journal of Psychoanalysis, 6*(2), 191–206.

Knox, A. (2013). *Waiting to be heard: A memoir*. New York, NY: Harper.

Kohlberg, L. (1963). The development of children's orientations toward a moral order: I. Sequence in the development of moral thought. *Vita Humana, 6*, 11–33.

Kozeny, E. (1962). Experimentelle Untersuchungen zur Ausdruckskundemittel photographisch—statistischer Methode. *Archiv fur die Gesamte Psychologie, 114*, 55–71.

Kraepelin, E. (1968). *Lectures in clinical psychiatry* (J. Johnstone, Ed.). New York, NY: Hafner. (Original work published in 1904)

Kurtzberg, R., Mandell, W., Levin, M., Lipton, D., & Shuster, M. (1978). Plastic surgery on offenders. In N. Johnston & L. D. Savitz (Eds.), *Justice and corrections*. New York, NY: Wiley.

Kutchinsky, B. (1973). The effect of easy availability of pornography on the incidence of sex crimes: The Danish experience. *Journal of Social Issues, 29*, 163–81.

Laskey, P., Bates, E. A., & Taylor, J. C. (2019). A systematic literature review of intimate partner violence victimisation: An inclusive review across gender and sexuality. *Aggression and Violent Behavior, 47*, 1–11.

Lavergne, G. (1997). *A sniper in the tower: The Charles Whitman murders*. Denton, TX: University of North Texas Press.

Lenz, W. (1988). A short history of thalidomide embryopathy. *Teratology, 38*, 203–15.

Levin, J., & Fox, J. (1985). *Mass murder: America's growing menace*. New York, NY: Plenum.

Levy, S. (1984). *Hackers: Heroes of the computer revolution*. New York, NY: Doubleday.

Lewis, D. O., Shanok, S. S., Grant, N. L., & Ritvo, E. (1983). Homicidally aggressive young children: Neuropsychiatric and experiential correlates. *American Journal of Psychiatry, 140*, 148–53.

Lewison, E. (1965). An experiment in facial reconstructive surgery in a prison population. *Canadian Medical Association Journal, 92*, 251–54.

Lichtenstein, P., Holm, N. V., Verkasalo, P. K., Iliadou, A., Kaprio, J., Koskenvuo, M., & Hemminki, K. (2000). Environmental and heritable factors in the causation of cancer—analyses of cohorts of twins from Sweden, Denmark, and Finland. *The New England Journal of Medicine, 343*(2), 78–85.

Liddick, D. (2009). The traffic in garbage and hazardous wastes: An overview. *Trends in Organized Crime, 13*(2–3), 134–46.

Lie, G., Schilit, R., Bush, J., Montague, M., & Reyes, L. (1991). Lesbians in currently aggressive relationships: How frequently do they report aggressive past relationships? *Violence and Victims, 6*(2), 121–35.

Liptak, A. (2008, May 25). U.S. voting for judges perplexes other nations. *New York Times*. Retrieved from https://www.nytimes.com/2008/05/25/world/americas/25iht-judge.4.13194819.html

Lista, M. (2018, January 2). The hacker king. *Toronto Life*. Retrieved from https://torontolife.com/city/crime/kid-made-millions-hacking-emails-fbi-took/

Lombroso, C. (1911). Introduction. In G. Lombroso-Ferrero (Ed.), *Criminal man, according to the classification of Cesare Lombroso* (pp. xi–xx). New York,

NY: G. P. Putnam's Sons. Retrieved from https://www.gutenberg.org/files/29895/29895-h/29895-h.htm

Lombroso, C. (2006). *Criminal man* (M. Gibson & N. H. Rafter, Trans. with new Intro.). Durham, NC: Duke University Press. (Original work published in Italian in 1876)

Long, H. (2018, May 20). China is winning Trump's trade war. *Washington Post*. Retrieved from https://www.washingtonpost.com/news/wonk/wp/2018/05/20/china-is-winning-trumps-trade-war/

Lykken, D. (2007). Psychopathic personality: The scope of the problem. In C. Patrick (Ed.), *Handbook of psychopathy*. New York, NY: Guilford Press.

Lysova, A. V., Dim, E. E., & Dutton, D. G. (2019). Prevalence and consequences of intimate partner violence in Canada as measured by the National Victimization Survey. *Partner Abuse, 10*(2), 199–221.

MacKinnon, C. A. (1989). *Toward a feminist theory of the state.* Cambridge, MA: Harvard University Press.

Mares, D. (2013). Climate change and levels of violence in socially disadvantaged neighborhood groups. *Journal of Urban Health: Bulletin of the New York Academy of Medicine, 90*(4), 768–93.

Mark, V. H., Ervin, F. R., & Sweet, W. H. (1972). Deep temporal lobe stimulation in man. In E. Eleftheriou (Ed.), *The neurobiology of the amygdala* (pp. 485–507). New York, NY: Plenum.

Markel, H. (2009, December 15). The child who put a face on abuse. *New York Times*, D5. Archived copy published online December 14 under different title available from https://www.nytimes.com/2009/12/15/health/15abus.html

Marrus, M. R. (1992). *Samuel Bronfman: The life and times of Seagram's Mr. Sam.* Lebanon, NH: University Press of New England.

Martin, S. (2008, July 2). Controversial abortion doctor faced a lifetime of persecution. *The Globe and Mail*. Retrieved from https://www.theglobeandmail.com/news/national/controversial-abortion-doctor-faced-a-lifetime-of-persecution/article20385281/

Massari, M., & Monzini, P. (2004). Dirty businesses in Italy: A case-study of illegal trafficking in hazardous waste. *Global Crime, 6*(3–4), 285–304.

McFadden, R. D. (1996, May 26). Prisoner of rage—A special report: From a child of promise to the Unabom suspect. *New York Times*. Retrieved from https://www.nytimes.com/1996/05/26/us/prisoner-of-rage-a-special-report-from-a-child-of-promise-to-the-unabom-suspect.html

McIntyre, J. (2011, July 25.). Anders Behring Breivik: A disturbing ideology. *The Independent*. Retrieved from https://web.archive.org/web/20120117051458/http://blogs.independent.co.uk/2011/07/25/anders-behring-breivik-a-disturbing-ideology/

Mead, G. H. (1913). The social self. *Journal of Philosophy, Psychology and Scientific Methods, 10*, 374–80.

Mead, G. H., & Morris, C. W. (Eds.). (1934). *Mind, self and society from the standpoint of a social behaviorist*. Chicago, IL: The University of Chicago Press.

Meakin, S. A. (1992, December). *Hazardous waste management: Canadian directions*. Background Paper No. BP-323E. Ottawa: Parliamentary Research Branch, Library of Parliament.

Mednick, S. A., Moffitt, T. E., & Stack, S. A. (1987). *The causes of crime: New biological approaches*. Cambridge, UK: Cambridge University Press.

Mehta, D. (Director & Screenwriter). (2015). *Beeba boys* [Motion picture]. Vancouver, BC: Hamilton Mehta Productions.

Merton, R. K. (1957). *Social theory and social structure*. Glencoe, IL: Free Press.

Michael, R. P., & Zumpe, D. (1986). An annual rhythm in the battering of women. *American Journal of Psychiatry, 143*, 637–40.

Milgram, S. (1963). Behavioral study of obedience. *The Journal of Abnormal and Social Psychology, 67*(4), 371–78. http://dx.doi.org/10.1037/h0040525

Miller, N. (1941). The frustration-aggression hypothesis. *Psychological Review, 48*, 337–42.

Mitrovica, A., & Mittelstaedt, M. (2000, November 13). Little done about mob ties to Ontario waste business. *Globe & Mail*, Monday, p. A1.

Moffitt, T. E. (1993). Adolescence-limited and life-course persistent antisocial behavior: A developmental taxonomy. *Psychological Review, 100*(4), 674–701.

Moffitt, T. E., Caspi, A., Rutter, M., & Silva, P. A. (2001). *Sex differences in antisocial behaviour: Conduct disorder, delinquency, and violence in the Dunedin longitudinal study*. Cambridge, UK: Cambridge University Press.

Montesquieu, Charles de Secondat, baron de. (1989). *Montesquieu: The spirit of the laws* (A. M. Cohler, B. C. Miller, & H. Stone, Eds. and Trans.). Cambridge texts in the history of political thought. Cambridge, UK: Cambridge University Press. Original work published in French in 1748.

Montgomery, M. (1995). Reassessing the waste trade crisis: What do we really know? *The Journal of Environment and Development, 4*(1), 1–28.

Morgan, R. (1980). Theory and practice: Pornography and rape. In L. Lederer (Ed.), *Take back the night: Women on pornography* (pp. 134–40). New York, NY: William Morrow.

Morse, B. (1995). Beyond the Conflict Tactics Scale: Assessing gender differences in partner violence. *Violence and Victims, 10*(4), 251–72.

Moulder, F. V. (1977). *Japan, China and the modern world economy: Toward a reinterpretation of East Asian development*. Cambridge, UK: Cambridge University Press.

Moyer, K. (1976). *The psychobiology of aggression*. New York, NY: Harper Row.

Mulgrew, I. (2011, October 3). Clifford Olson—Canada's national monster—dead at 71. *Vancouver Sun*. Retrieved from http://www.vancouversun.com/news/Clifford+Olson+Canada+national+monster+dead/5484826/story.html

Narabayashi, H., Nagao, T., Saito, Y., Yoshida, M., & Nagahata, M. (1963). Stereotaxic amygdalotomy for behavior disorders. *Archives of Neurology, 9*(1), 1–116.

National Institute on Drug Abuse. (2002). *Methamphetamine abuse and addiction.* NIH Research Report Series No. 02–4210. Retrieved from http://www.ehd.org/pdf/RRMetham.pdf

National Institute on Drug Abuse. (2007, March). *Methamphetamine addiction: Cause for concern—hope for the future.* Topics in Brief. Retrieved from https://casaa.unm.edu/ctn/ctn mod tool kit/General Information/Methamphetamine/NIDA Topics in Brief - Marijuana.pdf

National Institutes of Health. (2007). *Information about alcohol.* NIH Curriculum Supplement Series. Bethesda, MD: NIH. Retrieved from https://www.ncbi.nlm.nih.gov/books/NBK20360/

National Institutes of Health. (2011). *The teen brain: Still under construction.* NIMH Publication NO. 11-4929. Bethesda, MD: National Institute of Mental Health.

Neidig, P. (1993). *Family advocacy prevention/survey project.* Stony Brook, NY: Behavioral Science Associates.

Nelson, W. R. (2009*). Darwin, then and now: The most amazing story in the history of science.* Bloomington, IN: iUniverse.

Newcomer, D. J. (2015, August 25). Coping with Naples' toxic waste crisis. *Earth Island Journal.* Retrieved from http://www.earthisland.org/journal/index.php/articles/entry/coping_with_naples_toxic_waste_crisis/

Newman, G. (1976). *Comparative deviance: Perception and law in six cultures.* New York, NY: Elsevier.

Niccols, A. (2007). Fetal alcohol syndrome and the developing socio-emotional brain. *Brain and Cognition, 65*(1), 135–42.

Nilsson, K. W., Sjöberg, R. J., Damberg, M., Leppert, J., Öhrvik, J., Alm, P. O., & Oreland, L. (2006). Role of monoamine oxidase A genotype and psychosocial factors in male adolescent criminal activity. *Biological Psychiatry, 59*(2), 121–27.

Nisbett, R. E. (1993). Violence and U.S. regional culture. *American Psychologist, 48*, 441–49.

Nonato, S. D. (2012, March 29). Canadian torture survivor William Sampson dead: Report. *Vancouver Sun.* Retrieved from https://web.archive.org/web/20120401223507/http://www.vancouversun.com/news/canadian+torture+survivor+william+sampson+dead+report/6381327/

Norrie, A. (1983). Freewill, determinism and criminal justice. *Legal Studies, 3*(1), 60–73.

O'Brien, G., & Bartlett, J. (Eds.). (2014). *Bartlett's familiar quotations* (18th ed.) New York, NY: Little, Brown and Company.

O'Neill, K. (1997). Regulations as arbiters of risk: Great Britain, Germany, and the hazardous waste trade in Western Europe. *International Studies Quarterly, 41*(4), 687–717.

OECD. (2001). *Decision of the council concerning the transboundary movements of wastes destined for recovery operations.* Retrieved from http://www.ec.gc.ca/gdd-mw/default.asp?lang=en&n=6E36C8C4-1

Oliveira-Souza, R., Hare, R., Bramati, I. E., Garrido, G. J., Azevedo Ignácio, F., Tovar-Moll, F., & Moll, J. (2008). Psychopathy as a disorder of the moral brain: Fronto-temporo-limbic grey matter reductions demonstrated by voxel-based morphometry. *NeuroImage, 40*(3), 1202–13.

Olson, M. H., & Hergenhahn, B. R. (2009). *An introduction to theories of learning* (8th ed., pp. 201–03). Upper Saddle River, NJ: Prentice Hall.

Owens, G. (2001). *No kill, no thrill: The shocking true story of Charles Ng—one of North America's most horrific serial killers.* Markham, ON: Red Deer Press.

Paglia, C. (1991). *Sexual personae.* New York, NY: Vintage Books.

Pathak, E. B. (2018). Mortality among black men in the USA. *Journal or Racial and Ethnic Health Disparities, 5*(1), 50–61. doi: 10.1007/s40615-017-0341-5

Patrick, C. J. (2007). *Handbook of psychopathy.* New York, NY: Guilford Press.

Patterson, G. (1993). Orderly change in a stable world: The antisocial trait as chimera. *Journal of Consulting and Clinical Psychology, 61,* 911–19.

Pavlov, I. P. (1927). *Conditioned reflexes: An investigation of the physiological activity of the cerebral cortex.* London, UK: Oxford University Press.

Pelrine, E. W. (1983). *Morgantaler: The doctor who couldn't turn away.* Halifax, NS: Formac Publishing Company.

Phillips, D. P. (1986). Natural experiments on the effects of mass media violence on fatal aggression: Strengths and weaknesses of a new approach. In L. Berkowitz (Ed.), *Advances in experimental social psychology* (Vol. 19, pp. 207–50). New York, NY: Academic Press.

Physicians for a Smoke-Free Canada. (2003). *Tobacco in Canada.* Retrieved from http://www.smoke-free.ca/pdf_1/TOBACCOINCANADA2003.pdf

Pinel, P. (1962). *A treatise on insanity.* New York, NY: Hafner. (Originally published in 1806)

Press Trust of India. (2010, June 17). Union Carbide knew Bhopal would happen: Activists. *The Economic Times.* Retrieved from https://econo mictimes.indiatimes.com/news/politics-and-nation/union-carbide-knew -bhopal-would-happen-activists/articleshow/6059841.cms

Quay, H. C. (1986). Classification. In H. C. Quay & J. S. Werry (Eds.), *Psychopathological disorders of childhood.* New York, NY: Wiley.

Quay, H. C., & Werry, J. S. (Eds.). (1986). *Psychopathological disorders of childhood.* New York, NY: Wiley.

R. v. Morgentaler, [1988] 1 SCR 30.

R. v. Yaeck, [1991] 68 CCC (3d) 545.

Rabe, B. G., Becker, J., & Levine, R. (2000). Beyond siting: Implementing voluntary hazardous waste siting agreements in Canada. *The American Review of Canadian Studies, 30*(4), 479–96.

Rahm, D. (1998). Superfund and the politics of US hazardous waste policy. *Environmental Politics, 7*(4), 75–91.

Raine, A. (1993). *The psychopathology of crime: Criminal behavior as a clinical disorder*. San Diego, CA: Academic Press.

Raine, A. (2014). *The anatomy of violence: The biological roots of crime*. New York, NY: Pantheon Books.

Raine, A., Brennan, P., & Mednick, S. (1994). Birth complications combined with maternal rejection at age 1 year predispose to violent crime at 18 years. *Archives of General Psychiatry, 51*, 984–88.

Raine, A., & Yang, Y. (2006). The neuroanatomical bases of psychopathy: A review of brain imaging findings. In C. J. Patrick (Ed.), *Handbook of psychopathy* (pp. 278–312). New York, NY: Guilford Press.

Randall, C. L. (2001). Alcohol and pregnancy: Highlights from three decades of research. *Journal of Studies of Alcohol and Drugs, 62*, 554–61.

Rebovich, D. (1992). *Dangerous ground: The world of hazardous waste crime*. New Brunswick, NJ: Transaction Publishers.

Reifman, A. S., Larrick, R. P., & Fein, S. (1991). Temper and temperature on the diamond: The heat-aggression relationship in Major League Baseball. *Personality and Social Psychology Bulletin, 17*, 580–85.

Reuters. (2015, February 25). Tobacco companies to settle smoking lawsuits for $100 million. *CNBC*. Retrieved from https://www.cnbc.com/2015/02/25/tobacco-companies-to-settle-smoking-lawsuits-for-100-million.html

Rice, M. E. (1997). Violent offender research and implications for the criminal justice system. *American Psychologist, 52*(4), 414–23.

Rice, M. E. (1999). Review of *The abusive personality: Violence and control in intimate relationships*. *Canadian Psychological Association, 40*(3), 284–86.

Richler, M. (1968). *Cocksure; a novel*. Toronto, ON: McClelland and Stewart.

Robertson, H. (1981). *The flying bandit*. Toronto, ON: Lorimer.

Roe v. Wade, 410 US 113 (1973). Retrieved from Findlaw.com.

Rogers, M. K. (2011). The psyche of cybercriminals: A psycho-social perspective. In S. Ghosh & E. Turrini (Eds.), *Cybercrimes: A multidisciplinary analysis*. Heidelberg: Springer-Verlag.

Rogers, M. K. (2014). Cybercriminal taxonomies. In K. Seigfried-Spallar & M. Lanier (Eds.), *Essential readings in cybercrime theory and practice* (pp. 31–42). San Diego, CA: Cognella.

Saltman, J. (2018, November 14). Five people dead in Lower Mainland gang war in six weeks. *Vancouver Sun*. Retrieved from https://vancouversun.com/news/local-news/five-people-dead-in-lower-mainland-gang-war-in-six-weeks

Samenow, S. E. (1984). *Inside the criminal mind*. New York, NY: Times Books.

Samenow, S. E. (2007). *The myth of the out of character crime*. Santa Barbara, CA: Praeger.

Santayana, G. (1905). *The life of reason*. New York, NY: C. Scribner's Sons.

Sapkota, S. (2011). Violence against women: Focus on domestic violence. *Health Prospect, 10*, 48–50.

Sarbin, T. (1969). *The myth of the criminal type*. Middletown, CT: Center for Advanced Studies, Wesleyan University.

Scott, J. P., & Fuller, J. L. (1965). *Genetics and the social behavior of the dog*. Chicago, IL: University of Chicago Press.

Screamgates. (2007, March 23). *Ed Gein* [YouTube video]. Retrieved from www.youtube.com/watch?v=oVGv7BcqgVM

Selye, H. (1956). *The stress of life*. New York, NY: McGraw-Hill.

Senior, K., & Mazza, A. (2004). Italian "triangle of death" linked to waste crisis. *The Lancet Oncology, 5*(9), 525–27.

Seto, M. C. (2012). Is pedophilia a sexual orientation? *Archives of Sexual Behavior, 41*, 231–36.

Seto, M. C. (2018). Pedophilia and sexual offending against children: Theory, assessment, and intervention (2nd ed.). Washington, DC: American Psychological Association.

Shaw, C., & McKay, H. (1942). *Juvenile delinquency in urban areas*. Chicago, IL: University of Chicago Press.

Sherif, M., Harvey, O. J., White, B. J., Hood, W. R., & Sherif, C. W. (1961). *Intergroup conflict and cooperation: The Robbers Cave experiment*. Vol. 10. Norman, OK: University Oklahoma Book Exchange.

Shoalts, D. (2006, December 14). Bertuzzi and Moore attempt to reach out-of-court settlement. *The Globe and Mail*. Retrieved from https://www.theglobeandmail.com/sports/bertuzzi-and-moore-attempt-to-reach-out-of-court-settlement/article20417882/

Short, T., Thomas, S., Mullen, P., & Ogloff, J. R. (2013). Comparing violence in schizophrenia patients with and without comorbid substance-use disorders to community controls. *Acta Psychiatrica Scandinavia, 128*(4), 306–13.

Simister, J., & Van de Vliert, E. (2005). Is there more violence in very hot weather? Tests over time in Pakistan and across countries worldwide. *Pakistan Journal of Meteorology, 2*(4), 55–70.

Sinclair, G., Jr. (2010, March 17). Man who beheaded bus passenger could be freed in 5 years. *The Vancouver Sun*. Retrieved from http://www.vancouversun.com

Skinner, B. F. (1938). *The behavior of organisms: An experimental analysis*. New York, NY: Appleton.

Smith, M. D. (1990). Patriarchal ideology and wife beating: A test of a feminist hypothesis. *Violence and Victims, 5*, 257–73.

Sorenson, S. B., & Telles, C. A. (1991). Self-reports of spousal violence in a Mexican-American and non-Hispanic White population. *Violence & Victims, 6*, 3–15.

Sorokin, P. A. (2002). *The ways of power and love: Types, factors, and techniques of moral transformation*. Philadelphia, PA: Templeton Foundation Press.

Soyland, S. (2000, June). *Criminal organizations and crimes against the environment: A desktop study.* Turin, Italy: United National Interregional Crime and Justice Research Institute.

Special Committee on Pornography and Prostitution. (1985). *Pornography and prostitution in Canada: Report of the Special Committee on Pornography and Prostitution* (Vols. 1–2). Ottawa, ON: Canada, Department of Justice and Supply and Services Canada.

Spitz, R. A. (1965). *The first year of life: A psychoanalytic study of the development of normal and deviant object relations.* New York, NY: International Universities Press.

Stams, G. J. J. M., Brugman, D., Deković, M., Van Rosmalen, L., Van der Laan, P. H., & Gibbs, J. C. (2006). The moral judgment of juvenile delinquents: A meta-analysis. *Journal of Abnormal Child Psychology, 34,* 697–713.

Stets, J. E., & Straus, M. A. (1989). The marriage license as a hitting license: A comparison of assaults in dating, cohabiting, and married couples. *Journal of Family Violence, 41*(1), 37–54.

Sutherland, E. (1947). *Principles of criminology* (4th ed.). Philadelphia, PA: Lippincott.

Sylaska, K. M., & Edwards, K. M. (2014). Disclosure of intimate partner violence to informal social support network members: A review of the literature. *Trauma, Violence & Abuse, 15*(1), 3–21.

Szasz, A. (1986). Corporations, organized crime, and the disposal of hazardous waste: An examination of the making of a criminogenic regulatory structure. *Criminology, 24*(1), 1–27.

Tait, C. (2001/2002). Pregnant addicted women in Manitoba. *Canadian Women's Health Network Magazine, 4/5*(4/1). Retrieved from http://www.cwhn.ca/node/39573

Tajfel, H. (1982). *Social identity and intergroup behavior.* Cambridge, UK: Cambridge University Press.

Taylor, S. J. (1990). *Stalin's apologist: Walter Duranty, the* New York Times*'s man in Moscow.* Oxford, UK: Oxford University Press.

Taylor, W. C. (1910, July 20). Against Lombroso's theory: Thinks the law should not recognize the "born criminal." *New York Times,* p. 8.

Temple, J. R., Shorey, R. C., Tortolero, S. R., Wolfe, D. A., & Stuart, G. L. (2013). Importance of gender and attitudes about violence in the relationship between exposure to interparental violence and the perpetration of teen dating violence. *Child Abuse & Neglect, 37*(5), 343–52.

Thornton, G. (1939). The ability to judge crimes from photographs of criminals. *Journal of Abnormal and Social Psychology, 34,* 378–83.

Thrasher, F. (1926). The gang as a symptom of community disorganization. *Journal of Applied Sociology, 11*(1), 3–27.

Tottenham, N., Hare, T. A., Quinn, B. T., McCarry, T. W., Nurse, M., Gilhooly, T., … Casey, B. J. (2010). Prolonged institutional rearing is associated with atypically large amygdala volume and difficulties in emotion regulation. *Developmental Science, 13*(1), 46–61. doi: 10.1111/j.1467-7687.2009.00852.x

Trudeau, P. E. (1967, December 21). *CBC Television News*. Retrieved from https://www.cbc.ca/archives/entry/omnibus-bill-theres-no-place-for-the -state-in-the-bedrooms-of-the-nation

Tumulty, K., & Drogin, B. (1989, January 31). Steinberg convicted in girl's death: Jury returns manslaughter verdict, rejects murder count. *Los Angeles Times*. Retrieved from http://articles.latimes.com/1989-01-31/news/ mn-1236_1_elizabeth-steinberg

United Nations Environment Programme. (2006). *Handbook for the Montreal Protocol on substances that deplete the ozone layer* (7th ed.). Ozone Secretariat. Retrieved from http://ozone.unep.org/Publications/MP_Handbook/ Section_1.1_The_Montreal_Protocol/

United States National Advisory Commission on Civil Disorders. (1968). *Report of the National Advisory Commission on Civil Disorders*. New York, NY: Bantam Books.

Van Vugt, E., Gibbs, J., Stams, G. J., Bijleveld, C., Hendriks, J., & van der Laan, P. (2011). Moral development and recidivism: A meta-analysis. *International Journal of Offender Therapy and Comparative Criminology, 55*, 1234–47.

Vanyukov, M. M. (2004). Evolution, genes, and the environment: Neurobiological outcomes. In D. H. Fishbein (Ed.), *The science, treatment, and prevention of antisocial behaviors: Application to the criminal justice system* (Vol. 2, pp. 4.1–4.24). Kingston, NJ: Civic Research Institute.

Wallsten, P., & Riccardi, N. (2006, February 16). Cheney says he's to blame for shooting of fellow hunter. *The Los Angeles Times*. Retrieved from http:// articles.latimes.com/2006/feb/16/nation/na-cheney16

Walsh, A., Ellis, L., & Davis, M. (2007). *Criminology: An interdisciplinary approach*. Thousand Oaks, CA: Sage Publications.

Wasserman, U. (1981). Attempts at control over toxic waste. *Journal of Trade Law, 15*, 427–28.

Weatherburn, D., & Jones, C. (2001, August 23). Does prohibition deter cannabis use? *Crime and Justice Bulletin: Contemporary Issues in Crime and Justice, 58*. Retrieved from the NSW Bureau of Crime Statistics and Research, Department of Justice, Australia: https://www.bocsar.nsw.gov .au/Documents/CJB/cjb58.pdf

Wertham, F. (1954). *Seduction of the innocent*. New York, NY: Rinehart.

Whitaker, D. J., Haileyesus, T., Swahn, M., & Saltzman, L. (2007). Differences in frequency of violence and reported injury between relationships with reciprocal and nonreciprocal intimate partner violence. *American Journal of Public Health, 97*(5), 941–47.

White, P. (2009, March 5). Li found not criminally responsible in bus beheading. *The Globe and Mail*. Retrieved from https://www.theglobeand mail.com/news/national/li-found-not-criminally-responsible-in-bus -beheading/article714341/

Widom, C. S. (1989, April). The cycle of violence. *Science, 244*, 160–66.

Wilhelm, P. (2003). *Climate, corruption, fertility and religion: Implications for entrepreneurship and economy.* Retrieved online from http://citeseerx.ist .psu.edu/viewdoc/download?doi=10.1.1.531.5585&rep=rep1&type=pdf

Williams, S. L., & Frieze, I. H. (2005). Patterns of violent relationships, psychological distress, and marital satisfaction in a national sample of men and women. *Sex Roles, 52*, 771–85.

Wilson, E. O. (1975). *Sociobiology: The new synthesis.* Cambridge, MA: Harvard University Press.

Wilson, J. Q., & Herrnstein, R. J. (1985). *Crime and human nature.* New York, NY: Simon & Schuster.

Worthington, P. (2012). *Predator: The life and crimes of Clifford Olson.* Toronto: Rakuten Kobo.

Yasayko, J. (2010). *Attacks on transit drivers as a function of ambient temperature.* Unpublished master's thesis, Simon Fraser University, Burnaby, British Columbia, Canada.

Yochelson, S., & Samenow, S. (1976–1986). *The criminal personality* (Vols. 1–3). New York, NY: Jason Aronson.

Zajonc, R. B., Murphy, S. T., & Inglehart, M. (1989). Feeling and facial efference: Implications of a vascular theory of emotions. *Psychological Review, 96*(1), 395–416.

Zetter, K. (2014, November 3). An unprecedented look at Stuxnet, the world's first digital weapon. *Wired.* https://www.wired.com/2014/11/countdown -to-zero-day-stuxnet/

Zetter, K. (2015, January 9). Cyberattack causes physical damage for the second time ever. *Wired.* https://www.wired.co.uk/article/cyberattack -causes-physical-damage

INDEX

Italics indicate figures and tables.